THE BIBLE TIMELINE FOR MIDDLE SCHOOL

# ENCOUNTER

**LEADER'S GUIDE**

**Mark Hart with Colin and Aimee MacIver**

West Chester, Pennsylvania

The *Encounter: The Bible Timeline for Middle School* Leader's Guide has been submitted for ecclesial review and *imprimatur* to the Archdiocese of Philadelphia.



Ascension
PO Box 1990
West Chester, PA 19380
1-800-376-0520
ascensionpress.com

Cover design: Chris Lewis, BARITUS, LLC
Biblical character art: Chris Lewis, BARITUS, LLC

Printed in the United States of America
ISBN: 978-1-954882-51-5

# Contents

***Encounter* Program Overview** .....1
  **Tips for Introducing Young People to the Bible** ..... 2
  **Features Guide** ..... 3
  **Lesson Format** ..... 5
  **Lesson Plan Outlines** ..... 8
  **Fostering Family Catechesis** .....13
  **How to Use This Leader's Guide** .....13

***Encounter* Student Workbook with Leader's Notes and Steps**

**Lesson One**

INTRODUCTION TO THE BIBLE ..... 16

**Lesson Two**

EARLY WORLD ..... 34

**Lesson Three**

PATRIARCHS – EGYPT ..... 54

**Lesson Four**

EXODUS – DESERT WANDERINGS – CONQUEST AND JUDGES ..... 74

**Lesson Five**

ROYAL KINGDOM – DIVIDED KINGDOM ..... 94

**Lesson Six**

EXILE – RETURN – MACCABEAN REVOLT .....114

**Lesson Seven**

MESSIANIC FULFILLMENT: JESUS AND THE GOSPELS ..... 132

**Lesson Eight**

THE CHURCH (AND YOUR ROLE IN IT) ..... 154

Glossary ..... 172
Further Resources ..... 176
About the Author and Presenters ..... 196
Program Credits ..... 198

# *Encounter* Program Overview

*Encounter: The Bible Timeline for Middle School* is designed to provide an easy-to-understand overview of salvation history from Genesis through Revelation for your middle school students. In this adaptation of *The Great Adventure Bible Timeline*®, presenter Mark Hart unpacks God's Word in a dynamic way that makes Scripture come alive.

*The Bible Timeline*® Learning System organizes biblical history from Creation through the establishment of the Church by dividing the Old and New Testaments into twelve distinct time periods, each with a unique color. Within those periods, the timeline focuses on the fourteen narrative books of the Bible that outline salvation history. This focus makes the story of salvation easy to follow, and Mark's video presentations bring it to life for students today.

Each lesson focuses on facilitating students' engagement with the people, places, and events of specific biblical periods. Through video, thoughtful discussion, and group activities, *Encounter* aims to do more than simply impart an intellectual understanding of Sacred Scripture. The program ultimately strives to connect young people with their own salvation story, helping them better grasp God's personal love. The Scriptures themselves are meant to be a personal encounter with Jesus Christ that leads us to a conversion of heart.

This comprehensive, easy-to-use Leader's Guide equips you to accompany them. Over these eight lessons, your students will be invited to hear and then respond in faith to God's Word because "he first loved us" (1 John 4:19) and has called us to become his sons and daughters. *Encounter*'s vision for your classroom is not only a group of educated students but also a community of disciples.

## Tips for Introducing Young People to the Bible

Here are a few concrete ideas for introducing your students to the Bible:

- Recognize that the text-dense Bible often intimidates today's youth, who have grown up in an audiovisual world. Take advantage of the color-coded *Bible Timeline* chart located in the pocket at the back of each Student Workbook, and use the graphs, diagrams, and lists to help students better navigate the Bible. The more accessible the Bible becomes, the more "teachable" your students will be.
- When you will be reading aloud from the Bible, practice ahead of time so you can proclaim the Word with the clarity it deserves. Mark the pages before class to avoid losing time and momentum as you search for the Scripture passage. Also, you don't have to read a lengthy passage in its entirety. Students will retain more if you read just three or fewer verses at a time, and then pause for comments or questions before reading more. Finally, try to mix reading from the text with quoting from memory. Quoting from memory is a great way to model internalization.
- Use care and reverence with your words and tone when speaking about Scripture. For example, you might say "Some people find the Bible boring," but not "Hey, I know the Bible is boring." It is better to say "You will be confused at times" instead of "This is just too confusing." It is vital to acknowledge what the students are feeling but might be afraid to say aloud. It is equally important to turn negatives into positives, affirming the value of Scripture study and their ability to do it.
- Remember that you are cultivating not only minds but also hearts. It is great for students to know the words; it is more important that they are introduced to the Word. They need to know not only the characters but also the Author. Then, and only then, will the Scriptures resonate in their lives.
- When you do not know the answer to a question, don't be afraid to say so or delay answering until you can do so confidently and accurately. Many resources exist to help you find the correct answer. It is better to wait and give students a correct answer later than to risk giving incorrect or incomplete information.

Be sure to use a Catholic Bible for the program and explain to students why they should too. (See "Catholic Bibles" on page 16.) Catholic Bible translations approved for use in the United States include the following:

- The New American Bible (NAB) and the New American Bible, Revised Edition (NABRE)
- The Revised Standard Version–Catholic Edition (RSVCE) and the Revised Standard Version–Second Catholic Edition (RSV-2CE)
- The Jerusalem Bible (JB) and the New Jerusalem Bible (NJB)
- The English Standard Version–Catholic Edition (ESV-CE)

Always have a copy of the Bible and the *Catechism of the Catholic Church* (CCC) on hand for easy reference. The *Encounter* program uses Ascension's *Great Adventure Catholic Bible*, an RSV-2CE Bible that incorporates the color-coded tools of *The Bible Timeline* Learning System. You don't need the RSV-2CE, but if you use another translation, you'll notice differences in wording that may sometimes be confusing for students, along with differences in the numbering of verses in Daniel and Esther.

The Ascension app includes the full text of Ascension's *Great Adventure* Bible and can also be a helpful tool for quick reference. Catholic commentaries, a concordance, spiritual readings, and other approved texts may also provide answers. Having these resources on hand and using them shows students where to go for their own ongoing study and formation.

If you are feeling overwhelmed, remember: you are not alone! Christ is the true Teacher, not us. Christ is the Savior, not us. Pray with John 3:30 often: "You must increase, Lord, but I must decrease." If you feel intimidated, remember that the God of the universe called you to the awesome task of passing on the richness of the Catholic Faith in this way. He is in control and will provide. You can do it!

## Features Guide

Each lesson in *Encounter* includes the following features:

### The Big Picture

This text establishes the major ideas of the lesson. Consider inviting volunteers to read these sentences out loud to begin each session.

### Opening Prayer

This prayer helps students turn their focus to the Lord as the lesson begins. The prayer connects with the main theme of the lesson and helps set the tone for the class.

### Remember This! (memory verse and optional *lectio divina*)

To help set the context, this short memory verse is taken from Scripture readings associated with the lesson.

This verse may also be used optionally for *lectio divina,* a prayer practice in which students read the words closely and intentionally and listen for the Holy Spirit's prompting. Instructions for *lectio divina* can be found in the "Further Resources" section at the back of both the Leader's Guide and the Student Workbook.

### Warm Up (opening activity)

This activity starts each lesson and serves several functions. One, it helps engage students immediately in the content and themes. Two, it offers a way for you to assess what they already know about the lesson's characters and events.

### Time Period Overview

This section describes *The Bible Timeline* time periods and Scripture that will be covered in the lesson.

### If You Ask Me ... (discussion prompts)

These open-ended questions give students an opportunity to connect personally to the events of the time period.

### Main Content Teaching

This section presents the lesson's main subject matter. It has four parts: a video, text, discussion prompts, and a quick quiz.

### Dive In video

Mark Hart presents the main subject matter of the lesson in a way designed to grab the attention of the students.

### Dive In text

This section goes further into the lesson's main teaching. It can be read aloud in class or assigned for quiet reading.

### If You Ask Me (discussion prompts)

These open-ended questions prompt discussion and help students relate personally to the characters and events they are learning about in the lesson.

### Got It?

This quiz consists of multiple-choice questions to help you check students' understanding.

### Dive In Activity

This activity offers a hands-on application of the lesson's main ideas and themes. This repetition of material helps students internalize the content by engaging different senses and tasks.

### Biblical Character Video

The presenter in this video introduces one of the main characters from the time period and offers a personal story that connects that character's experience to modern, everyday life.

### Biblical Character Profile and Exercise

This text and activity bring the biblical character to life, helping students relate to the character and offering them a way to apply the character's experience to their own lives.

### Find Out More

These Bible passages provide additional stories about characters and events from the time periods covered in the lesson. They will be of special interest to students who like to read. These passages can also be used for *lectio divina*.

### Living It Out

These at-home activities help students move from a head knowledge of Sacred Scripture to a conversion of heart so that they are motivated to change their personal decisions and actions and share these truths with others. This section offers ideas for a personal action plan for the coming week—and beyond.

### Closing Prayer

This prayer recaps the main theme of the lesson and turns students' thoughts to the Lord as they are sent forth from the classroom.

## Lesson Format

The following steps show the basic structure of the lessons and explain what to do at each step. *Encounter* is designed to be flexible, so you can adapt the steps to suit your group's needs.

### Welcome – The Big Picture

**Welcome:** Before the students arrive, make sure you have all the supplies needed for the lesson, such as Student Workbooks, Bibles, copies of *The Bible Timeline* chart, materials for activities, paper, and pens or pencils. Set up the equipment for the video presentations and queue the first video so that it is ready to play.

Greet the students as they arrive. This helps create a warm and inviting atmosphere where everyone is comfortable and feels welcome. Consider asking an ice-breaker question to get them talking. Take attendance so that you can follow up later with students who are absent.

**The Big Picture:** Read this together to prepare students for the major idea of the lesson. Consider inviting students to rotate the reading.

### Opening Prayer

Pray the opening prayer in the Student Workbook, beginning and ending the prayer with the Sign of the Cross. You may lead the prayer yourself, ask a volunteer to read it, or pray it aloud together as a class.

### Remember This! (memory verse and optional *lectio divina*)

**Memory Verse:** After explaining the context and importance of the verse, ask the students to memorize it, and then remind them that you will ask about it when you meet for the next class. Consider offering a small prize at your next session to those who have memorized the verse.

***Lectio divina* (optional):** Invite the students to eliminate distractions and open their hearts and minds to the Holy Spirit. Using the memory verse (or, alternatively, using one of the Scripture passages from the lesson's "Find Out More" section), read the Scripture passage slowly and prayerfully to the class. After a short silence, ask the students to read the passage silently to themselves and reflect on it. Encourage them to focus on a specific word, phrase, or idea that strikes them. What is God trying to say to us through his Word?

After a minute or two, ask if anyone would like to share a thought or reflection with the class. If no one answers, you can mention what stood out to you and why you think it is important. More information about *lectio divina* can be found in "Further Resources" at the back of this guide (p. 183).

### Warm Up (opening activity)

Make sure the group has all the necessary materials. Go over the instructions carefully and answer questions. When they have finished, ask them to share what they learned from the activity.

## STEP 5 Time Period Overview

Review the key words (in blue capital letters) and their meanings, which you can find in the "Wordplay" section of each lesson in the workbook. (A complete list of key words also appears in the Glossary at the back of the workbook and this guide.) Then read the text in the workbook out loud. You can select students to read different paragraphs to increase class participation.

Next, using *The Bible Timeline* chart, review together the key events of the time periods, any covenants covered in the lesson, the approximate dates in history, and the world power at the time to give additional context to the lesson.

## STEP 6 Main Content Teaching

**Dive In video:** Make sure that the video and sound system are set up beforehand. Ask students to put away phones, close laptops, and avoid other distractions so that they can give their full attention to the video presentation. Play the video, which presents the main subject matter of the lesson and is designed to grab the attention of the students. Be prepared to pause the videos and open your Bibles when Mark mentions it!

**Dive In text:** Review the key words (in blue capital letters) and their meanings, referring to the "Wordplay" section of the lesson. Then read the "Dive In" section in the Student Workbook, which covers the main subject and complements the video presentation. You may ask students to read it quietly to themselves or, to increase class participation, select students to read different paragraphs out loud.

**If You Ask Me (discussion prompts):** Use these open-ended questions to spark conversation and encourage students to think about how the lesson applies to their daily lives. Lead the students in small group discussion and, if time permits, answer their spontaneous questions.

**Got It?** Ask students to complete the questions in the Student Workbook. Review the answers together.

## STEP 7 Dive In Activity

These activities offer a hands-on application of the lesson's main ideas and themes. This repetition of material helps them internalize the content by engaging different senses and tasks. Make sure the group has all the necessary materials. Go over the instructions carefully and answer questions. When they have finished, ask them to share what they learned from the activity.

## STEP 8 Biblical Character Profile

**Biblical Character Video:** Make sure that the video and sound system are set up beforehand, and ask students to put away phones, close laptops, and avoid other distractions so that they can give their full attention to the video presentation. Play the video. Ask students to pay special attention to what the character's words, actions, and experiences teach us about God and ourselves.

**Biblical Character Profile:** Read the text in the Student Workbook, which tells us more about the biblical character introduced in the video. You can select students to read different paragraphs aloud to increase class participation.

**Biblical Character Exercise:** This section offers students a personal way to apply what they learned from the biblical character's experience. Make sure the group has all the necessary materials. Go over the instructions carefully and answer questions. When they have finished, ask them to share what they learned from the activity. You can also implement these prompts as group discussion, journaling prompts, or homework.

## Find Out More & Living It Out

**Find Out More:** For students who are well-motivated and like to read, mention the stories that appear in this list, which they can read on their own. (These Scripture selections can be used for *lectio divina* as well.)

**Living It Out:** Read this together as a class to give the students ideas for putting what they have learned into practice, or you can assign this section as homework. Encourage students to turn the ideas in this section into a personal action plan for the coming week—and beyond.

This section also provides a good opportunity for family catechesis. Remind students and parents that the Student Workbook is available on Thinkific, and consider asking parents to review the "Living It Out" activities so they can support their child during the week.

## Closing Prayer

Remind the students about assignments for the next lesson, if any, and lead them in the closing prayer. Begin and end the prayer with the Sign of the Cross.

## Lesson Plan Outlines

The following tables provide outlines for classes that run 45, 60, and 90 minutes. Features in the light gray rows are optional and can be assigned as homework, depending on the needs of the group.

| 45-Minute Lesson Plan | | | |
|---|---|---|---|
| STEP 1 | **Welcome—The Big Picture** | • Before session: set up and prepare.<br>• Welcome students.<br>• Call on one or two students to share briefly how their "Living It Out" plan from the previous session went.<br>• Read aloud "The Big Picture" for this lesson. | 5 min |
| STEP 2 | **Opening Prayer** | Pray aloud as a group. | 1 min |
| STEP 3 | **Remember This! (memory verse)** | Read the memory verse aloud. Ask students to memorize it and remind them you will check at the next session. | 3 min |
| STEP 4 | **Warm Up (opening activity)** | Optional | |
| STEP 5 | **Time Period Overview** | Review key words. Read the text aloud. Use the "If You Ask Me" prompts to lead a short discussion. | 5 min |
| STEP 6 | **Main Content Teaching** | **Dive In video (ranges from 6 to 13 minutes):** Make sure that the video and sound system are set up beforehand, and ask students to put away phones, close laptops, and avoid other distractions so that they can give their full attention to the video presentation. Play the video.<br>**Dive In text:** Review the key words. Read the section in the Student Workbook.<br>**If You Ask Me (discussion prompts):** Depending on the video length, choose one to three discussion questions and call on one or two students to share their responses.<br>**Got It? (quick quiz):** Complete the quiz question by question, allowing students about ten seconds to choose their response. Then review the answers aloud. | 20 min |

| | | | |
|---|---|---|---|
| STEP 7 | **Dive In Activity** | Optional | |
| STEP 8 | **Biblical Character Profile** | **Biblical Character Video (5 min):** Make sure that the video and sound system are set up beforehand, and ask students to put away phones, close laptops, and avoid other distractions so that they can give their full attention to the video presentation. Play the video.<br>**Biblical Character Profile:** Read aloud the text in the Student Workbook.<br>**Biblical Character Exercise (optional)** | 8 min |
| STEP 9 | **Find Out More & Living It Out** | Choose one activity to assign. Remind students that you will check in at the next session. | 2 min |
| STEP 10 | **Closing Prayer** | Pray aloud as a group. | 1 min |
| | | **Total Time:** | **45 Minutes** |

| **60-Minute Lesson Plan** | | | |
|---|---|---|---|
| STEP 1 | **Welcome—The Big Picture** | • Before session: set up and prepare.<br>• Welcome students.<br>• Call on one or two students to share briefly how their "Living It Out" plan from the previous session went.<br>• Read "The Big Picture" aloud. | 5 min |
| STEP 2 | **Opening Prayer** | Pray aloud as a group. | 1 min |
| STEP 3 | **Remember This! (memory verse)** | Read the memory verse aloud. Ask students to memorize it and remind them you will check at the next session. | 3 min |
| STEP 4 | **Warm Up (opening activity)** | Give instructions and complete the activity. | 8 min |
| STEP 5 | **Time Period Overview** | Review key words. Read the text aloud. Use the "If You Ask Me" prompts to lead a short discussion. | 5 min |

| | | | |
|---|---|---|---|
| STEP 6 | **Main Content Teaching** | **Dive In video (ranges from 6 to 13 minutes):** Make sure that the video and sound system are set up beforehand, and ask students to put away phones, close laptops, and avoid other distractions so that they can give their full attention to the video presentation. Play the video.<br>**Dive In text:** Review the key words. Read the section in the Student Workbook.<br>**If You Ask Me (discussion prompts):** Depending on the video length, choose one or more discussion questions and call on one or two students to share their responses.<br>**Got It? (quick quiz):** Complete the quiz question by question, allowing students about ten seconds to choose their response, then review the answers aloud. | 15–20 min |
| STEP 7 | **Dive In Activity (optional)** | **Option choice:** Choose this activity *or* the "Biblical Character Exercise." Some activities may be conducted as a discussion, asking students how they will complete the exercise. | 7 min |
| STEP 8 | **Biblical Character Profile** | **Biblical Character Video (5 min):** Make sure that the video and sound system are set up beforehand, and ask students to put away phones, close laptops, and avoid other distractions so that they can give their full attention to the video presentation. Play the video.<br>**Biblical Character Profile:** Read aloud the text in the Student Workbook.<br>**Biblical Character Exercise:** Choose the exercise *or* the "Dive In Activity." Some activities may be conducted as a discussion, asking students how they will complete the exercise. | 15 min |
| STEP 9 | **Find Out More & Living It Out** | Choose one activity to assign. Remind students that you will check in at the next session. | 2 min |
| STEP 10 | **Closing Prayer** | Pray aloud as a group. | 1 min |
| | | **Total Time:** | **60 Minutes** |

| 90-Minute Lesson Plan | | | |
|---|---|---|---|
| STEP 1 | **Welcome—The Big Picture** | Before the session: set up and prepare.<br>Welcome students.<br>Call on several students to share briefly how their "Living It Out" plan from the previous session went.<br>Read "The Big Picture" aloud. | 8 min |
| STEP 2 | **Opening Prayer** | Pray aloud as a group. | 1 min |
| STEP 3 | **Remember This! (memory verse)** | Read aloud the memory verse. Ask students to memorize it and remind them you will check at the next session. | 3 min |
| STEP 4 | **Warm Up (opening activity)** | Give instructions and complete the activity. | 8 min |
| STEP 5 | **Time Period Overview** | Review key words. Read the text aloud. Use the "If You Ask Me" prompts to lead a short discussion. | 12 min |
| STEP 6 | **Main Content Teaching** | **Dive In video (ranges from 6 to 13 minutes):** Make sure that the video and sound system are set up beforehand, and ask students to put away phones, close laptops, and avoid other distractions so that they can give their full attention to the video presentation. Play the video.<br>**Dive In text:** Review the key words. Read the section in the Student Workbook.<br>**If You Ask Me (discussion prompts):** Depending on the video length, choose one or more discussion questions and lead a discussion.<br>**Got It? (quick quiz):** Ask students to complete the quiz in their workbooks, allowing about three minutes for the quiz, then review the answers aloud. | 15–30 min |
| STEP 7 | **Dive In Activity** | Give instructions and complete the activity. Some activities may be conducted as a discussion, asking students how they will complete the exercise. | 10 min |

| | | | |
|---|---|---|---|
| STEP 8 | **Biblical Character Profile** | **Biblical Character Video (5 min):** Make sure that the video and sound system are set up beforehand, and ask students to put away phones, close laptops, and avoid other distractions so that they can give their full attention to the video presentation. Play the video.<br>**Biblical Character Profile:** Read aloud the text in the Student Workbook.<br>**Biblical Character Exercise:** Review the exercise and either give time to complete it during the session or conduct a discussion asking students how they will complete the exercise. | 15 min |
| STEP 9 | **Find Out More & Living It Out** | Choose one activity to assign. Remind students that you will check in at the next session. | 2 min |
| STEP 10 | **Closing Prayer** | Pray aloud as a group. | 1 min |
| | | **Total Time:** | **90 Minutes** |

## Fostering Family Catechesis

Let parents know that all the student materials are available on Thinkific.

Parents' involvement in their children's faith formation is vital and lasting—the single most important factor in fostering the ongoing faith of children throughout their lives.*

*Encounter* encourages family catechesis in several ways. Parents can lead the whole program comfortably at home if they choose.

Alternatively, they may wish to use *Encounter* at home to supplement a parish-based program. Parents can watch the videos independently or with their child and then talk with their child about them. In addition, the "Living It Out" activities are specially designed to be done at home. When parents and children do them together, the whole family benefits.

## How to Use This Leader's Guide

This Leader's Guide is designed to walk you through each lesson in ten easy steps. The guide features lesson overviews, objectives, and ideas for facilitating each part of the lesson. For some lessons, it also provides suggestions for optional leader-guided discussion topics and questions.

We recommend that leaders and facilitators read through the entire lesson plan and watch the videos before the lesson. When this is not possible, however, the lesson overview and lesson objectives will provide a basic outline of the themes and topics to be addressed.

### Lesson plans

The Leader's Guide reproduces the pages of the Student Workbook and provides easy-to-follow steps and notes to help you deliver an effective lesson. The numbered steps under the workbook pages explain and guide you through the lesson. Simply follow these steps for a fruitful and engaging classroom experience.

The lesson plan outlines on pages 8–12 of this Leader's Guide indicate how much time to spend on the steps during 45-, 60-, and 90-minute classes and identify which steps are optional and can be assigned as homework. Students can also access course materials on Thinkific.

### Activities

The activities listed for each lesson address the lesson content and show how the lesson content applies to our individual faith journeys.

### Video lesson notes

Video notes for each lesson will help you better understand the teaching content of the videos.

### Quizzes

The Got It? quizzes in the Student Workbook help increase students' comprehension. Answers to the quizzes for each lesson are provided in the Leader's Guide.

*John Roberto, "Partnering with Parents to Nurture Family Faith – Insights from Research," *USCCB*, September 8, 2020, usccb.org.

THE BIBLE TIMELINE FOR MIDDLE SCHOOL

# ENCOUNTER

STUDENT WORKBOOK

*with*

LEADER'S NOTES AND STEPS

# Lesson One

## INTRODUCTION TO THE BIBLE

### LESSON OVERVIEW

The first lesson in *Encounter* is an opportunity to establish a learning community where students trust their catechists and one another so that they can come to understand Scripture as God's Word to them—relevant to their own lives and situations.

This lesson also introduces students to *The Bible Timeline* and makes clear that Sacred Scripture is God's Word—and God's Word to the students specifically. They should be able to understand the narrative structure of the program and see how it is relevant to their own lives, even and especially as middle schoolers.

This lesson also provides a framework that students will be able to follow through the whole series of lessons. Ultimately, the lesson sets the stage for the program as a whole. Leaders should take care to create a welcoming tone and a space where students know that they are seen, heard, and cared for.

### LESSON OBJECTIVES

Students will

- **Understand** that the Bible isn't just a book about God. It is God's own Word.
- **Become** familiar with *The Bible Timeline* so that they are equipped to follow the narrative of salvation history as it is presented in Sacred Scripture.
- **Engage** the notions of inspiration and Divine Revelation to see that Scripture is God's Word to us.
- **Appreciate** the relevance of Scripture to their own stories, lives, and experiences.

### CATHOLIC BIBLES

Lesson One gives you an opportunity to explain the difference between Catholic and Protestant Bibles.

The Catholic Church assembled the first Christian Bible. It is the same Bible we use today. Before then, the early Christians had the Hebrew Scriptures (our Old Testament) and hand-written copies of the Gospels, the Acts of the Apostles, and letters from the Apostles to the new Christian churches. These documents were circulated among the Christian communities, were read aloud during the Liturgy, and eventually became the books of our New Testament.

All Christians share a great love for the Bible, and all Christian Bibles have the same twenty-seven New Testament books. But not all Bibles are the same: the differences are in the Old Testament. In Catholic Bibles, the Old Testament contains forty-six books, but Protestant Bibles only have thirty-nine. The seven books omitted from Protestant Bibles are Tobit, Judith, Baruch, Sirach, 1 Maccabees, 2 Maccabees, and Wisdom, along with some passages from Esther, Daniel, and Baruch. Some Protestant Bibles call these missing books the Apocrypha and include them in a separate section between the Old and New Testaments.

If you hand out Bibles to your class, you can show your students how to tell whether they have a Catholic Bible. Ask them to open their Bibles to the copyright page (the page after the full title page in the front) and look for the Latin words "*nihil obstat*" and "*imprimatur*." When they are present, the *nihil obstat* and *imprimatur* indicate that a book is an approved edition for the Catholic faithful.

## VIDEO LESSON NOTES

### DIVE IN VIDEO – **INTRODUCTION TO THE BIBLE** – MARK HART

- Mark tells us about how he grew up Catholic but had no real knowledge of the Faith and didn't know how to read the Bible.

### The Bible

- The Bible is hard to read and full of big names, but in these videos Mark will cut through that to help make the Bible make sense.
- Scripture (the Bible) is relevant to our lives now. It is not just words *about* God. It is the Word *of* God. It is God's way of speaking directly to each of us about his plan for our lives.

> Mark says, "Here's what you have to understand: the Bible's not just words *about* God. The Bible's the word *of* God. It's not just the words about him; it's the words *from* him. This is how you come to know God and how you really come to figure out yourself. ... This is God speaking to you, about you. The Bible is how you're going to find your way through life and find your way to eternal life, to everlasting life."

- Mark explains the basic structure of the Bible: It's actually a collection of seventy-three books: forty-six in the Old Testament, and twenty-seven in the New Testament. Mark will be focusing on stories from the fourteen narrative books that together tell the overarching story of salvation history.

### St. Timothy and Your Students

- Even though your students are young, God can speak to and through them. Mark gives the example of 1 Timothy 4:12 (this week's memory verse, which reads, "Let no one despise your youth, but set the believers an example in speech and conduct, in love, in faith, in purity").
- St. Timothy was a young man who was trying to live a holy life among people who were older and thought they were a lot smarter and holier than he was. But St. Paul saw something in St. Timothy and wrote this letter to encourage him—the same way that you as a leader see something in your students.
- Mark looks ahead to the book of Genesis and reminds us that the Bible is a really wild and wonderful story.

### BIBLICAL CHARACTER VIDEO – **YOU!** – FR. FRANKIE CICERO

It is easy to think that the Bible is ancient history, but the truth is that our middle schoolers are important characters in the epic story of God's love. God calls people today!

Fr. Frankie tells about a time when God called him to share the good news with a woman in an unexpected place—a grocery store! His story reminds us that encounters with God happen anywhere, anytime, to everyone.

God is writing our unique part of the story now. Great adventures with God await us.

As we study God's Word, we will learn how to listen for God's invitation.

## BEFORE- AND AFTER-CLASS REMINDERS

### Before students arrive:

Make sure you have all the supplies needed for the lesson, such as Student Workbooks, Bibles, copies of *The Bible Timeline* chart, materials for activities, paper, and pens or pencils.

If you are handing out Bibles, place one at each student's place.

Review the video notes above and take note of anything you would like to mention to the class before they watch the video presentations.

Set up the equipment for the video presentations and queue the first video so that it is ready to play.

### After class:

Follow up with students who missed the lesson.

Learn your students' names.

**NOTES**

## Lesson One

### Introduction to the Bible

2 | ENCOUNTER

## STEP 1 Welcome – The Big Picture

Greet the students as they arrive, and take attendance. Make sure they have all the supplies they need for today's lesson, such as Student Workbooks, Bibles, *The Bible Timeline for Teens*, paper, and pens or pencils.

Consider asking students something simple to help put them at ease when they're seated—for example, if they could live anywhere in the world, where would it be? When you are ready to begin, read "The Big Picture" aloud.

# The Big Picture

The Bible isn't just a book *about God*. The Bible is God's own Word—the Word *of God*. There is a huge difference between a book that describes God and a book that is a direct message from him to us.

Even better, that message from God is about how deeply he loves us—then, now, always. Sacred Scripture isn't just a history lesson; it wasn't meant only for people who lived long ago. When you learn the story of God's people, you are learning your own story as well.

**THE BIG PICTURE**

"The Big Picture" prepares students for the major idea of the lesson. Consider inviting a student to read it aloud to get started.

For this first lesson, it is a good idea to have your Bible ready! Hold it up and ask students to have their Bibles out on their desks. The Bible is a core component of this study. Students will hear and read the Word of God.

**OPENING PRAYER**

"God our Father, you gave us your Word so that we could know and encounter you. You also gave us your Word so that we could know our own story—who we are and how to grow close to you. Speak to us through your Word. Make this encounter real and lasting in our lives. In Jesus' name, we pray. Amen."



## STEP 2 Opening Prayer

Before you pray, ask your students to settle, take a deep breath, and quiet their minds. Then pray the opening prayer in the Student Workbook, beginning and ending with the Sign of the Cross. If you want students to follow along, ask them to open their workbooks.

**MEMORY VERSE**

Read **1 Timothy 4:12** aloud. Talk about St. Timothy, St. Paul, and what the verse might mean to young people today, as described in the Student Workbook. What opportunities do they have in their everyday lives to set examples for others—friends, siblings, even parents?

***LECTIO DIVINA* (OPTIONAL)**

To pray with the memory verse, invite your students to eliminate distractions and open their hearts and minds to the Holy Spirit. Read **1 Timothy 4:12** slowly and prayerfully to the class.

Pause and then read the verse again. Ask students to reflect on it silently, focusing on a specific word, phrase, or idea that strikes them. What is God trying to say to them through his Word?

After a minute or two, ask if anyone would like to share a thought or reflection with the class. Consider mentioning what stood out to you and why you think it is important.

More information about *lectio divina* can be found in "Further Resources" on page 183 in this guide.

**REMEMBER THIS!**

"Let no one despise your youth, but set the believers an example in speech and conduct, in love, in faith, in purity."

—1 Timothy 4:12

You are young, just like St. Timothy was when St. Paul wrote to him. Paul was reminding Timothy that holiness does not depend on age.

When Paul wrote these words almost two thousand years ago, God knew that you would read them today. God wanted to give you a personal message with these words: *He's calling* you, *and you are capable of teaching and inspiring everyone around you.*

In the same way that I (Mark) learned this verse long ago, you can memorize it and, more importantly, live by it as an example for others. How?

- In the way you talk, text, and post
- In the way you act 24/7
- In the way you put others ahead of yourself
- In the way you honor your body and everyone around you
- In the way you believe in God and trust him

4 | ENCOUNTER

## Remember This!

The memory verse is taken from a Scripture reading associated with the lesson. To help set the lesson context, read it aloud and talk about it together.

Even though the verse is written in their workbooks, this is a good opportunity to have students open their Bibles and find 1 Timothy 4:12. Some students may not be familiar with how to use a Bible, so the more practice, the better!

Ask them to memorize the verse, and remind them that you will ask them about it at your next class. You may also use the verse for *lectio divina*, an ancient prayer practice based in Scripture.

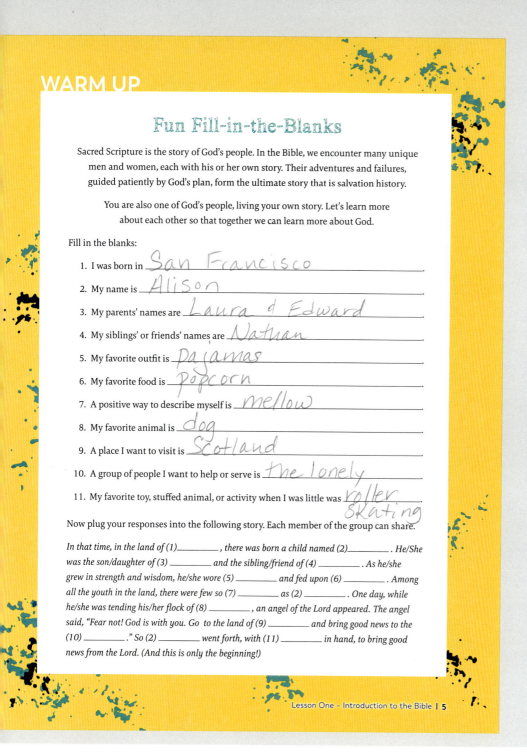

WARM UP

## Fun Fill-in-the-Blanks

Sacred Scripture is the story of God's people. In the Bible, we encounter many unique men and women, each with his or her own story. Their adventures and failures, guided patiently by God's plan, form the ultimate story that is salvation history.

You are also one of God's people, living your own story. Let's learn more about each other so that together we can learn more about God.

Fill in the blanks:

1. I was born in San Francisco.
2. My name is Alison.
3. My parents' names are Laura & Edward.
4. My siblings' or friends' names are Nathan.
5. My favorite outfit is Pajamas.
6. My favorite food is Popcorn.
7. A positive way to describe myself is mellow.
8. My favorite animal is dog.
9. A place I want to visit is Scotland.
10. A group of people I want to help or serve is the lonely.
11. My favorite toy, stuffed animal, or activity when I was little was roller skating.

Now plug your responses into the following story. Each member of the group can share.

*In that time, in the land of (1)________, there was born a child named (2)________. He/She was the son/daughter of (3) ________ and the sibling/friend of (4) ________. As he/she grew in strength and wisdom, he/she wore (5) ________ and fed upon (6) ________. Among all the youth in the land, there were few so (7) ________ as (2) ________. One day, while he/she was tending his/her flock of (8) ________, an angel of the Lord appeared. The angel said, "Fear not! God is with you. Go to the land of (9) ________ and bring good news to the (10) ________." So (2) ________ went forth, with (11) ________ in hand, to bring good news from the Lord. (And this is only the beginning!)*

### STEP 4 Warm Up: *Fun Fill-in-the-Blanks*

This activity is a light-hearted way for students to have fun and get to know one another. Make sure each student has a copy of the blank activity and something to write with. Go over the instructions carefully and answer questions. (Notice that for #4, we ask for the names of siblings or friends. Encourage children who don't have brothers or sisters to name a friend or two.)

When students have finished the activity, ask them to share their fractured stories with a partner or with the whole group.

## TIME PERIOD OVERVIEW

### *The Bible Timeline*

In *The Great Adventure* Bible Study Program, *The Bible Timeline* Learning System arranges the key people, places, and events of the Bible into twelve color-coded periods. The chart in the back pocket of this workbook uses the same system to show you how the books of the Bible fit together to tell the story of **SALVATION HISTORY**. *The Bible Timeline* teaches the "big picture" of the Bible and gives us the tools to really understand our story as God's people.

The twelve periods of *The Bible Timeline* are shown in the banner across the bottom of the page and on your timeline chart.



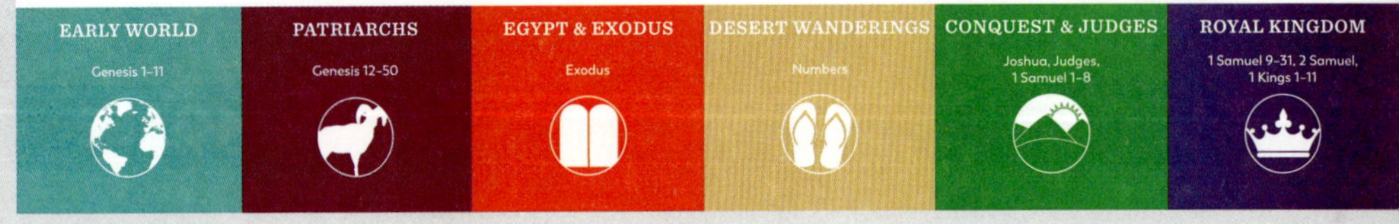

## Time Period Overview: *The Bible Timeline*

Invite students to take out their *Bible Timeline* charts and open them to show the side with the period panels.

In the workbook text, notice the key word in blue capital letters, and make sure students understand its meaning. (See "Wordplay" on p. 15 of the workbook.) Then read the "Time Period Overview" text out loud. Consider selecting students to read different paragraphs to increase class participation.

Look at your *Bible Timeline* chart to get familiar with the different periods. Notice especially where the books of the Bible appear on the chart and how the flow of people and events relates to those books.

You may already be familiar with some of the key events, like "The Flood" (Noah's ark), "David kills Goliath," and "Nativity of the Lord." Find those three stories on your chart. For each one, pay attention to the name of the time period, along with its color and dates. These will help you remember the stories later.

"All Scripture is inspired by God."

—2 Timothy 3:16

# If You Ask Me

- Do you know some other Bible stories already? What Bible story has really stuck with you since you first learned it? What makes it so memorable?
- Which *Bible Timeline* period is already familiar to you? What do you know about it? Where did you learn about it?
- Which people in the Bible can you remember? What do you remember about them?

Lesson One – Introduction to the Bible | 7

| DIVIDED KINGDOM | EXILE | RETURN | MACCABEAN REVOLT | MESSIANIC FULFILLMENT | THE CHURCH |
|---|---|---|---|---|---|
| 1 Kings 12–22<br>2 Kings 1–16 | 2 Kings 17–25 | Ezra<br>Nehemiah | 1 Maccabees | Luke | Acts |
| 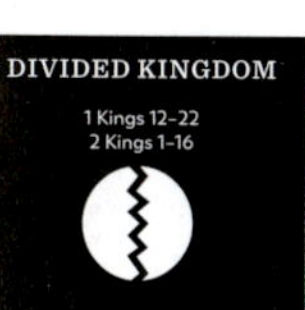 |  |  |  |  | 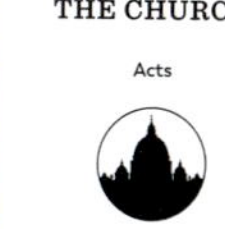 |

## IF YOU ASK ME

These questions prompt students to think about what they already know about the Bible. Choose one or more questions to talk about in class. Full-class discussions can be challenging, especially for students who do not know each other well yet, so consider asking students to think about each question and discuss responses with a partner or small group first.

Remember to walk around the room and be available to answer questions and engage in conversations. Your students' answers to the questions will give you a helpful sense of how familiar they already are with the Bible.

Pause to point out the main features of the chart: the twelve time periods, their colors, and the narrative books listed for each. Notice too the key events in each time period, the covenants, the approximate dates in history, and the world powers.

Use the "If You Ask Me" questions to get students talking about what they've learned.

**DIVE IN VIDEO**

Make sure the video and sound system are already set up. Before you play the video, ask students to put away phones, close laptops, and avoid other distractions so they can give it their full attention. Also consider reviewing together the "Got It?" questions on page 10 of the workbook so they can be alert to the answers as they watch.

**DIVE IN TEXT**

The text in the workbook complements the video presentation. Review the key words and then invite students to read the text to help familiarize themselves with their Bibles. You can read the text aloud with them in class or ask them to read it quietly to themselves.

Help your students understand that while Scripture is *about* God, it is also the Word *of* God—God's own Word spoken directly to each one of us!

DIVE IN VIDEO

**Introduction to the Bible . . . . . . . . . . . . . . . . . . Mark Hart**

"Scripture is God's way of speaking directly to all of us." —Mark H.

# DIVE IN

The **BIBLE** may look like one book, but it is actually a collection of seventy-three different books. These books were written over the course of thousands of years by many authors in many places. The books have different writing styles, purposes, audiences, and literary forms.

Sometimes **SACRED SCRIPTURE** describes certain events as they happened in history. Other times, symbols and creative writing are used to communicate the truth in other ways. Across this variety of books, remember:

- All of Scripture is the story of God's great love for his people throughout history. (The Bible is *about* God.)
- All of Scripture is the ***INSPIRED*** Word *of* God. (The Bible is God's own words.)
- All of Scripture is God's ***REVELATION*** to us. (The Bible is *from* God.)
- In all of Scripture, God is speaking personally to you, about you. (The Bible is *your* story, too.)

Sometimes people find the Bible confusing because it contains so many books and so many kinds of writing: histories, laws, poems and songs, love letters, wise sayings, visions, Gospels, and personal letters. God speaks to us through all these books. But how can we make sense of everything?

8 | ENCOUNTER

## STEP 6 Main Content Teaching

This step involves watching Mark Hart's teaching video and reading together the text in the Student Workbook. Three more "If You Ask Me" questions follow the text along with a quick "Got It?" quiz.

Detailed notes on the video content start on page 17 of this Leader's Guide.

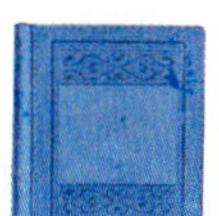

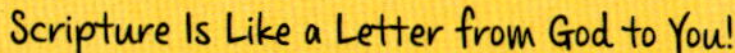

**Scripture Is Like a Letter from God to You!**

St. Gregory the Great was a pope a long time ago. We call him "the Great" because he was a wonderful leader, teacher, and writer. Gregory called the Scriptures "a letter from Almighty God to his creature"—a letter directly from God to me and you!

The *Encounter* program helps you make sense of the Bible by looking at the one big story that's woven through it: the story of **SALVATION**. The **OLD TESTAMENT** tells us how God made us to love him and how we turned away from him. It tells us how sin entered our lives and how much we need a savior. The **NEW TESTAMENT** tells us the story of our Savior, Jesus. It tells us about his life on earth two thousand years ago, his Resurrection from the dead, and the beginnings of his **CHURCH**. Together the Old and New Testaments tell us the story of salvation from the beginning of time until now.

Take another look at your *Bible Timeline* chart. Notice which narrative books are listed for each time period. In upcoming lessons, we'll focus on key events from these fourteen books that tell God's story and ours—the story of salvation.

## If You Ask Me

- Have you ever related to a book, movie, show, or song as if it were telling your own story or describing your own feelings, even though it was created by someone else? How did that make you feel?
- When have you felt inspired? What was the situation? Who or what inspired you? What were you inspired to notice, do, feel, or change?
- Who or what makes you think about God? Why?



**IF YOU ASK ME**

These open-ended questions are intended to spark conversation and encourage students to think about how the lesson applies to their daily lives. The questions in today's lesson prompt students to think about how God communicates with us.

The questions can be covered in a class discussion or in pairs or small groups with class discussion to follow. Lead the group discussion and, if time permits, answer students' spontaneous questions.

If you are asking students to talk in pairs or small groups, stay consistent within a class period. The next time you meet, you can switch up the groups so more students get to know one another.

**Notes**

## GOT IT?

Ask students to complete the multiple-choice questions in the Student Workbook, and review the answers together.

# Got It

1. **How many books are there in the Bible?**
   a. 27
   b. 46
   c. 73
   d. 14

2. **How many books will we be focusing on in this program?**
   a. 27
   b. 46
   c. 72
   d. 14

3. **All of Scripture is ________ and is God's ________ to us. It is God's Word.**
   a. nice, nugget
   b. inspired, Revelation
   c. Revelation, inspiration
   d. wordy, puzzle

10 I ENCOUNTER

**Notes**

DIVE IN ACTIVITY

## Bible Race

For this program, you need to know how to find your way around the Bible. The only way to get better is to practice—so let's do it! Below are several verses. Your leader will give a signal to begin the search for each. The first person to find and read the verse wins the round. May the fastest Bible searcher win!

- [ ] John 3:16
- [ ] Ephesians 4:24
- [ ] John 14:6
- [ ] Genesis 3:15
- [ ] Psalm 63:1
- [ ] Deuteronomy 17:18
- [ ] 1 Samuel 3:4
- [ ] 1 John 4:8
- [ ] John 4:8
- [ ] 1 Corinthians 13:13

Which verse got you thinking? Why? Write your answer here.

________________________________________

________________________________________

________________________________________

________________________________________

________________________________________

Lesson One – Introduction to the Bible | 11

### BIBLE RACE

Make sure everyone has a Bible. Go over the instructions carefully and answer questions. Review the table of contents in the Bible before getting started so that students have a general idea of the order of the books. The graphic of the Old and New Testament books on page 6 of their workbook may also help.

To start, call out the first verse ("John 3:16") and say "Go!" The first person or team to find the verse shouts "Got It!" and reads the verse out loud.

If students are working with partners or as teams, make sure they take turns looking up passages. Prizes go a long way—consider giving each winner a small prize or treat.

## STEP 7 Dive In Activity

This activity will get students to notice where some books are in the Bible. Students can work independently, as partners, or as teams.

**BIBLICAL CHARACTER VIDEO**

Ask students to put away phones, close laptops, and avoid other distractions so that they can give their full attention to the video presentation. In this video, Fr. Frankie talks about how, like the people in the Bible, each of us is an important character in salvation history. Ask students to pay special attention to what Fr. Frankie's story teaches us about God and about ourselves.

**BIBLICAL CHARACTER PROFILE**

Read the text in the workbook aloud. You can select students to read different paragraphs to increase class participation.

BIBLICAL CHARACTER VIDEO

**You! . . . . . . . . . . . . . . . . . . . . . . . . . . . Fr. Frankie Cicero**

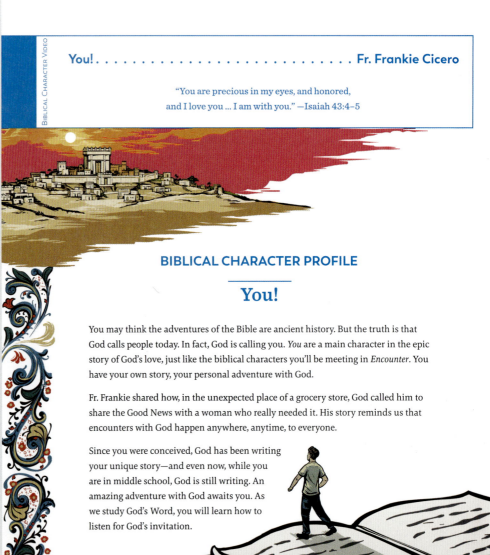

"You are precious in my eyes, and honored, and I love you ... I am with you." —Isaiah 43:4–5

## BIBLICAL CHARACTER PROFILE

# You!

You may think the adventures of the Bible are ancient history. But the truth is that God calls people today. In fact, God is calling you. *You* are a main character in the epic story of God's love, just like the biblical characters you'll be meeting in *Encounter*. You have your own story, your personal adventure with God.

Fr. Frankie shared how, in the unexpected place of a grocery store, God called him to share the Good News with a woman who really needed it. His story reminds us that encounters with God happen anywhere, anytime, to everyone.

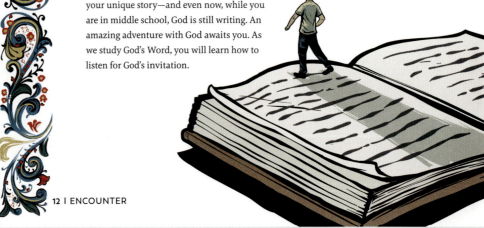

Since you were conceived, God has been writing your unique story—and even now, while you are in middle school, God is still writing. An amazing adventure with God awaits you. As we study God's Word, you will learn how to listen for God's invitation.

12 I ENCOUNTER

## STEP 8 Biblical Character Profile: YOU

This step features a short video by Fr. Frankie, a read-aloud profile of "you," and an exercise for students to do during class or at home.

Make sure the video and sound system are already set up. After you play the video, review the video notes on page 18 of this Leader's Guide, and ask students about specific points of interest. Then read the "You!" profile aloud and give your students time to do the exercise, "Sharing What You Love."

## Sharing What You Love

God wants us to share our faith. In the Gospel of Matthew, Jesus gives his **APOSTLES**—and us!—a mission: to tell other people about him. He commands us to "go ... and make disciples of all nations" (Matthew 28:19–20).

Fr. Frankie had an adventure—a chance to share his faith in an unexpected way in an unexpected place. We never know when God will give us an opportunity to tell someone else about him. Thinking about what to share helps us prepare for the opportunities God gives us.

What are three things about God and our **CATHOLIC** Faith that you think are worth sharing? Examples are knowing Jesus, the Mass, the Eucharist, Adoration, the Blessed Mother, the Rosary, *lectio divina* (praying with Scripture), works of mercy, grace before meals, praise and worship, youth group, retreats, Advent and Christmas, Lent and Easter, the saints, Gregorian chant, and on and on. Can you think of more? What is special to you? Write three things here:

1. ______________________

2. ______________________

3. ______________________

Now think about specifically where and how you could share these things with others. For example, "In the morning before school, I could tell my sister, 'I'm praying for you today.'" Or "I could tell my friend who is having a hard time, 'In my hard times, Jesus has always been there. He is here for you too!'"

______________________

______________________

______________________

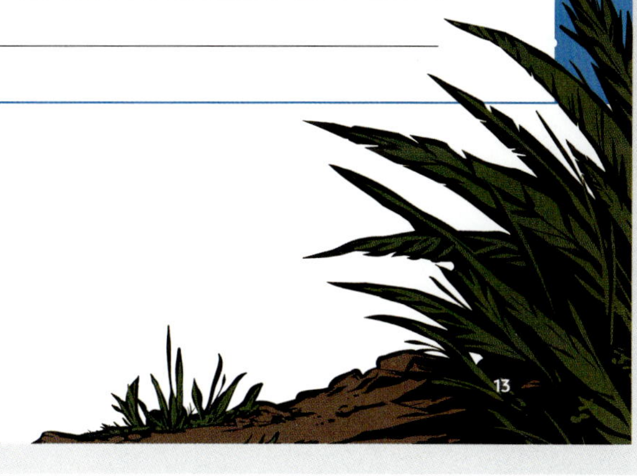

13

**BIBLICAL CHARACTER EXERCISE**

"Sharing What You Love" asks students to think about what they value about their Catholic Faith and what they think is worth sharing. Make sure they have their workbooks and something to write with. Read the instructions aloud and spend some time brainstorming together. Then ask students to write down the three things they each value most about their Catholic Faith. If there's time, invite them to keep going and write down specifically how they can share these things with someone else.

**Notes**

______________________

______________________

______________________

______________________

______________________

______________________

______________________

**LIVING IT OUT**

This section gives students ideas for habits that can make their faith (and this study!) more meaningful to them. Encourage them to develop a personal action plan for praying, getting to Mass, or talking to a friend about their faith in the coming week.

For this lesson, let students know the Mass times at your parish.

**FAMILY CATECHESIS**

"Living It Out" provides a good opportunity for family catechesis. Remind students and parents that the Student Workbook is available on Thinkific, and consider asking parents to review the "Living It Out" activities so they can support their child during the week.

Specifically, parents can help a child make time to pray every day, and they can pray together as a family. They can help their child get to Mass by going together. And if their child wants to talk to a friend about what he or she is learning, practicing first with a parent or sibling will make it much easier.

## Living It Out

As we start the *Encounter* program, consider the three habits below that you can practice over the next weeks and months that will make the study more meaningful, powerful, and effective in your life. Are you ready for the challenge?

1. Commit to praying every day. This can be very simple. Think of a few specific ways you could pray daily.

2. Go to Mass every Sunday. Beforehand, go to the USCCB website (usccb.org), click on "Daily Readings," and read the Sunday Mass readings *before* Mass. This little habit will dramatically improve how much you remember from the readings. By the end of this program, you will also know much more about what these readings mean.

3. Talk to a friend about what you are learning, wondering, and thinking. It might be awkward at first, but talking about your faith helps both your faith and your friendships grow.

### Find Out More & Living It Out

There is no "Find Out More" section in the first lesson.

"Living It Out" activities are specially designed to be done at home. Read the text in the workbook together as a class to give your students ideas for putting what they have learned into practice, and ask them each to choose one activity for the week. Remind them that you will check in with them the next time you meet to see how they did.

## WORDPLAY

**Apostle**: From a Greek word meaning "one who is sent." The original twelve Apostles were chosen by Jesus to preach the Gospel and make disciples of all nations.

**Bible:** From the Greek word *biblia*, which means "collection of books." The Bible contains seventy-three books of many different types.

**Catholic**: A word meaning "universal"; the name for the Church instituted by Jesus and passed down through the successors of the Apostles.

**Church (capital "C")**: The whole assembly of believers in Jesus Christ throughout the world.

**inspired**: From a Latin word meaning "to breathe into," referring (for example) to how the Holy Spirit guided the human authors of the Bible as they wrote the truth God wants us to know for our salvation.

**New Testament**: The latter part of the Bible, which details the life, death, and Resurrection of Jesus Christ, along with the early history of his Church.

**Old Testament**: The first part of the Bible, which describes Creation, the Fall, and God's ongoing attempts to repair his relationship with humanity.

**Revelation**: Divine truth that God communicates to us through his Word (Scripture) and the teachings handed down to us (Tradition).

**Sacred Scripture**: The collection of ancient biblical texts that are inspired by God and reveal his nature and presence to his people.

**salvation**: Our deliverance, through Jesus Christ, from the powers of sin and death.

**salvation history:** God's redemptive plan in human history, culminating in Jesus Christ, who completely reveals the Father to us.

## CLOSING PRAYER

"Thank you, Father, for the chance to discover more about the great story that we are a part of. Thank you for helping us see our own unique places in the story. Thank you for the community of faith that surrounds us and strengthens us. Help us to grow as we learn about your Word. In Jesus' name, we pray. Amen."

## Closing Prayer

Remind students about their homework assignments. Then lead the class in the closing prayer. Begin and end the prayer with the Sign of the Cross.

**THIS WEEK'S HOMEWORK**

1. Memorize the memory verse: 1 Timothy 4:12.
2. Do your "Living It Out" assignment.

# Lesson Two

## EARLY WORLD

### LESSON OVERVIEW

Lesson Two launches into the story itself—from the beginning. This lesson seeks to stoke the fires of imagination for middle schoolers and invite them into the narrative of the Early World. We begin in Eden and stretch out into the world as it was through the Flood. We see God's goodness and the ugly consequences of sin through the tragic story of Cain and Abel.

Middle schoolers have a growing capacity to grasp the relationship between Scripture, history, and science. This lesson will help them see that the story of salvation history is not in conflict with the claims of modern science.

Whether these stories are familiar or brand new to students, it is important for middle schoolers to consider them in light of their own lives and progressing stories. In the context of the whole program, this lesson begins to build a biblical framework in the minds and hearts of young learners. They can see themselves in these stories (we all can!), and they can see God's plan as it unfolds—not only in the distant past, but in their lives here and now.

### LESSON OBJECTIVES

Students will

- **Understand** that the story of salvation history begins with Creation.
- **Remember** the narrative of the Early World as the start of a biblical framework they can build on in the future.
- **Understand** that Scripture seeks to tell a story rather than teach science.
- **Envision** the consequences of sin as the consequences of human decisions in the larger plan of God's love, rather than as an arbitrary punishment.
- **Understand** that from the very beginning, our story was driven by God's overarching plan for our salvation.

### VIDEO LESSON NOTES

#### DIVE IN VIDEO – **EARLY WORLD** – MARK HART

Mark will prompt you to pause the video to read these passages:

**Genesis 3:1–13, The Fall**
**Genesis 4:1–10, Cain and Abel**

- Mark tells us that the Early World is the old family photo album portion of the Bible. Like a family album, it tells the story of our family's love and shows us how we got here.

## Creation

- In Genesis, we hear that God created and separated all the different parts of creation over six days:

  Day 1: Day from night

  Day 2: Sea from sky

  Day 3: Land from sea

  Day 4: Sun from moon

  Day 5: Birds (creatures of the air) from fish (creatures of the sea)

  Day 6: Animals (creatures of the land) from human beings

- God's final act of creation is his greatest: a man and a woman, Adam and Eve. He gave them Paradise, the Garden of Eden, for their home—a perfect, sinless world made just for them.
- Mark explains that people get tangled up because they're looking for science in the Book of Genesis. But Genesis is telling us the *why* of creation, not the *how*.

  Creation points to a Creator, to the God who made it all. He made us, he knows us, he loves us, and he wants the best for us. Unfortunately, we human beings sometimes have other ideas.

## The Fall

- The serpent tempts Adam and Eve to eat the fruit God asked them not to eat.

  "Serpent" in the original Hebrew is actually better translated as "dragon." The serpent is the devil, the fallen angel we call Satan.

- The thought of eating the fruit is really attractive to Adam and Eve because sin is attractive. The devil asks, "Did God really tell you not to eat it?" Notice how he plants seeds of doubt about what God said. Adam and Eve eat the fruit, are filled with guilt and shame, and hide from God. (This is the Fall.) So why does God punish them? Because he loves them, just as your students' parents might ground them for playing video games instead of doing homework—for their own good.
- Mark reminds us that God doesn't abandon Adam and Eve—or us. He loves us and wants the best for us, even when we fall short. This is where we introduce the recurring theme of God's promises, through an explanation of the *protoevangelium*, "the first Gospel" (Genesis 3:15). This is where God promises that
  - he will send a savior. This is the first prophecy about Jesus, which will be fulfilled on the Cross.
  - Satan's victory will only be temporary. Satan will not have the last word.

## Abel

- Mark makes the point that the ripples of sin don't stop with Adam and Eve. Their two sons, Cain (a farmer) and Abel (a shepherd), prepare sacrifices to God. God prefers Abel's sacrifice to Cain's, though the story doesn't tell us why. God says to Cain, "If you do well, will you not be accepted? And if you do not do well, sin is lurking at the door; its desire is for you, but you must master it" (Genesis 4:7).

- We can infer from this that Cain did not do well in some way when he offered his sacrifice. Perhaps he gave out of duty while Abel gave out of love. We don't know. But we do know that God still loves Cain and wants to teach him to do well and master sin. But Cain doesn't like that lesson, and he kills Abel instead.
- The story of Cain and Abel is an example of something we will see often in Genesis 1–11:
    - » God gives everything; we give something.
    - » God gives everything; we become selfish.
    - » God gives everything; we become prideful.
- Mark briefly mentions the story of Noah and the Flood, when people had become so terrible that God had to intervene.

## The Takeaway

- The lesson is always the same: we're supposed to be a family, and we're supposed to have our hearts set on God. Instead, we become prideful. So God has to intervene and save us from ourselves.
- Things to understand:
    - » God created you because he loves you.
    - » God has an amazing plan for your life if you stay in right relationship with him.
    - » The key is to find yourself in the story. God is the author who is writing the script of your life.

### BIBLICAL CHARACTER VIDEO – **ABEL** – TANNER KALINA

Tanner tells us about a time when he was competing to be the starting shortstop on the varsity baseball team. He and his competitor were equal in skill and ability in every way except for one: Tanner was hungry for victory and excellence. He was the first person on the field and the last one off. He was all in.

In the Bible story in Genesis 4, Abel offers the firstlings of his flock—his very best—to God. It's possible that Abel's sacrifice was more acceptable because it came from his heart. Abel did not hold back from God. Abel was invested, dialed in, and committed. What Cain offers is less pleasing to God. Perhaps Cain did only the bare minimum, just enough to check a box.

Remember that the Bible's Early World time period teaches us a lot about our own stories. Abel shows us what God really wants from us: our hearts.

# BEFORE- AND AFTER-CLASS REMINDERS

## Before students arrive:

Make sure you have all the supplies needed for the lesson, such as Student Workbooks, Bibles, copies of *The Bible Timeline* chart, materials for activities, paper, and pens or pencils.

If you are handing out Bibles, place one at each student's place.

Review the video notes above and take note of anything you would like to mention to the class before they watch the video presentations.

Set up the equipment for the video presentations and queue the first video so that it is ready to play.

## After class:

Follow up with students who missed the lesson.

Continue to learn your students' names.

**NOTES**

# Lesson Two

## Early World

EARLY WORLD GENESIS 1–11 

16 | ENCOUNTER

## Welcome – The Big Picture

As they arrive, greet students by name (from memory, if possible). Take attendance so that you can follow up later with students who are absent. Consider asking students something simple to help put them at ease when they're seated—for example, to share a positive experience they had since the previous class.

## The Big Picture

To fully experience any great story, we must start at the beginning. Whether it's the origin of a hero's superpowers, an epic love story, or the story of our own lives, the beginning is critical. This is especially true of the greatest story of all time: salvation history.

It's easy to settle for a vague sense of Genesis as a simple story about a man and a woman in a garden with a snake and some fig leaves—and then quickly move on. But the beginning—*our* beginning—goes far deeper than that. So, let's go deeper.

### OPENING PRAYER

"Lord God, we ask you to draw us into our human story as we enter this lesson. Help us to understand more about how you made us, how sin hurt us, and how you enacted a plan for our salvation. May we see how the stories of the Bible are like our own stories. May we learn and grow from everything you reveal. In Jesus' name, we pray. Amen."



**THE BIG PICTURE**

Read the text to introduce the major ideas of the lesson on the Early World: Creation, Adam and Eve, and God's plan for our salvation from the beginning. It will be helpful to bookmark Genesis 3 and Genesis 4. Ask students to bookmark their Bibles as you are bookmarking yours.

## STEP 2 Opening Prayer

Before praying, ask your students to settle, take a deep breath, and quiet their minds. Invite them to share personal intentions. Personal intentions are simply prayer requests, offering prayers for the good of a specific person or event or cause—for example, "for my grandfather," "for my big sister's wedding," "for peace in the world." Invite students to name their intention aloud or to themselves.

Pray the opening prayer in the workbook, beginning and ending with the Sign of the Cross. You may lead it yourself, pray it together as a class, or ask someone to volunteer to read it.

**MEMORY VERSE**

Read **Genesis 3:15** aloud. Talk about Adam and Eve and how sin changed the world, as described in the Student Workbook. Who is the "you" in the verse? Who are the woman and her seed? What hope do we have in a world broken by sin?

***LECTIO DIVINA* (OPTIONAL)**

Invite your students to close their eyes and open their hearts and minds to the Holy Spirit. Read **Genesis 3:15** slowly and prayerfully out loud. Pause and then read the verse again. Ask students to reflect on it silently, focusing on a specific word, phrase, or idea that seems important to them. (This will be different for different students.) What is God saying to them? After a minute or two, invite them to share their thoughts.

If you want to use a longer passage for *lectio divina*, consider one listed in "Find Out More" on page 30 of the workbook.

## REMEMBER THIS!

"I will put enmity between you and the woman, and between your seed and her seed; he shall bruise your head, and you shall bruise his heel."

—Genesis 3:15

Genesis 3 tells the story of Adam and Eve, who are freshly created, enjoying bodies without any pain or imperfection. They are in Paradise. They are in love. They are living without shame in God's presence. It can be tough to believe that, just one chapter later—after a disastrous encounter with the serpent—Adam and Eve end up hiding behind fig leaves, ashamed, blaming each other for their failures, and facing the terrible consequences of sin.

Yet, even in the distressing confusion of sin, hope remains. Adam and Eve stumbled and suffered because of their disobedience, but God already has a plan to save them: he will give his only begotten Son. The "new Adam"—Jesus—will be born of the "new Eve"—Mary—who is the crown of creation. His sacrifice and her obedience will crush the serpent. (Notice what's under Mary's foot in the image on the right.)

God's plan and promise were at work from the very beginning. Genesis 3:15 is a verse for your heart because it declares that even when suffering and brokenness seem endless, God has a plan! Trust him.

*The Immaculate Conception*
by Giovanni Battista Tiepolo

18 | ENCOUNTER

## STEP 3 Remember This!

Ask your students if they can recite the memory verse from the last class (1 Timothy 4:12). Award small prizes if you are offering them.

This lesson's memory verse is taken from the story of Adam and Eve and the Fall. To help set the context, read it aloud and talk about it together.

Invite students to open their Bibles and navigate to Genesis 3:15. Ask them to memorize the verse, and remind them that you will ask them about it at the next class. You may also (optionally) use the verse for *lectio divina*.

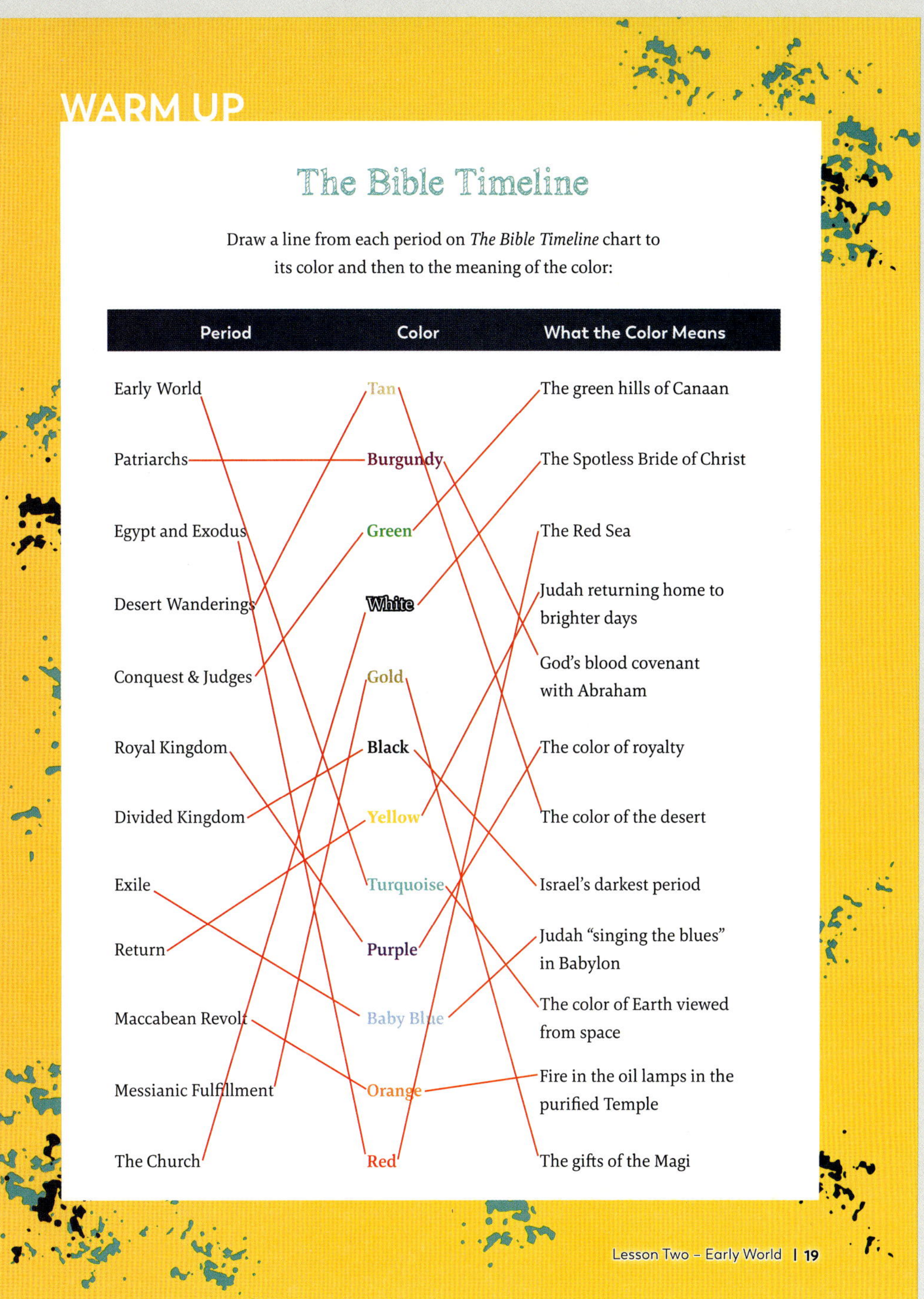

WARM UP

## The Bible Timeline

Draw a line from each period on *The Bible Timeline* chart to its color and then to the meaning of the color:

| Period | Color | What the Color Means |
|---|---|---|
| Early World | Tan | The green hills of Canaan |
| Patriarchs | Burgundy | The Spotless Bride of Christ |
| Egypt and Exodus | Green | The Red Sea |
| Desert Wanderings | White | Judah returning home to brighter days |
| Conquest & Judges | Gold | God's blood covenant with Abraham |
| Royal Kingdom | Black | The color of royalty |
| Divided Kingdom | Yellow | The color of the desert |
| Exile | Turquoise | Israel's darkest period |
| Return | Purple | Judah "singing the blues" in Babylon |
| Maccabean Revolt | Baby Blue | The color of Earth viewed from space |
| Messianic Fulfillment | Orange | Fire in the oil lamps in the purified Temple |
| The Church | Red | The gifts of the Magi |

Lesson Two – Early World | 19

## STEP 4 Warm Up: *The Bible Timeline*

Make sure your students have their workbooks, *Bible Timeline* charts, and something to write with. Go over the instructions carefully and answer questions.

When they have finished the activity, start with the Early World period and ask a student to name its color and the meaning of the color. Do this with all twelve timeline periods.

This activity is a good way to familiarize students with the *The Bible Timeline*, which they will explore throughout the *Encounter* program.

## TIME PERIOD OVERVIEW

### Early World

*Adam and Eve in the Garden of Eden* by Johann Wenzel Peter

If you miss the beginning of a story, you might seriously misunderstand the rest. Here, we aren't talking about just any story. We are talking about *the* story: who God is, who we are, how we got here, what life means, and where we're headed. We want to get the beginning of this story right.

Remember that the Bible isn't trying to explain science or math or give a detailed history. The Bible is trying to reveal our true identity and purpose. Maybe you've looked at a family photo album that does something similar: it shows you where you came from, which helps you understand your place in a story that is bigger than you are. The Bible tells us the greatest story of all—and our personal stories have a place in it.

**20** | ENCOUNTER

## Time Period Overview: Early World

Draw students' attention back to the turquoise panel of their *Bible Timeline* chart, and review the key events. This lesson focuses on the Fall. ("Find Out More" provides Scripture references for the events not covered in the overview.)

Read the "Time Period Overview" text out loud. You can select students to read different paragraphs to increase class participation. Then use "If You Ask Me" to get students talking about the Early World period.

The essential takeaway here is how the beginning of the story in Genesis sets up everything that follows in salvation history, including God's never-ending efforts to redeem us.

On your *Bible Timeline* chart, find the Early World panel (turquoise). Notice that the narrative book for the Early World is Genesis (the word means "beginning"). This lesson takes us into the book of Genesis and the beginning of our human family story. We will follow God's love as it brings everything in the universe into existence—including Adam and Eve, our first parents. We will also learn about the catastrophe of sin.

Genesis contains some wild stories: people who live for hundreds of years, a worldwide flood, murder, scandal, and more names than you could possibly remember. (Don't worry. The point isn't for you to remember them all.) Ultimately, the *Encounter* program wants to teach you about *your* story. A good look into Genesis can help you understand more about your past, your current experience, and even your family. (You think *you* have issues with your siblings? Wait until you meet Cain and Abel.) As you go deeper into the Bible, you will see your own joys and struggles reflected in the stories.

> "I praise you, for I am wondrously made. Wonderful are your works! You know me right well."
>
> —Psalm 139:14

## If You Ask Me

- Genesis means "beginning." What are some important events in your own personal Genesis story? What has happened in your life up to today that has shaped who you are?
- Adam and Eve fell into temptation and chose sin. What modern temptations do you and your friends face? How can you resist temptation and avoid falling into sin?
- One of the big stories in the early world is about Cain and Abel. Cain allowed his feelings of jealousy to grow into hatred, and Abel became his target. Can you relate to either Cain or Abel? Have you ever been jealous of a sibling? Has anyone ever been jealous of you? Have you ever taken out your feelings on someone who had done nothing wrong? What can you learn from your experiences?

Lesson Two – Early World | 21

DIVIDED KINGDOM
1 Kings 12–22
2 Kings 1–16

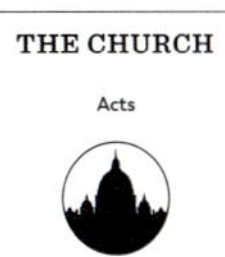

**IF YOU ASK ME**

These questions prompt students to think about their lives in the light of the Bible stories. Lead the students in discussion using one or more questions. Your students may still be getting to know one another, and some may be uncertain about speaking up in front of the whole group, so consider breaking them up into pairs or smaller groups before you go over the questions as a large group.

## Notes

### DIVE IN VIDEO

Make sure the video and sound system are already set up. Mark will ask students to read **Genesis 3:1–13** and **Genesis 4:1–10** during the presentation, so ask them to find and bookmark those passages in their Bibles now. Also consider reviewing together the "Got It?" questions on page 26 of the workbook so they can be alert to the answers as they watch.

Before playing the video, ask students to put away phones, close laptops, and avoid other distractions so they can give it their full attention. Be prepared to pause the video when prompted for Bible reading.

### DIVE IN TEXT

After watching the video, review the key words in the "Dive In" text in the workbook. Then read the text, which complements the video presentation and covers the main ideas of the lesson: Creation, Adam and Eve, and the Fall. You can read it aloud, ask students to read different paragraphs, or assign it for quiet reading.

DIVE IN VIDEO

**Early World . . . . . . . . . . . . . . . . . . . . . . . . . . Mark Hart**

"When we go way back to the beginning, we see where we all come from. And we see that we're born out of love." —Mark H.

*During the video, Mark will ask you to pause and read two Bible stories. Find and mark them in your Bibles now so that you can open to them quickly when you need to:*

- *Genesis 3:1–13, The Fall*
- *Genesis 4:1–10, Cain and Abel*

In the beginning, there was nothing ... except God. There was no air, no space, no light, no creature of any kind. Only God existed, and he existed as the **TRINITY**—one God in three Persons: Father, Son, and Holy Spirit. Within the Trinity, the Father loves the Son, and the Son loves the Father. The fruit of their love is the Holy Spirit.

God's love always overflows. So, in the nothingness, God's love overflowed into Creation. He created light first, and then he continued to create. He made the day and the night, the sky, the land and the sea, the sun and the moon, the creatures of the sea and air, and the creatures of the land.

Then, at last, God made his greatest work: a man and a woman, in his image!

**The Six Days of Creation***

| GOD BRINGS FORM | GOD FILLS THE FORM |
|---|---|
| Day 1: light and dark | Day 4: sun, moon, stars |
| Day 2: water and sky | Day 5: fish and birds |
| Day 3: land (and plants) | Day 6: land animals, human beings |

*Based on a table in *The Bible Timeline: The Story of Salvation*, by Jeff Cavins, Sarah Christmyer, and Tim Gray (West Chester, PA: Ascension, 2019), 19.

22 | ENCOUNTER

## Main Content Teaching

Now it's time to watch Mark's teaching video and read together the text in the Student Workbook. Three more "If You Ask Me" questions follow the text along with a quick "Got It?" quiz. Detailed notes on the video content start on page 34 of this Leader's Guide.

All creation came from God's goodness and shares in his goodness. "And God saw everything that he had made, and behold, it was very good" (Genesis 1:31). And then, at last, God rested—which is the reason we rest on Sunday, the Lord's Day.

The man and the woman were Adam and Eve, our first parents. God gave them a paradise, the **GARDEN OF EDEN**, as their home. Everything they needed and wanted was there, and they lived without shame or suffering, in close friendship with God and in harmony with each other.

God asked them not to eat the fruit of one tree: "Of the tree of the knowledge of good and evil you shall not eat, for in the day that you eat of it you shall die" (Genesis 2:17).

You'd think they could follow one simple rule, right? Not so much.

Satan, appearing as a cunning serpent, lied to Adam and Eve. He made them distrust God's love for them. Surrounded by God's goodness, you'd think they would ignore Satan's lies. But Adam and Eve faced what we all face: temptation. Sin seems attractive and can be hard to resist. We are tempted and tricked into doubting God's goodness and love. We are tricked with lies.

Adam and Eve disobeyed God and ate the fruit. Immediately, their sinful act filled them with guilt and shame. For the first time ever, they wanted to hide from God. When God asked them what happened, Adam blamed Eve and Eve blamed the serpent.



## Notes

Adam and Eve had to leave Paradise. They would now experience pain, struggle, suffering, and death. But why did God make them leave? Did God stop loving them? Was he punishing them?

No. Think of a parent telling a child not to touch a hot stove. If the child touches the stove anyway and is burned, the burns are not a punishment but a consequence. Similarly, it wasn't that God no longer loved Adam and Eve. Of course he loved them. But their sin had wounded them and made them afraid, distrustful, and disobedient. It had robbed them of the original justice and holiness they'd had when God created them. That is why this event is called **THE FALL**, because Adam and Eve fell away from the grace of God. Without that, they couldn't live in Paradise. It was impossible.

Adam and Eve passed on the wound of sin to their children and to everyone who came after them. Their sin is called **ORIGINAL SIN**, and it affected all creation. Because of it, we have all inherited a condition of sin, which we call the fallen state. We see its effects every day in the way we drift toward sin.



## Notes

We were created in God's image, but because of Original Sin, our desire for what is good and true is weak. We go crooked when we mean to go straight. We prefer a lie to the truth. The Church has a big word for this tendency to sin: **CONCUPISCENCE**. It's the way we imagine sin to be easy and fun—easier and more fun than doing what is truly good for us and for others. It's the way we want to rely on ourselves rather than on God.

From Genesis 4 on, we see the terrible damage concupiscence causes: lies, jealousy, betrayal, and murder. But we also see hope. God promises Adam and Eve that he will send a savior one day. And while the world waits for its **SAVIOR**, we will meet Abel and Abraham, Moses and Miriam, David and Esther, and many others—good people who show us that all is not lost for humanity.

**We Are Made in God's Image**

"So God created man in his own image, in the image of God he created him; male and female he created them. And God blessed them, and God said to them, 'Be fruitful and multiply, and fill the earth and subdue it; and have dominion over the fish of the sea and over the birds of the air and over every living thing that moves upon the earth. ... And God saw everything that he had made, and behold, it was very good.'"

—Genesis 1:27–28, 31

## If You Ask Me

- List some details that stand out to you from the Creation story in Genesis. Why do you think those details stay with you? What about them is important to you?
- Can you think of a time when you gave in to a temptation that had negative consequences? What was that like?
- Has a consequence ever helped you in the long run? What did you learn from it?



**IF YOU ASK ME**

Use these open-ended questions about temptation and consequences to spark conversation and encourage students to think about how the lesson applies to their daily lives. To help students continue to get to know one another, consider having them sit in small groups. Lead them in small group discussion and, if time permits, answer their spontaneous questions.

**Notes**

1. **Human beings arrived on the __________ day of creation.**
   a. sixth
   b. fifth
   c. first
   d. seventh

2. **God asked Adam and Eve not to eat the fruit to __________.**
   a. control and limit them
   b. show his power over everything
   c. protect them
   d. test whether they were good

3. **Sin tricks us into __________.**
   a. doubting God's love
   b. thinking we know better than God what is good for us
   c. doubting God's goodness
   d. all of the above



**GOT IT?**

Ask students to complete the multiple-choice questions in the Student Workbook, and review the answers together.

## Notes

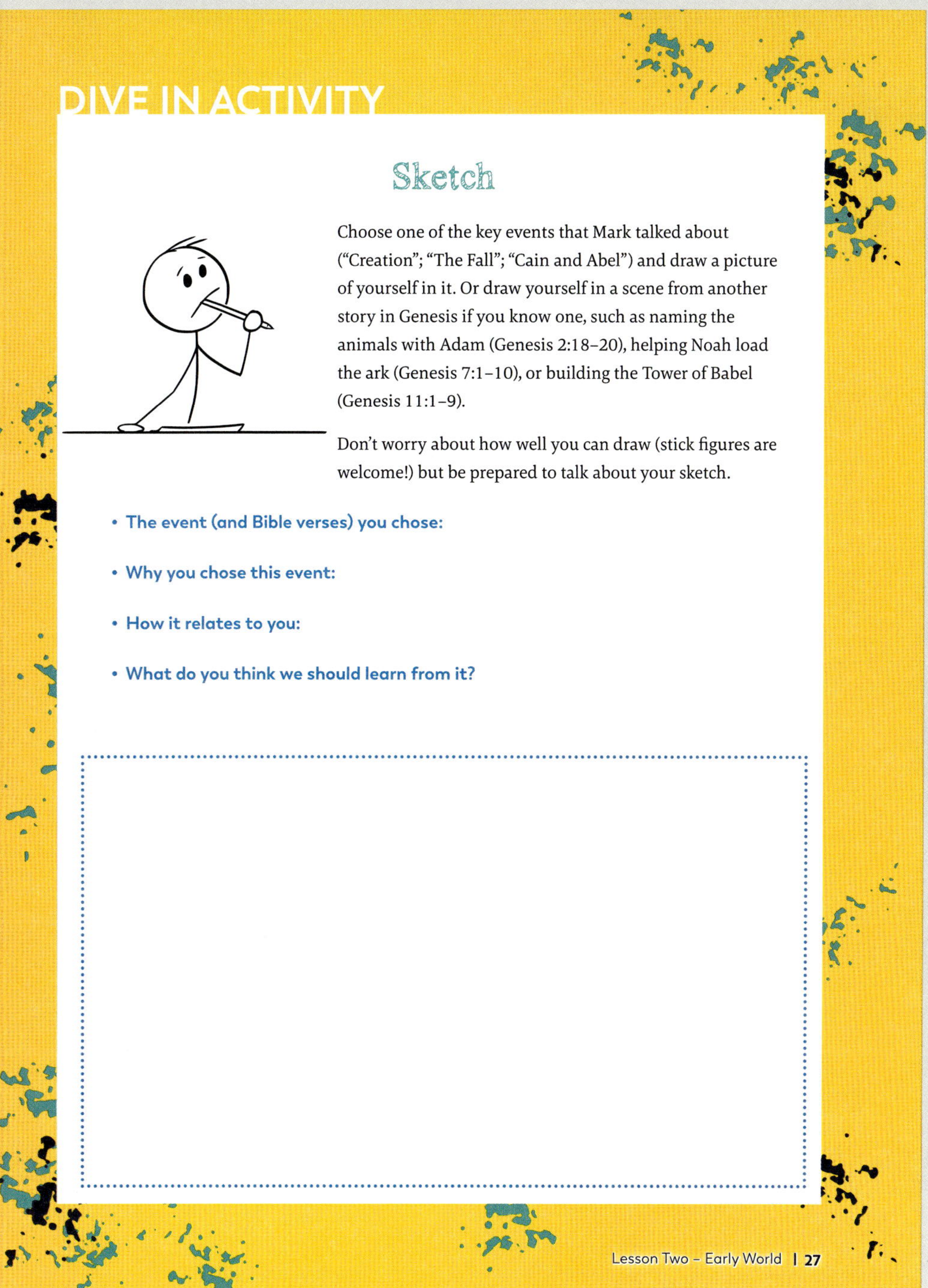

# DIVE IN ACTIVITY

## Sketch

Choose one of the key events that Mark talked about ("Creation"; "The Fall"; "Cain and Abel") and draw a picture of yourself in it. Or draw yourself in a scene from another story in Genesis if you know one, such as naming the animals with Adam (Genesis 2:18–20), helping Noah load the ark (Genesis 7:1–10), or building the Tower of Babel (Genesis 11:1–9).

Don't worry about how well you can draw (stick figures are welcome!) but be prepared to talk about your sketch.

- **The event (and Bible verses) you chose:**
- **Why you chose this event:**
- **How it relates to you:**
- **What do you think we should learn from it?**

Lesson Two – Early World | 27

**SKETCH**

Drawing comes more naturally to some people than others, so reassure students that this activity isn't about artistic skill. It's about making an imaginative, personal connection with some key events in Scripture.

Brainstorm with students about the Early World event they might choose. Encourage them to talk about how the events relate to them.

When your students have finished, ask them to describe the event they chose and why they chose it. If there's time, talk together about what it can teach us.

## STEP 7 Dive In Activity

This activity offers a hands-on application of the lesson's main ideas and themes. Make sure the group has drawing paper and colored pencils or markers. Go over the instructions carefully and answer any questions.

BIBLICAL CHARACTER VIDEO

**Abel** . . . . . . . . . . . . . . . . . . . . . . . . . . . . . . **Tanner Kalina**

"The Lord had regard for Abel and his offering,
but for Cain and his offering he had no regard." —Genesis 4:4–5

**BIBLICAL CHARACTER VIDEO**

As before, ask students to put away phones, close laptops, and avoid other distractions so that they can give their full attention to the video presentation. Ask students to pay special attention to Tanner's experience. What do Tanner's experience and the story of Abel and his brother teach us about what God wants from us?

**BIBLICAL CHARACTER PROFILE**

Read the text about Abel and his brother in the workbook. You can select students to read different paragraphs aloud to increase class participation. Focus on the importance of self-giving.

### BIBLICAL CHARACTER PROFILE

## Cain and Abel

Tanner shared his experience of competing to be the starting shortstop on the varsity baseball team. He and his competitor were equal in skill and ability in almost every way except for one thing: Tanner was the first on and last off the field. He was passionate about playing. He was hungry for victory and excellence. He was all in.

Tanner's story gives us insight into Cain and Abel, the brothers in Genesis 4. Abel offers God the firstlings of his flock, including "the fatty portions"—the most delicious parts—while Cain offers God just a portion of his harvest. God accepts Abel's offering, but not Cain's.

Is the point that God has food preferences? No. The Bible doesn't tell us exactly why Abel's sacrifice is more pleasing to God, but it suggests that Abel gives God his best, while Cain does not. Abel gives from his heart. He does not hold back. He is invested, dialed in, and committed.

God challenged Cain to give more of himself, saying, "If you do well, will you not be accepted?" (Genesis 4:7). But instead of trying to do better, Cain gave in to his anger and jealousy and murdered his brother.

## Biblical Character Profile: CAIN AND ABEL

This step features a short video by Tanner Kalina about Cain and Abel, a read-aloud profile, and an exercise for students to do during class or at home.

After the video, review the video notes on page 36 of the Leader's Guide and ask students about specific points of interest. Then read the "Cain and Abel" profile text aloud, and give your students time to do the "All In" exercise.

Remember that the Bible teaches us a lot about our own stories. You probably aren't a shepherd like Abel. You may or may not play baseball like Tanner. But you have the same choice: to give with passion or to do only the minimum. This choice is most important in your relationship with God, but it also matters at school, at home, and everywhere else.

Abel shows us what God really wants from us: our hearts. Are we giving God our best? Are we really showing up for our family and friends? Let's live, pray, and really invest ourselves in self-offering like Abel.

**BIBLICAL CHARACTER EXERCISE**

"All In" asks students to make deeper commitments to their faith.

Make sure everyone has a *Bible Timeline* chart, workbook, Bible, and something to write with. Invite them to find Cain and Abel on the chart. Then navigate to Genesis 4:1–16 and read the story.

Go over the exercise prompts in the workbook and answer students' questions. Brainstorm with them about areas where they can make real commitments.

When they have finished writing, invite them to share their responses. Ask them to think about people in their lives who will help them commit and hold them accountable.

## All In

Find Cain and Abel on your *Bible Timeline* chart, and then read their story in **Genesis 4:1–16**.

Tanner's baseball story—which is really about Abel's sacrifice—reminds us that God wants us to be all in. He wants us to give from our hearts. It can be tempting to do the minimum in school, in sports, in our activities, and in our faith. But you're made for more than the minimum.

In what areas of your faith can you commit to going all in? Maybe you can pay better attention at Sunday Mass. Maybe you can offer a certain prayer as soon as you wake up. Maybe you can commit to going to Confession once a month. What are three things you can do to really go all in?

1. ______________________________

2. ______________________________

3. ______________________________

29

**Notes**

______________________________

______________________________

______________________________

______________________________

______________________________

______________________________

______________________________

### LIVING IT OUT

Ask students how last week's "Living It Out" activities went. Then, after reading the "Living It Out" section for this week, encourage them to choose a new activity and turn it into a personal action plan.

For this lesson, let students know when Confession is available at your parish. An examination of conscience for young people is available in "Further Resources," on page 186 in this guide.

### FAMILY CATECHESIS

"Living It Out" provides a good opportunity for family catechesis. Remind students and parents that the Student Workbook is available on Thinkific, and consider asking parents to review this lesson's "Living It Out" activities so they can support their child during the week.

Specifically, parents can help their children examine their consciences and make time to go to Confession. Even better, parents can go to Confession at the same time! Parents' support and participation make a crucial difference as their children learn to live the Faith.

### Find Out More

The Flood .......... Genesis 6–9

People Scattered at the Tower of Babel .......... Genesis 11:1–9

**Early World**

Your *Bible Timeline* chart mentions two more Early World stories, which you might know already: the story of Noah's ark ("The Flood") and a story about what happened when people tried to build a tower to heaven.

## Living It Out

The stories of Adam and Eve and of Cain and Abel show us what sin looked like from the very beginning. Sin is a trick and a lie every time. If we want to be truly free and happy, we must avoid sin. When we sin, we can ask God to heal us and help us do better in the future.

- At bedtime, examine your conscience for the day. Think about the day: what you did, what you said, the interactions you had with others. Is there anything good from the day that you wish to offer back to God in thanksgiving? Is there anything you should not have done or could have done better? Be honest with yourself and ask God to help you tomorrow.
- Go to Confession. This sacrament is truly amazing: God never gets tired of forgiving us when we go to him. If you are nervous, ask a family member or friend to go with you. In Confession, through the sacrament of the priesthood, you are talking to the priest who is representing Jesus—and Jesus is thrilled that you are there! (To help yourself prepare for Confession, you can use the **Examination of Conscience for Middle School** in the back of your workbook, starting on p. 138.)
- Sharing our lives makes us stronger in faith. Ask a family member or friend to be your faith partner. Once a week, talk about how you're doing in your faith life.

30 I ENCOUNTER

## Find Out More & Living It Out

For students who are interested and like to read, mention the extra Early World stories in "Find Out More" for them to read at home. You may also consider using one of these passages for *lectio divina*.

The "Living It Out" activities are specially designed to be done at home. Read the workbook text together to give your students ideas for putting what they have learned into practice. Remind them that you will check in with them the next time you meet to see how they are doing.

## WORDPLAY

**concupiscence**: The desire or inclination to commit sin.

**Fall, the**: The event in Genesis when Adam and Eve disobeyed God and "fell" from grace.

**Garden of Eden**: Also called "Paradise." God made this special place for Adam and Eve to live in before the Fall.

**Original Sin**: The "stain" of sin we inherited from Adam and Eve, which means we are born in a "state of sin" and require redemption.

**Savior**: Jesus Christ, the one who delivers us from the consequences of sin and death.

**Trinity**: The three distinct Persons who make up the single divine nature of God: the Father, the Son, and the Holy Spirit.

## CLOSING PRAYER

"Lord God, we see our story in the story of Genesis. From the beginning, you loved us and wanted to be with us. When we chose sin, you still loved us and opened the way back to you. Help us to see how our own story is in the story of Scripture. As we study your Word, show us how to grow, trust, and make our way back to you. Open our eyes and ears to see and hear what you want to reveal. In Jesus' name, we pray. Amen."

Lesson Two – Early World | 31

## Closing Prayer

Remind students of their homework assignments. Then lead the class in the closing prayer. Begin and end the prayer with the Sign of the Cross.

**THIS WEEK'S HOMEWORK**

1. Memorize the memory verse: Genesis 3:15
2. Do your "Living It Out" assignment.
3. In Lesson Three, students will learn about patriarchs, matriarchs, and family trees. Ask them to find time this week to ask their parents about their family history: stories about their grandparents, who their great-grandparents were, where their ancestors came from, and so on.
4. Students will also learn about names and what they mean in Lesson Three. Ask them to find out what their own names mean and whether they were named for someone in their family.

# Lesson Three

## PATRIARCHS – EGYPT

### LESSON OVERVIEW

Lesson Three introduces students to the story of the Patriarchs, beginning with Abraham and continuing through Isaac, Jacob, and Jacob's sons. These narratives help us understand how God drew a people to himself, beginning with the promises he made to Abraham.

Students will see how faith in God can lead us into unexpected adventures that figure into the bigger plan that he has for us (and sometimes for our descendants). This lesson focuses on a few key narrative events that will be relatable to middle schoolers and their personal challenges. This lesson will also give them a memorable way to envision the time of the Patriarchs as they grow in their understanding of salvation history in years to come.

Finally, this lesson will introduce Moses and set the stage for the larger story of the Exodus, which is so important for understanding who Jesus is and what he came to do in the "New Exodus" so many generations later.

### LESSON OBJECTIVES

Students will

- **Explore** the narrative from the lives of the Patriarchs to Moses.
- **Learn** the names and stories of the key figures of this period of salvation history.
- **Understand** what a covenant is and the significance of God's covenant with Abraham.
- **Make real-life connections** between the descendants of the Patriarchs and the importance of their own families.
- **Appreciate** the relevance of Miriam's story in their own lives.

### VIDEO LESSON NOTES

#### DIVE IN VIDEO – **PATRIARCHS AND EGYPT** – MARK HART

Mark will prompt you to pause the video to read these passages:

**Genesis 45:1–10, Joseph Makes Himself Known to His Brothers**

**Exodus 3:2–14, Moses and the Burning Bush**

We saw how, over and over again, the people forgot about God and turned prideful, and God humbled them. But God never breaks his promises.

## The Patriarchs: Abraham and the Twelve Tribes

- The story picks up in Genesis 12 when God makes a covenant with a holy, righteous man named Abraham.
- Abraham is the first of the Patriarchs. *Patriarch* means "father figure." In his covenant with Abraham, God promises to give Abraham land and many descendants.
- Even though Abraham and his wife are very old, Sarah gives birth to Isaac. Then Isaac marries and has two sons. Later, Isaac's younger son, Jacob (who gets his name changed by God to Israel), has twelve sons. Ten of them (along with two of Jacob's grandsons) become heads of the twelve tribes of Israel, the twelve groups that make up the Jewish nation.
- God's family starts to grow, and the covenant starts to grow. Here we pick up the story again with one of Jacob's twelve sons, Joseph. "What a dreamer, that kid," Mark says.

## Joseph

- Joseph is Isaac's second youngest son and his father's favorite. He dreams that one day his brothers will all bow down to him, and he tells them the dream. Jealous and angry, they throw Joseph into a pit and sell him into slavery in Egypt. After many trials over many years, he becomes a high-ranking official in Egypt—Pharaoh's right-hand man.
- Drought strikes the whole land, and Joseph's brothers come to Egypt to buy grain from Pharaoh. They end up in the royal court, standing before Joseph, but they don't recognize him. He recognizes them, but he doesn't say anything. As in his dream from long ago, they bow down to him.
- Instead of taking revenge, Joseph provides them with grain. Eventually, he tells them who he is and offers them forgiveness.

## Slavery in Egypt

- The brothers and their families (all the Israelites) move to Egypt. Their numbers grow and grow. Joseph dies, and eventually, a less-friendly pharaoh comes to power. He enslaves the Israelites. Then he gets paranoid about how many Israelites there are, and he orders the murder of all male Israelite babies.
- At this time, a new hero arrives: Moses. Moses is an Israelite, born to slaves in Egypt. His mother hides him (so he won't be killed) by putting him in a wicker basket and floating him down the Nile River. He gets picked up by Pharaoh's daughter and raised as part of the Egyptian royal family. He's living the good life until one day he kills an Egyptian who is mistreating an Israelite slave. Moses flees into the wilderness.

## Moses Meets God

- Moses starts a new life as a shepherd. One day he comes across a miraculous sight: a bush on fire that is not consumed. Moses is standing before the God of the Universe. God tells him to take off his shoes—because Moses is on holy ground. God also tells him that he has heard the cry of his people. God wants Moses to tell Pharaoh to let the people go. Moses resists and makes excuses, but God insists.

- Moses asks God for his name, and God says his name is "I AM WHO I AM." This exchange is important. Relationships start with the exchange of names. By telling Moses his name, God is showing him that he wants to establish a relationship with him.
- Even though the Israelites are enslaved in Egypt, God has a plan, and it's just getting started.

### BIBLICAL CHARACTER VIDEO – **MIRIAM** – ASHLEY HINOJOSA

Ashley tells us that when she was young, she was always comparing herself to her older brother. Everything seemed easier for him. He was good at school, had a ton of friends, and got to do things and go places she couldn't. He was a talented musician, too. She spent many years wanting to be like him and trying to be someone she wasn't. Comparing herself to her brother always made her feel disappointed and insecure.

Ashley tells us about Miriam the prophet. Miriam was the sister of two men with great callings—Moses and Aaron—but there is another way to see her. She is introduced in Exodus 15 as a prophet in her own right. She has her own story. She has her own role to play. Miriam led the Israelite women in praising God after they left Egypt. We can still read her song of praise thousands of years later!

Who are you? What are you being called to? We don't discover the answers by comparing ourselves to others but by listening to God's voice and answering his call.

## BEFORE- AND AFTER-CLASS REMINDERS

### Before students arrive:

Make sure you have all the supplies needed for the lesson, such as Student Workbooks, Bibles, copies of *The Bible Timeline* chart, materials for activities, paper, and pens or pencils.

If you are handing out Bibles, place one at each student's place.

Review the video notes above and take note of anything you would like to mention to the class before they watch the video presentations.

Set up the equipment for the video presentations and queue the first video so that it is ready to play.

### After class:

Follow up with students who missed the lesson.

Continue to learn your students' names.

## NOTES

**WELCOME**

Consider using ice-breaker questions to engage students when they arrive and help them get comfortable. You can ask about an upcoming event they are excited about, for example, or who their favorite superhero is and why.

# Lesson Three

## Patriarchs – Egypt

PATRIARCHS GENESIS 12–50 

EGYPT EXODUS 1–3

32 | ENCOUNTER

## STEP 1 Welcome – The Big Picture

Greet students by name as they arrive, and take attendance so that you can follow up later with students who are absent. When everyone has settled, read "The Big Picture" text together.

## The Big Picture

God is truth, so he never lies. He honors his covenants. He never breaks his promises. But his timing doesn't always fit our desires or expectations. We often look for an instant result, not realizing that God usually plays the long game when carrying out his work. He always comes through—but it's on his perfect timetable, not ours.

And sometimes God makes really interesting choices in forming his team. He picks the least likely players and still wins, every single time. He levels up with old game controllers. He creates masterpieces with broken crayons.

**THE BIG PICTURE**

"The Big Picture" introduces the major ideas of this lesson: the Patriarchs, the Israelites in Egypt, and God's call to Moses. It will be helpful to bookmark Genesis 12, Genesis 45, Exodus 3, and Exodus 15 for this lesson. Ask students to bookmark their Bibles as you are bookmarking yours.

### OPENING PRAYER

"Lord God, from the beginning you took our broken world and broken hearts into your fatherly heart and worked wonders. You drew a family together, slowly mended their brokenness, and worked through even their worst mistakes and failures. As we learn the story of your people, show us how you want to do the same in our personal stories. Give us great trust, open hearts, and belief in your promise. In Jesus' name, we pray. Amen."

Lesson Three – Patriarchs – Egypt | 33

Ask your students to settle and quiet their minds before you pray. Invite them to share personal intentions.

Pray the opening prayer in the Student Workbook, beginning and ending with the Sign of the Cross. You may lead it yourself, pray it together as a class, or ask a volunteer to read it.

**MEMORY VERSE**

Read **Genesis 12:3** aloud. Who is the "you" in this verse? Talk about God's promises to Abram and Sarai (who became Abraham and Sarah), as described in the Student Workbook. Why is it surprising that God promised them many descendants?

***LECTIO DIVINA*** **(OPTIONAL)**

Invite your students to close their eyes and open their hearts and minds to the Holy Spirit. Read **Genesis 12:3** slowly and prayerfully out loud. Pause and then read the verse again. Ask students to reflect on it silently, focusing on a specific word, phrase, or idea that seems important to them. What is God saying to them in this verse? After a minute or two, invite them to share their thoughts.

If you want to use a longer passage for *lectio divina*, consider one listed in "Find Out More" on page 46 of the workbook.

## REMEMBER THIS!

"By you all the families of the earth shall bless themselves."

—Genesis 12:3

SARAH

These words are God's first promise to Abram. God also promised to give Abram and his wife, Sarai, many descendants, even though they were already old—too old to have children. God gave them new names to confirm his promise. To Abram he gave the name Abraham, meaning "father of many nations," and to Sarai he gave the name Sarah, meaning "mother of many nations." Over many generations, God fulfilled all his promises to them.

34 | ENCOUNTER

## Remember This!

Ask "Who can recite the memory verse from the last class?" (It's Genesis 3:15.) Award small prizes if you are offering them.

This lesson's memory verse is God's first promise to Abram (who became Abraham!). The verse is written in their workbooks, but you may want to ask students to open their Bibles and navigate to Genesis 12:3. Ask them to memorize the verse, and remind them that you will ask them about it at the next class. You may also (optionally) use the verse for *lectio divina*.

## WARM UP

### Coats

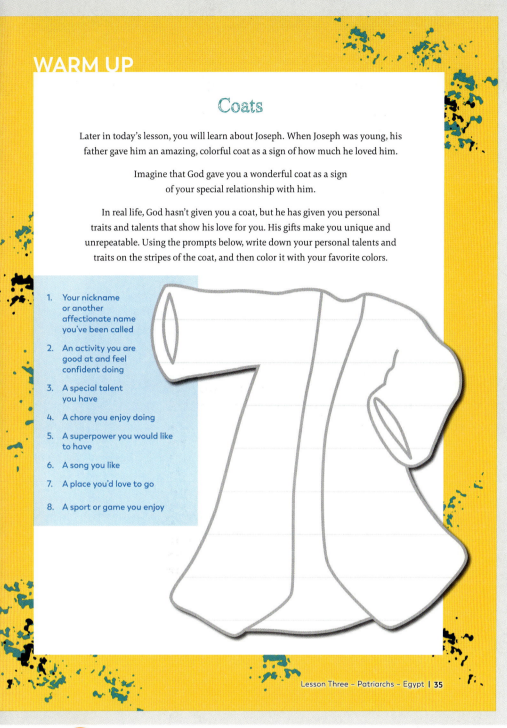

Later in today's lesson, you will learn about Joseph. When Joseph was young, his father gave him an amazing, colorful coat as a sign of how much he loved him.

Imagine that God gave you a wonderful coat as a sign of your special relationship with him.

In real life, God hasn't given you a coat, but he has given you personal traits and talents that show his love for you. His gifts make you unique and unrepeatable. Using the prompts below, write down your personal talents and traits on the stripes of the coat, and then color it with your favorite colors.

1. Your nickname or another affectionate name you've been called
2. An activity you are good at and feel confident doing
3. A special talent you have
4. A chore you enjoy doing
5. A superpower you would like to have
6. A song you like
7. A place you'd love to go
8. A sport or game you enjoy

Lesson Three – Patriarchs – Egypt | 35

## STEP 4 Warm Up: *Coats*

Joseph is one of the biblical characters students will meet today. His story is a popular one, and some of them may have already heard or read about his coat of many colors. This activity is based on the idea of being, like Joseph, a valued child with a wonderful coat.

Make sure your students have their workbooks and something to color with. Go over the instructions in the workbook and answer questions. Brainstorm possible answers to the numbered prompts, and encourage students to use their favorite colors for their coats.

When they have finished, invite them to share their coats and their answers to the prompts.

## TIME PERIOD OVERVIEW

### Patriarchs and Egypt

*Abraham's Journey from Ur to Canaan by Jozsef Molnar*

Look on your *Bible Timeline* chart and find the **Patriarchs** period (burgundy) and Egypt, the first part of the **Egypt and Exodus** period (red). The narrative books for these periods are Genesis and Exodus.

These periods show how God gathered a people to himself and freed them so they could know him and **WORSHIP** him. It begins with a **COVENANT** that God made with Abraham. In his covenants, God promises to be with us. He reminds us that he isn't just watching us from far away without caring. Covenants are God's solemn promises that unite us with him, as a family. Sometimes they include promises we make to him.

## Time Period Overview: Patriarchs and Egypt

Invite students to take out their *Bible Timeline* charts and open them to the burgundy and red period panels. Review together the key events and people of these periods and the approximate dates in history to give additional context to the lesson. Notice especially the covenant with Abraham. The world power at this time is still Egypt.

In their workbooks, review the key words in the "Time Period Overview" text and then read the text aloud. To increase class participation, you could select students to read different paragraphs.

The key takeaway here is the concept of covenant—a promise between God and man. God always lives up to his end of the bargain. He never breaks his promises.

What a story! A very old man without any children leaves his own people and makes a dangerous journey to the land of Canaan (hundreds of miles away!) to settle among strangers. Why? Because God asks him to. Abraham trusts God, and he trusts God's promises: land, more descendants than there are stars, and the blessing of all the families on earth.

The covenant passed from Abraham to his son Isaac, and then to his grandson Jacob. One night when Jacob was grown, he wrestled with an angel. They wrestled all night, and in the morning God changed his name to Israel ("wrestled with God") and blessed him. Jacob became the father of the twelve tribes of Israel.

These men—Abraham, Isaac, and Jacob—are known as the **PATRIARCHS**. They are the father figures of both **JEWS** (also called **ISRAELITES**) and **CHRISTIANS**.

One of Jacob's sons was Joseph, whose beautiful coat we mentioned earlier. Joseph's brothers sold him into slavery (really!). But after many adventures, Joseph became a powerful figure in Egypt. He forgave his brothers, and he brought them and their families to live in Egypt during a famine, where they had plenty of food.

Later, another Egyptian pharaoh enslaved Joseph's descendants. Now they were trapped in a land that wasn't their own among people who worshiped false gods. They had lost their identity, their community, and their friendship with God. That's when God called Moses to lead them out of Egypt to freedom, to the land he had promised Abraham: the **PROMISED LAND**.

The story is really about God's plan and God's initiative. You'll notice that Abraham's adventures weren't Abraham's idea; Joseph's adventures weren't Joseph's idea; Moses' adventures weren't his idea, either. Their adventures were God's idea. God chose Abraham, Joseph, and Moses for *his* plan: to bless his people there, here, and ultimately, through the Church, everywhere in the world.

## If You Ask Me

- Who are the patriarchs and matriarchs in your family? What do you know about your grandparents (or great-grandparents and generations beyond)? Are any of your ancestors from places far away from where you live now?
- What are your family's most important places? Where does your family gather for important moments, vacations, or traditions? What do you like about these places?



DIVIDED KINGDOM
1 Kings 12–22
2 Kings 1–16

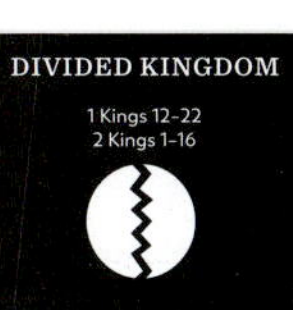

EXILE
2 Kings 17–25

RETURN
Ezra
Nehemiah

MACCABEAN REVOLT
1 Maccabees

MESSIANIC FULFILLMENT
Luke

THE CHURCH
Acts

**IF YOU ASK ME**

These questions are about students' family stories. Consider grouping students in pairs or smaller groups to talk over their answers before you gather as a larger group. To begin the large group discussion, invite students to share surprising or interesting facts they learned about their family history.

## Notes

**DIVE IN VIDEO**

Make sure the video and sound system are set up. Mark will ask students to read **Genesis 45:1–10** and **Genesis 3:2–14** during the presentation, so ask them to find and bookmark those passages in their Bibles before they watch the video. Consider reviewing the "Got It?" questions together (on page 42 of the workbook) so they can be alert to the answers.

Before you play the video, ask students to put away phones, close laptops, and avoid other distractions so they can give it their full attention. Be prepared to pause the video when prompted for Bible reading.

**DIVE IN TEXT**

After the video, review the key words in the "Dive In" text. Then read the text, which complements the video presentation and covers the subject of Abraham's family tree. You can read it aloud, ask students to read different paragraphs, or assign it for quiet reading.

DIVE IN VIDEO

**Patriarchs and Egypt . . . . . . . . . . . . . . . . . . . . .Mark Hart**

"Taking revenge is easy. ... Rising above all that to show mercy, that's true strength." —Mark H.

*During the video, Mark will ask you to pause and read two Bible stories. Find and mark them in your Bibles now so that you can open to them quickly when you need to:*

- *Genesis 45:1–10, Joseph Makes Himself Known to His Brothers*
- *Exodus 3:2–14, Moses and the Burning Bush*

## DIVE IN

The Patriarchs, whose stories aren't so different from our own, were part of a greater plan that was ultimately fulfilled in Jesus. We've seen how, over time, God was making himself known to more and more people—first to Adam and Eve; later to Abraham, Isaac, and Jacob; and then to the families of Jacob's sons, the twelve tribes of Israel.

A family tree helps us keep the story straight. One of God's promises to Abraham was that he would have more descendants than there are stars in the sky. Look at Abraham's family tree on pages 40–41. You can see already how it grows with each generation. Notice especially the long row of Jacob's twelve sons. All of them, except Reuben and Joseph, became heads of the tribes (Reuben lost his share, and Joseph received a double share that went to his two sons, Ephraim and Manasseh). The twelve tribes were named for Jacob's sons or grandsons: Simeon, Levi, Judah, Dan, Naphtali, Gad, Asher, Issachar, Zebulun, Benjamin, Ephraim, and Manasseh.

Notice too, below them, that Moses, Aaron, and Miriam are Levites, members of the priestly tribe of Levi's descendants.

"You shall be my people, and I will be your God."

—Jeremiah 30:22

38 | ENCOUNTER

STEP 6 **Main Content Teaching**

This step involves watching Mark's teaching video and reading the text in the Student Workbook together. Three more "If You Ask Me" questions follow the text along with a quick "Got It?" quiz. Detailed notes on the video content start on page 54 of this Leader's Guide.

In the Gospels, Matthew traces Jesus' ancestry back to Abraham. Luke traces it even further, all the way back to Adam. Don't worry about memorizing every detail or branch on that tree. Just become familiar with the overall picture so that you can follow the greater plan.

The family tree helps us visualize the key figures in Mark's tour through the time periods so we can see how God began fulfilling his promises to Abraham in a growing family. It also helps us see how, when the Israelites became enslaved in Egypt, God set in motion the plan for their freedom.

## If You Ask Me

- Names are important to God. As Mark says, that's where a relationship starts—with learning someone's name. Why do you think God changed the names of Abraham, Sarah, and Israel? What does your name mean?
- Think about God's promise to give Abraham many descendants. How does the family tree above show how God fulfilled it?
- Remember that all events of salvation history ultimately lead to Jesus. What traits does Moses have in common with Jesus?



**IF YOU ASK ME**

These questions are about names and generations of family. You can cover them in a class discussion or in small groups with class discussion to follow. To help students transition into large group discussion, invite them to share the meaning of their own names. Lead the discussion and, if time permits, answer their spontaneous questions about what they're learning.

**Notes**

# ABRAHAM'S FAMILY TREE

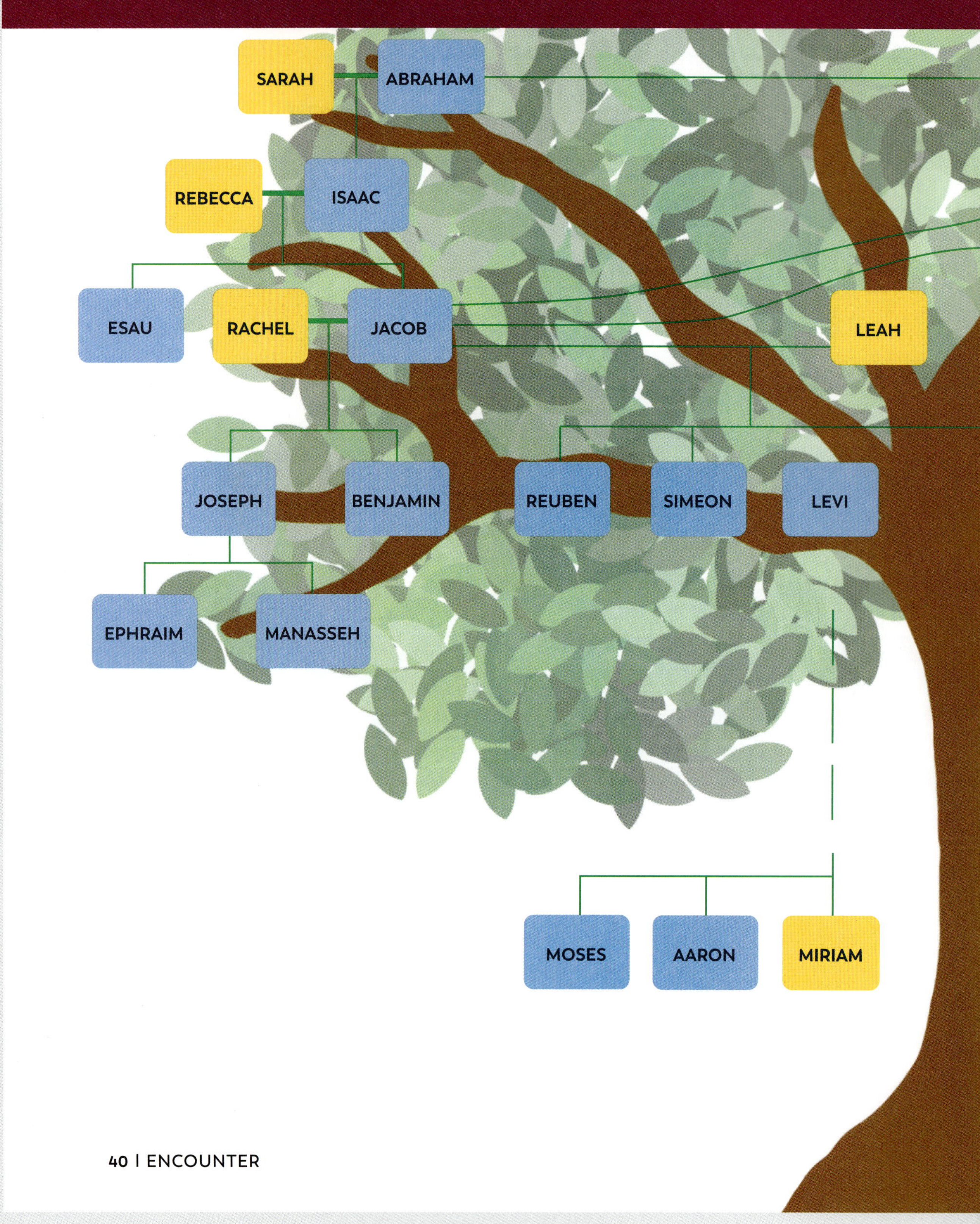

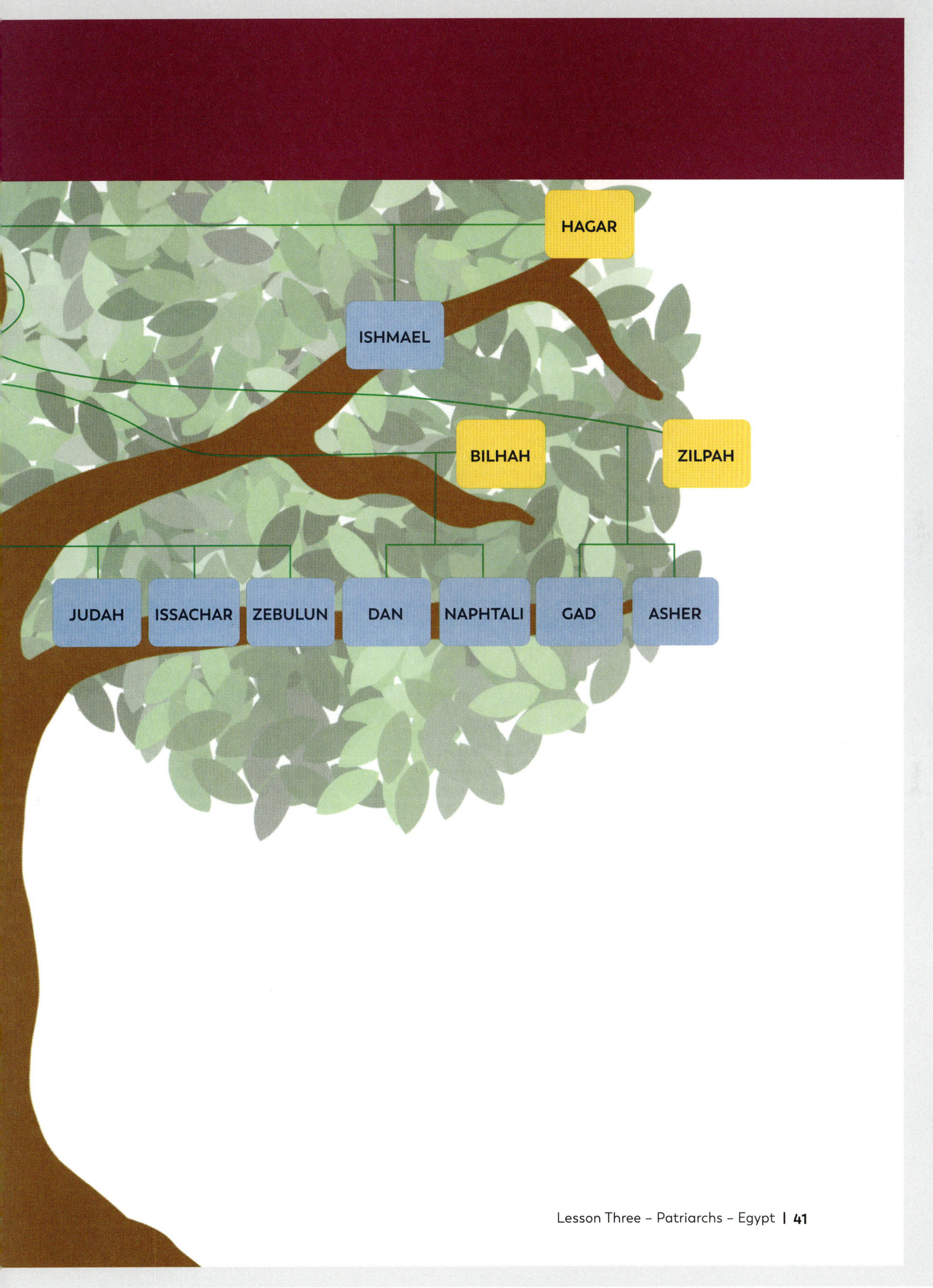
HAGAR
ISHMAEL
BILHAH
ZILPAH
JUDAH
ISSACHAR
ZEBULUN
DAN
NAPHTALI
GAD
ASHER
Lesson Three – Patriarchs – Egypt | 41

# Got It

1. **A patriarch is __________.**

   a. a priest

   b. a father figure or leader of a family or tribe

   c. a prophet

2. **Abraham, Isaac, and Jacob are the ancestors of __________.**

   a. everyone in the world

   b. Matthew and Luke, the Gospel writers

   c. Jesus

3. **The family tree of Genesis is not just a family history. It also shows the history of __________.**

   a. God's plan to save us

   b. the Egyptian pyramids

   c. the whole ancient world



**GOT IT?**

Ask students to complete the multiple-choice questions in the workbook, and review the answers together.

As an extra-credit question, consider asking "What is a mother figure or leader called?"

## Notes

## DIVE IN ACTIVITY

### Promise

Choose a verse from Genesis that you find meaningful—
one of the verses below or another that strikes you:

- Genesis 1:1
- Genesis 1:3-4
- Genesis 1:27
- Genesis 1:31
- Genesis 4:6-7
- Genesis 12:3
- Genesis 50:20

How does the verse you chose remind you of God's love and promise? Write your verse below and then decorate it. If you like, take a picture of it, print it, and hang it where you can see it every day.

*Verse:*



**PROMISE**

Before class, consider finding examples of Scripture verses written in calligraphy or artistic handwriting. Or consider doing the activity ahead of time to share as an example.

Make sure the group has what they need to decorate their verses in their workbooks. Go over the instructions and answer questions. Then look up the verses together and read them aloud. Remind students that they may choose another verse if they wish.

When they have finished writing and decorating their verses, ask students to share the verse they chose and why they chose it.

## Dive In Activity

This activity offers a hands-on application of the lesson's main ideas and themes. Make sure everyone has a Bible, their workbook, and colored pencils or markers. Go over the instructions carefully and answer students' questions.

BIBLICAL CHARACTER VIDEO

**Miriam . . . . . . . . . . . . . . . . . . . . . . . . . . Ashley Hinojosa**

"And Miriam sang to them." —Exodus 15:21

### BIBLICAL CHARACTER VIDEO

As before, ask students to put away phones, close laptops, and avoid other distractions so that they can give their full attention to the video presentation. Ask them to pay special attention to Ashley's experience. What do Ashley and Miriam teach us about comparing ourselves to others?

### BIBLICAL CHARACTER PROFILE

Read the text about Miriam in the workbook. You could select students to read different paragraphs aloud to increase class participation.

## BIBLICAL CHARACTER PROFILE

# Miriam

Ashley Hinojosa struggled with comparing herself to her older brother. He had more friends than she did, played multiple instruments, and was always first chair in the band. Ashley was in the band, too, but she was never first chair. Because he was older, he got to sit in the front seat of the car and was invited to do things that she couldn't. He seemed to know more, do more, and get noticed more.

Comparing herself to her brother was always a source of disappointment and insecurity for Ashley. But then she discovered that the points of comparison weren't the full truth about who she was or her abilities. She came to see that she was special in her own ways.

Enter Miriam the prophet. Miriam was the sister of two men with great callings—Moses and Aaron—but she is introduced in Exodus 15 as a prophet in her own right.

We don't know many details of Miriam's life, but her story is her own. After the Israelites crossed the Red Sea on dry land, Miriam led all the Israelite women in thanksgiving and song. We know that she later had

44 | ENCOUNTER

## STEP 8 Biblical Character Profile: MIRIAM

This step features a short video by Ashley Hinojosa, a read-aloud profile of Miriam, and an exercise for students to do during class or at home.

After you play the video, review the video notes on page 56 of the Leader's Guide and ask students about specific points of interest. Then read the profile text aloud, and give your students time to do the exercise, "Loved, Not Compared."

leprosy but was cured of it, and she died before the Israelites reached the Promised Land.

Miriam's story reminds us to stop comparing ourselves to other people. Sometimes we think we're better than someone else; on the flip side, we often think we don't measure up. Either way, the comparison steals our joy and sense of belonging.

So, who are you? What are you being called to do? You won't discover the answers by comparing yourself to others. Only by listening to God's voice and answering his call can you discover who you really are in his eyes.

## Loved, Not Compared

Find Miriam on your *Bible Timeline* chart. Which period is she in? Now read about her in **Exodus 15:19–21**.

Comparing ourselves to others usually makes us feel bad about ourselves and blocks us from seeing the wonderful way God has made us. Remember that when God looks at you, he doesn't compare you to another person. He loves you for being *you*.

Ask your family and friends to name several things they love about you, then write down their responses below. You will begin to get just a glimpse into God's great love for you.

__________________________________________

__________________________________________

__________________________________________

__________________________________________

__________________________________________

__________________________________________

45

### BIBLICAL CHARACTER EXERCISE

"Loved, Not Compared" invites students to reflect on the importance of being the people God made them to be and not comparing themselves to others. It is designed to be done at home, but you can get started in class.

Make sure everyone has their *Bible Timeline* chart and invite them to find Miriam on it. Then navigate to Exodus 15:19–21 in the Bible and read it aloud. Talk about the difference for Miriam between being Moses' sister and being a prophet and leader in her own right. Ask students about their experiences of being compared with someone else. How does it make them feel?

If your students know one another pretty well, consider trying the exercise in class. Choose a student to start, and ask the person in the next seat to say something they like about that student. Share something that you like about that student, too. Then move to another student, and repeat the exercise until everyone has spoken up for others and heard positive things about themselves.

Afterward, return to the activity in the workbook and go over the instructions for doing it at home.

### Notes

__________________________________________

__________________________________________

__________________________________________

__________________________________________

__________________________________________

__________________________________________

__________________________________________

**LIVING IT OUT**

Ask students how last week's activities went. Then read the "Living It Out" text in the workbook together as a class to give the students ideas for putting what they have learned about families into practice.

For this lesson, you may want to invite students to brainstorm about family members they can pray for and helpful things they can do at home. Encourage them to turn the ideas into a personal action plan for the coming week—and beyond.

**FAMILY CATECHESIS**

Remind parents that the "Living It Out" section is available on Thinkific and is excellent for family catechesis. Parents' help with this week's activities makes all the difference. They can help their child find time to pray for other family members or make the prayers a family activity! And each morning they can brainstorm with their children different ways they can all help one another during the day.

### Find Out More

**Patriarchs and Egypt**

Here are more stories about the Patriarchs, and one story that you might know already about Moses when he was a baby.

God Calls Abram out of Ur. . . . . . . . . . . . . . . . . . . . Genesis 12:1–7
Jacob Steals His Brother's Blessing. . . . . . . . . . Genesis 27:1–39
Joseph's Brothers Sell Him into Slavery . . . . . Genesis 37:12–36
Joseph Saves the Egyptians from Famine . . . . . . . . . . . . . . . . . . . . . . Genesis 41:46–49, 53–57
Joseph Forgives His Brothers . . . . . . . . . . . . . . Genesis 50:15–21
Moses in the Bulrushes. . . . . . . . . . . . . . . . . . . . Exodus 1:15–2:10

### Living It Out

As you have seen, the theme of family is huge in God's plan. God the Father uses our human families to teach us about his love and about our identity as his sons and daughters.

- Choose one family member to pray for with special focus. At the beginning of the week, ask for the intentions of the person you've chosen and say that you will be offering prayers and sacrifices for them this week. Set reminders for yourself to follow through on praying for this family member's intentions.

  After a week (or a few days if your family is very large), move on to another family member until you have covered everyone.

- Each day, do one helpful or kind thing for another family member without being asked. Maybe you can put away laundry for someone else. Maybe you can bring someone a drink or snack. Maybe you can take out the trash. Maybe you can create a card or drawing that says how much you love and appreciate the other person. Maybe you can serve another person's plate before yours at lunch or dinner.

46 | ENCOUNTER

## Find Out More & Living It Out

For students who are interested and like to read, mention the stories in "Find Out More," which they can read at home. You may also consider using one of these passages for *lectio divina.*

The "Living It Out" activities are specially designed to be done at home. Read the workbook text together to give your students ideas for putting what they have learned into practice. Remind them that you will check in with them the next time you meet to see how they are doing.

## WORDPLAY

**Christians**: A follower of Christ who has been baptized in his name.

**covenant**: From a Latin word meaning "to agree on." More than a contract, a covenant is an exchange of persons that helps establish an ongoing relationship.

**Israelites**: The descendants of the Patriarch Jacob (whose other name was Israel). Jacob's twelve sons were the ancestors of the twelve tribes of Israel.

**Jews**: Another name for the Israelite people, or "men of Judah," used in the period of the Exile and after.

**patriarch**: The male head of a family or tribe, often the eldest or most respected man in the family. A **matriarch** is the female head of a family or tribe.

**Promised Land**: The region that God promised to give to Abraham and his descendants as an inheritance.

**worship**: To honor or show reverence to God alone.

## CLOSING PRAYER

"Thank you, God, for being our good and loving Father. Thank you for always doing what is best for us and for always keeping your promises. Help us to know you better as a father. Help us to see one another as sisters and brothers. Give us patience with our family members and help us grow in love together. In Jesus' name, we pray. Amen."

## STEP 10 Closing Prayer

Remind students of their homework assignments. Then lead the class in the closing prayer. Begin and end the prayer with the Sign of the Cross.

**THIS WEEK'S HOMEWORK**

1. Memorize the memory verse: Genesis 12:3.
2. Do the "Loved, Not Compared" exercise at home with family and friends.
3. Do the "Living It Out" activity they chose.

# EXODUS – DESERT WANDERINGS – CONQUEST AND JUDGES

## LESSON OVERVIEW

In this lesson, we journey with the Israelites from slavery to freedom and see that, as it turns out, it's a long ride. The students will get a chance to consider the encounter that the Israelites, as a people, had with God as they were led out of Egypt and purified in the desert.

Both familiar and unfamiliar elements of this story are likely to touch the experience of middle schoolers in powerful ways. They will be called to consider their own idols, their own struggles with obedience, and even the struggle of long-delayed gratification as they walk with the Israelites through the hot days and years of wandering in the desert. This lesson also explores the entry of the Israelites into the Promised Land with Joshua as their leader.

## LESSON OBJECTIVES

Students will

- **Explore** the stories of the first Passover, the Exodus, and the desert wanderings of the Israelites as they prepare to enter the Promised Land.
- **Appreciate** the significance of the Ten Commandments and God's covenant with Moses.
- **Make** real-life connections between the Israelites and their own struggles with trusting God.
- **Explore** how the Israelites' desire for a king is connected to their own struggles with peer pressure.
- **Find** connections between Gideon's story and their own stories.

## VIDEO LESSON NOTES

### DIVE IN VIDEO – **EXODUS, DESERT WANDERINGS, CONQUEST AND JUDGES** – MARK HART

Mark will prompt you to pause the video to read these passages:

**Exodus 32:1–6, The Golden Calf**

**Joshua 3:8–17, The Israelites Cross the Jordan on Dry Land**

- The Israelites are enslaved in Egypt. God wants Moses to persuade Pharaoh to free them. Moses doubts his abilities but says yes because he trusts God. But that doesn't mean it's going to be easy.

## The Exodus: Moses and Pharoah

- Moses goes to Pharaoh and tells him, "The God of Israel says, 'Let my people go.'" Pharaoh says back, "I'm sorry, who?"
- Pharaoh refuses to let the Israelites go, so God curses Egypt with ten plagues. God does this not simply to punish Pharaoh but also to demonstrate his power.

  The Egyptians were polytheists, which means they believed in many false gods. Each plague showed the power of God over a specific false god. Unfortunately, many Israelites had also started worshiping the false Egyptian gods.

- After ten plagues, Pharaoh relents and lets the Israelites go. Moses leads them out of Egypt; then Pharaoh changes his mind and sends his army to chase them. At the Red Sea, God parts the waters miraculously so the Israelites can cross safely on dry land. But the waters close back over the Egyptians, and Pharaoh's army is destroyed.

## Desert Wanderings: The Ten Commandments

- Moses leads the Israelites in the desert. At Mount Sinai, God gives Moses the Ten Commandments and renews his covenant. God promises the Israelites that they will be his own people if they keep his commandments.
  - » The Ten Commandments are guardrails. They keep us going in the right direction instead of sideways or backward.
  - » They don't restrict our freedom; they give us freedom. They free us from the distractions of false gods (popularity, success, etc.) so that we can focus on God—because that's how we become the people God made us to be.
- The Israelites build the Ark of the Covenant to hold the commandments.

  The Ark is the tangible presence of God with them. The Tabernacle is a portable tent that houses the Ark. It is where they worship God and offer sacrifices to him.

## The Golden Calf—and Our Own False Gods

- Moses is on the mountain with God for such a long time that the Israelites are worried that he has died. They think God has abandoned them, even though he just brought them out of slavery, out of Egypt, and through the Red Sea. But they still don't trust that God will take care of them! So they make a golden calf and worship it instead.

  Mark says, "You gotta be thinking to yourself ... 'I would never worship a golden calf!' Well, maybe you would—but golden calves look a little bit different in the twenty-first century."

  A false god is whatever takes your attention away from God, like fame ... money ... your phone ... video games ... popularity.

- Jesus says, "Where your treasure is, there will your heart be also" (Luke 12:34). God wants to be the center of our lives, just as he wanted to be the center of the Israelites' lives. For forty years in the desert, God teaches the Israelites to worship him, love him, and trust him. He's getting them ready for the Promised Land.

- God does the same for us today. The false gods couldn't help the Israelites, and they won't help us either. We are created for so much more.

## Conquest: Into the Promised Land

- When Moses dies, God chooses Joshua to lead the Israelites. Eventually, Joshua leads the people to the edge of the Jordan River, the border of the Promised Land. But the Promised Land isn't empty. Lots of big, powerful tribes live there.
- The Israelites are scared, but God says once again, "Hey, trust me. Like, for real this time! You missed trusting me with the plagues, with the golden calf. Seriously, trust me now."
- God doesn't just say they should trust him—he shows them *why* they should trust him. They carry the Ark to the Jordan River, and he rolls back the river (just like the Red Sea) so they can cross on dry land to the Promised Land. Later, as they carry the Ark into battle, God brings down the walls of the enemy's most powerful city, Jericho.
- What about now? From then to now, God is saying, "I've never left you. I am with you." Just as the Israelites knew that God was with them in the Ark, in the Tabernacle, we too know that God is with us. Where? In the Eucharist. In the Blessed Sacrament, reserved in the Tabernacle of your own church and in every Catholic church in every country of the world.

## The Judges

- Now that the Israelites are finally home, in the Promised Land, we move into the time of Judges. The Judges are leaders who oversee and direct the nation. Some are good; some are not so good. But the people are not content. They want a king like other nations. God tells them that having kings won't go well for them; it's a bad idea. But they want a king anyway. Mark says, "Some people never learn."

### BIBLICAL CHARACTER VIDEO – **GIDEON** – TANNER KALINA

In high school, Tanner struggled with self-confidence. Then one day the school counselors asked him to lead a small group on an upcoming retreat.

At first, Tanner didn't want to do it because he didn't think he had what it took. Him? Talking about Jesus and being a role model? But the counselors persuaded him, and Tanner ended up leading the retreat group. To his surprise, it went so well that some of the other students said Tanner's leadership was a highlight of the whole retreat.

Gideon was also insecure and uncertain when God called him. Gideon also questioned his own ability. But when God called Gideon and instructed him to do bold things, like destroy the altars of a false god, Gideon followed and obeyed.

God is calling you, too. Maybe you're thinking, "Why me? Doesn't God know that I'm not as smart or holy as my friends? What if people think I'm weird? What if God asks me to do something I'm afraid to do?"

You—yes, you!—are called to be a saint. God wants to use you to show others more about him. Remember, God doesn't call the equipped; he equips the called. The Lord invites you to say yes to a mission that only you can do. God knows you even better than you know yourself, so you can trust him even when you're unsure or afraid.

God worked through Tanner and Gideon, and he will work through you! Go forward with confidence and strength.

## LEADER-GUIDED DISCUSSION (OPTIONAL)

If you have a few minutes after the "Time Period Overview" (step 5), use the following prompt to talk about the role of the Judges in freeing the Israelites from sin, and compare it with the role of the sacraments in freeing us from sin.

### The 7x Cycle

On the Conquest and Judges panel of your *Bible Timeline* chart, the circle marked "7x" refers to the cycle of sin and deliverance that occurs seven times during the time of the Judges. The cycle is described in Judges 2:11–19.

- **Sin**—The people disobey God and worship idols.
- **Servitude**—they become their enemies' servants or slaves.
- **Supplication**—They cry out, asking God for help.
- **Salvation**—God raises up a judge (a warrior hero) to save them.
- **Silence**—The judge saves them, and they are faithful while the judge is alive. But when the judge dies, they fall into sin again, and the cycle starts over.

Things are not so different today: we still fall easily into sin and need help to get free of it. What gift do we have today, given to us by Jesus Christ, that helps us break the cycle of sin?

## BEFORE- AND AFTER-CLASS REMINDERS

### Before students arrive:

Make sure you have all the supplies needed for the lesson, such as Student Workbooks, Bibles, copies of *The Bible Timeline* chart, materials for activities, paper, and pens or pencils.

If you are handing out Bibles, place one at each student's place.

Review the video notes above and take note of anything you would like to mention to the class before they watch the video presentations.

Set up the equipment for the video presentations and queue the first video so that it is ready to play.

### After class:

Follow up with students who missed the lesson.

**WELCOME**

Some suggested ice-breaker questions:

- Name something you really like about yourself.
- If you could travel into the past or the future, which would it be? Why?
- What is the strangest thing you've ever eaten?

# Lesson Four

## Exodus – Desert Wanderings – Conquest & Judges

Exodus — Exodus 4–40 

Desert Wanderings — Numbers 

Conquest & Judges — Joshua, Judges, 1 Samuel 1–8

48 I ENCOUNTER

### Step 1 Welcome – The Big Picture

Greet students by name as they arrive, and take attendance so that you can follow up later with students who are absent. Ask an ice-breaker question to put students at ease. Then read "The Big Picture" text together.

## The Big Picture

A home, an identity, a community, a quest, an adventure, freedom: we are made for these. And these are what God gives his people in the books of Exodus, Numbers, and Joshua. As slaves in Egypt, the Israelites had lost their true identity, their community, and their close relationship with God. But through Moses, God has freed them. Now God will give them a new covenant—to bring them to the Promised Land—and he gives them his commandments to protect their freedom. Only as a free people can they come to know him again, worship him, and finally find their home.

**THE BIG PICTURE**

This lesson's "The Big Picture" introduces students to the Exodus from Egypt, the Ten Commandments, the Israelites' desert wanderings and conquest of the Promised Land, and the time of the Israelite judges. For this lesson, it will be helpful to bookmark Exodus 20 and 32, Joshua 3, and Judges 6. Students can bookmark their Bibles as you bookmark yours.

### OPENING PRAYER

"Lord God, our liberator, you call us out of the slavery of sin into freedom. You call us to leave behind the ways of thinking and acting that lead to misery. You call us into a life of joy as your people. Show us how we, like the Israelites, are on a journey from captivity to the place you have prepared for us. Help us listen to your voice and to grow daily along the way. In Jesus' name, we pray. Amen."

## STEP 2 Opening Prayer

Invite students to settle and share their prayer requests. Then pray the opening prayer in the Student Workbook, beginning with the Sign of the Cross. You may lead the prayer yourself, pray it aloud as a class, or ask a student to read it.

Consider ending the prayer with a Hail Mary or Glory Be. Students who are not familiar with these prayers can find them in the "Further Resources" section at the back of their workbook. End with the Sign of the Cross.

**MEMORY VERSE**

Read **Exodus 20:2–3** aloud. What are some of the "other gods" people worship today?

***LECTIO DIVINA* (OPTIONAL)**

Invite your students to close their eyes and open their hearts and minds to the Holy Spirit. Read **Exodus 20:2–3** slowly and prayerfully out loud. Pause and then ask the students to read and reflect on the passage themselves. Encourage them to focus on a specific word, phrase, or idea that seems important.

To encourage conversation, you can invite a willing student to share the word or phrase that stood out for them. Then ask whether it resonated with anyone else, and invite others to share.

If you want to use a longer passage for *lectio divina*, consider one listed in "Find Out More" on page 62 of the workbook.

## REMEMBER THIS!

"I am the Lord your God, who brought you out of the land of Egypt, out of the house of bondage. You shall have no other gods before me."

—Exodus 20:2–3

The First Commandment might seem obvious. God is God, right? But the Israelites needed this commandment because they had been so immersed in Egyptian beliefs that they had lost sight of God himself, the one true God. In fact, it was very hard for them to separate themselves from what they'd known in Egypt, and they kept returning to the worship of false gods even after God showed them his power, rescued them from slavery, and gave them this commandment.

Few of us have actual pagan statues on our nightstands. But we should ask ourselves: Is God first in our hearts and lives, or do we allow other things to come before him? Who, or what, do we actually place on the throne of our hearts?

50 | ENCOUNTER

## STEP 3 Remember This!

Ask "Who can recite the memory verse from the last class?" (It's Genesis 12:3.) Be ready to award small prizes to those who can recite it successfully!

This lesson's memory verse is the First Commandment. The verse is written in their workbooks, but you may want to ask students to read it in their Bibles at Exodus 20:2–3. Ask them to memorize the verse, and remind them that you will ask them about it at the next class. You may also (optionally) use the verse for *lectio divina*.

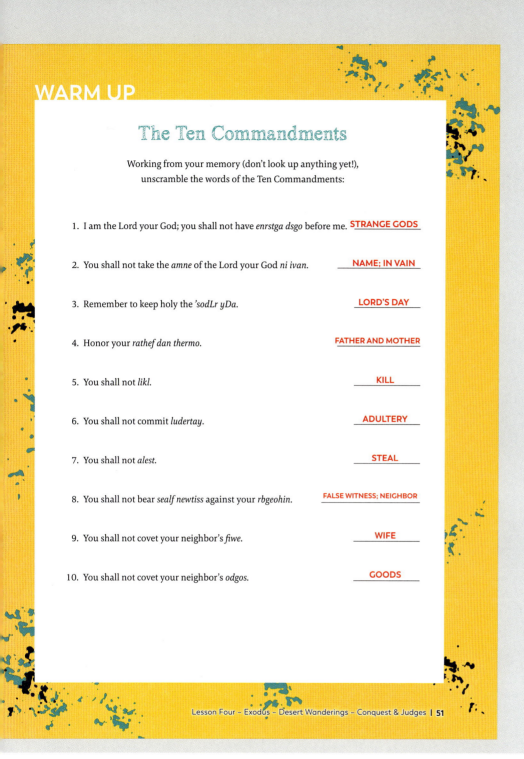

WARM UP

## The Ten Commandments

Working from your memory (don't look up anything yet!), unscramble the words of the Ten Commandments:

1. I am the Lord your God; you shall not have *enrstga dsgo* before me. STRANGE GODS
2. You shall not take the *amne* of the Lord your God *ni ivan*. NAME; IN VAIN
3. Remember to keep holy the *'sodLr yDa*. LORD'S DAY
4. Honor your *rathef dan thermo*. FATHER AND MOTHER
5. You shall not *likl*. KILL
6. You shall not commit *ludertay*. ADULTERY
7. You shall not *alest*. STEAL
8. You shall not bear *sealf newtiss* against your *rbgeohin*. FALSE WITNESS; NEIGHBOR
9. You shall not covet your neighbor's *fiwe*. WIFE
10. You shall not covet your neighbor's *odgos*. GOODS

Lesson Four – Exodus – Desert Wanderings – Conquest & Judges | 51

### STEP 4 Warm Up: *The Ten Commandments*

Make sure everyone has a workbook and something to write with. Go over the instructions together, and encourage students to do their best to unscramble the words on their own. When they have finished, go over the unscrambled commandments one at a time and ask students if they have any questions.

*NOTE: The wording of the commandments in this exercise is the traditional catechetical formula from the* Catechism of the Catholic Church. *It is different in places from the wording in the Book of Exodus.*

## TIME PERIOD OVERVIEW

### Exodus, Desert Wanderings, Conquest & Judges

Have a look at your *Bible Timeline* chart. Today we'll cover a lot of ground with the Israelites—from **Exodus (red)** through **Desert Wanderings (tan)** and into the Promised Land in **Conquest & Judges (green)**.

When God's people were enslaved in Egypt, God chose Moses to set them free. Moses cooperated with God's call. He went to Pharaoh and demanded that he let the Israelite people go. It was a dangerous, difficult mission. Pharaoh was the ruler of an empire, a powerful king, like a god himself—so why should he listen to this scruffy messenger? He refused.

Because of Pharaoh's refusal, the Egyptians suffered ten **PLAGUES**. Each of the plagues represented one of the false gods that the Egyptians worshiped. God showed that he was the true God by defeating the Egyptian gods one by one.

Before the tenth and final plague, God warned Moses that all the firstborn in the land of Egypt would die. He told the Israelites to sacrifice a lamb and use its blood to mark the doorposts of their homes. That evening, the Israelites ate the lamb with their shoes on and their belongings ready to go. Then, at midnight, all the firstborn in Egypt died—except for the Israelites, whose houses were marked with the

52 | ENCOUNTER

## Time Period Overview: Exodus, Desert Wanderings, Conquest & Judges

Invite students to take out their *Bible Timeline* charts and open them to the red, tan, and green period panels. Review the key events and people of these time periods and the approximate dates in history to give additional context to the lesson. Notice especially the covenant with Moses and the approximate dates in history. If you have time, explain the 7x circle under Conquest and Judges (see Leader-Guided Discussion on page 77 of the Leader's Guide).

The key lesson here is that God not only freed his people from slavery, but he also continued to dwell among them and teach them how to live in freedom. He is God-with-us!

blood of the lamb. This was the first **PASSOVER**, because when God came down to take the firstborn, he saw the blood and "passed over" those houses.

After the tenth plague, Pharaoh finally relented, and the Israelites fled from Egypt. But Pharaoh quickly changed his mind. He sent the Egyptian army to chase the Israelites into the sea and be destroyed. But through Moses, God saved his people again; he divided the sea so they could walk across on dry land, with walls of water on either side. Pharaoh and his army were the ones who were destroyed in their pride and rage. The Israelites passed through the water into freedom—freedom in the desert.

The Israelites were free, but they were not ready to go into the land that God had promised to Abraham. They disobeyed and complained. They still had Egypt's false gods in their hearts and minds.

God used their time in the desert to turn their hearts to him. He performed miracles to feed them—bread from heaven, quails, and water from a rock. Most importantly, God established a covenant with Moses and all the Israelites. In it, he gave Moses the **TEN COMMANDMENTS** and the whole Law (the Torah), and he promised to make the Israelites his own people (see Exodus 19:5–6).

God also gave the people detailed instructions for building the Tabernacle and the beautiful Ark of the Covenant. The **TABERNACLE**, or tent of the covenant, was where God dwelt. Inside was the **ARK OF THE COVENANT**, the golden chest that held the stone tablets with the Ten Commandments. On the lid of the Ark was the mercy seat, the throne where God's presence rested.

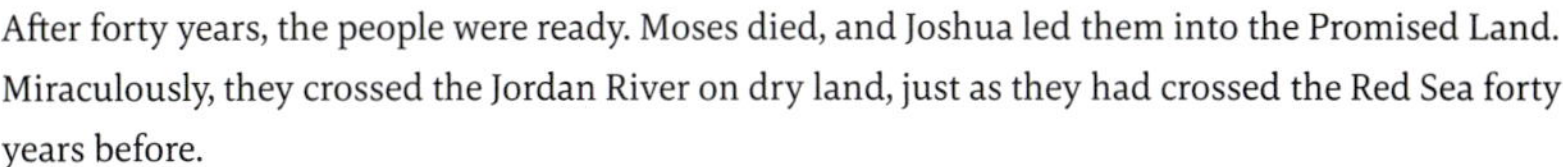

After forty years, the people were ready. Moses died, and Joshua led them into the Promised Land. Miraculously, they crossed the Jordan River on dry land, just as they had crossed the Red Sea forty years before.

Now came the time of conquest. With God leading them, the Israelites conquered their enemies and divided the land among the twelve tribes. God's people were finally home, in the land God had promised to Abraham.

## If You Ask Me

- Who are the most powerful people in our society? What makes them powerful? Which individuals can you think of who use their power and authority for good?
- The Israelites were enslaved for generations in Egypt. What are we "enslaved" to today? What do we allow to control our time and focus?
- When do you find it hard to obey the people you should obey, like parents and teachers? What happens when you do not obey them?



| DIVIDED KINGDOM | EXILE | RETURN | MACCABEAN REVOLT | MESSIANIC FULFILLMENT | THE CHURCH |
|---|---|---|---|---|---|
| 1 Kings 12–22<br>2 Kings 1–16 | 2 Kings 17–25 | Ezra<br>Nehemiah | 1 Maccabees | Luke | Acts |
|  | 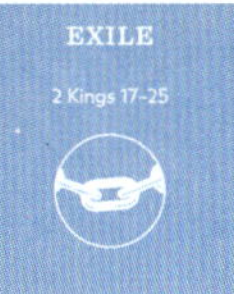 |  |  |  | 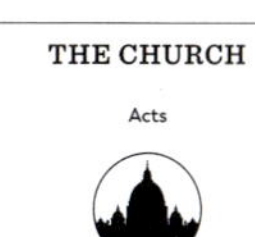 |

**IF YOU ASK ME**

These questions are about power, slavery, and obedience. To ease students into a whole-class conversation, consider starting them off in pairs or small groups and then transition to a large group discussion.

**Notes**

**DIVE IN VIDEO**

Make sure the video and sound system are set up. Mark will ask your students to read **Exodus 32:1–6** and **Joshua 3:8–17** during the presentation, so invite them to find and bookmark those passages in their Bibles before they watch the video. Also consider reviewing the "Got It?" questions together on page 58 of the workbook so they can be alert to the answers.

Finally, ask students to put away phones, close laptops, and avoid other distractions so they can give the video their full attention. Be prepared to pause the presentation when prompted for Bible reading.

**DIVE IN TEXT**

Review the key words, and then read this section in the workbook, which covers the Israelites' experiences in the desert, their entrance into the Promised Land, and the period of the judges. You can read it together in class or assign it for quiet reading.

DIVE IN VIDEO

Exodus, Desert Wanderings, Conquest & Judges . . . . . . . . . Mark Hart

"Guardrails help guide us in the right direction and keep us safe. And that's what the commandments do. They guide us in the right direction. They keep us safe." —Mark H.

*During the video, Mark will ask you to pause and read two Bible stories. Find and mark them in your Bibles now so that you can open to them quickly when you need to:*

- *Exodus 32:1–6, The Golden Calf*
- *Joshua 3:8–17, The Israelites Cross the Jordan on Dry Land*

Freedom from slavery! A dramatic, miraculous rescue! Did the Israelites rejoice and trust God with grateful hearts?

Not for long. The desert was vast, hot, and dry. There were no comfortable homes and little food. The Israelites quickly began to complain about God and doubt his plan. This was not a new problem. While they were still enslaved in Egypt, they had also doubted God. Many had even worshiped the false Egyptian gods.

In the desert, God provided for them, but they complained at every point. When they were hungry, he gave them **MANNA** (bread from heaven) and wild quail. They moaned because it wasn't the food they were used to. When they were thirsty, God made water spring out of desert rocks. They groaned that it wasn't cold enough. Sometimes they even grumbled aloud that they wished they had never left Egypt!

**God's Name**

In the video, Mark talks about the burning bush, where God appeared to Moses and asked him to lead his people to freedom. Moses asked God to tell him his name that day, and God said his name is "**I AM WHO I AM**" (Exodus 3:14). God's name is so holy that the people would not speak it aloud. They called God *Adonai* (which means "LORD") instead.

54 | ENCOUNTER

## Main Content Teaching

This step involves watching Mark's teaching video and reading the text in the Student Workbook together. Three more "If You Ask Me" questions follow the text along with a quick "Got It?" quiz. Detailed notes on the video content start on page 74 of this Leader's Guide.

God gave the Israelites the Ten Commandments at Mount Sinai to protect them and show them how to worship him and live together peacefully. But the people almost immediately broke the commandments; they even made a golden calf to worship as a new god! Their disobedience and their stony hearts kept them wandering for forty years.

What does this story about the Israelites thousands of years ago have to do with you? You didn't melt down your family's jewelry to create a false idol, but you've probably struggled with putting other things before God. You may not moan about having to eat manna, but you might complain instead of being grateful for God's constant gifts. On a bad day, you too might have doubted that God has an amazing plan for you.

We sometimes behave like the whining Israelites in the desert. But God keeps calling us back to him, showing his love for us, drawing us back to his commandments so we can enter heaven—the Promised Land that he has prepared for us.

If you have time, read and talk about the importance of the Ten Commandments. See "Further Resources," page 184, in this guide.

**The Great Commandment**

"Hear, O Israel: The LORD our God is one LORD; and you shall love the LORD your God with all your heart, and with all your soul, and with all your might."

—Deuteronomy 6:4–5

*Moses Receiving the Ten Commandments* by Gebhard Fugel

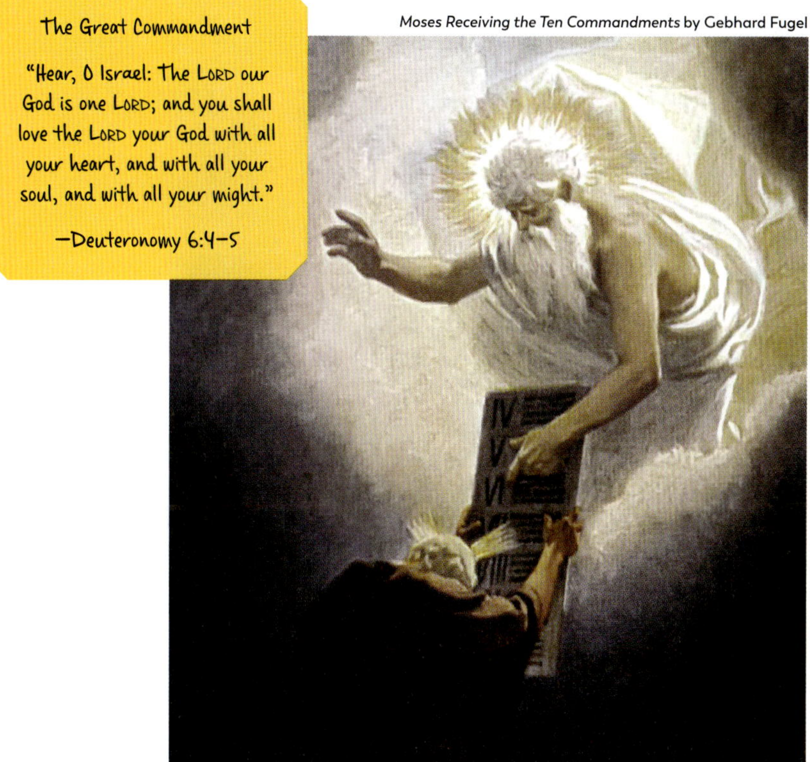

**Notes**

As the Israelites settled into the Promised Land, the period of **Judges** began. God wanted his people to be different from other nations and set apart. He didn't want them to worship false gods and celebrate sinful behavior. He gave them commandments that taught them to live differently, and he gave them judges instead of a king to guide them.

The Israelite **JUDGES** weren't like our judges today, who decide in court how laws should be applied. These judges were leaders or champions, often good warriors, who were chosen by God to deliver the people from their enemies. But the Israelites didn't want judges. They begged God for a king so they could be more like their neighbors, who all had kings to rule over them.

Maybe you can relate. Have your parents ever said no when you wanted something everyone else seemed to have or when you wanted to do something everyone else seemed to be doing? Maybe you argued with them, but your parents were firm in setting a different standard for you. Your parents do this because they want what is best for you. That is also why God set boundaries for the Israelites.

But, as you'll see in the next lesson, when the Israelites finally got what they wanted and had kings, they found even more trouble.

**IF YOU ASK ME**

These questions are about being different and standing up for what's right. Consider talking about them in small groups, with class discussion to follow.

## If You Ask Me

- What is something your family does differently than everyone else? Why does your family have this different standard? How do you feel about it?
- What is something you see everyone else doing or having that you don't think is good or healthy? What problems do you think this thing causes? What is a different, better choice?
- Why do you think it is so hard for the Israelites to trust God, even though they experience miracles and his divine intervention? What causes them to constantly drift away from trusting God's goodness?



**Notes**

## Gratitude Notes

| | | |
|---|---|---|
| I'm grateful for<br>**Example:**<br>my dog, Spot | I'm grateful for | I'm grateful for |
| I'm grateful for | I'm grateful for | I'm grateful for |
| I'm grateful for | I'm grateful for | I'm grateful for |
| I'm grateful for | I'm grateful for | I'm grateful for |

Lesson Four – Exodus – Desert Wanderings – Conquest & Judges | 57

## Notes

**GOT IT?**

Ask students to complete the multiple-choice questions in the workbook, and review the answers together. After you've gone over the answers, consider checking in to see if your students have any other questions about the lesson so far.

# Got It

1. The Israelites sinned and broke the Ten Commandments by ________.
   a. writing a new set of commandments
   b. making a golden calf statue that they worshiped
   c. going back to Egypt
   d. stealing from other groups they met

2. For ________ years, the Israelites wandered in the desert because they were not yet ready for the Promised Land.
   a. 5
   b. 25
   c. 40
   d. 100

3. When they were settled in the Promised Land, the Israelites were ruled by ________ instead of kings like other nations.
   a. prophets
   b. pharaohs
   c. priests
   d. judges



**Notes**

DIVE IN ACTIVITY

## Grumbling and Gratitude

Like the Israelites, we all struggle with our own grumbling. God wants to help us become grateful and to trust in his goodness.

Think about the things or people you often grumble about: chores, homework, rules, a neighbor. What else can you think of? Be specific and write them down. Then, focus on one or two of them and think about them again. Is there something about that situation or person that you can be grateful for instead? Is there something important about them that you've been missing?

| What do I grumble about? | What is something about the situation or person that I can be grateful for instead? |
|---|---|
| Example: Setting the table for dinner. | All of us get to be together at dinner. I get to help out. I get to make things a little easier for Mom and Dad. |
| | |
| | |
| | |



**GRUMBLING AND GRATITUDE**

Make sure the group has all the necessary materials. Go over the instructions carefully and answer students' questions. It might be helpful to brainstorm as a group about the things they often grumble about. Are there opportunities for gratitude hiding in those same situations or people?

When students are ready to fill in the chart, do an example together to help them get started. Or do the whole activity together as a class, filling in the chart on a whiteboard.

When the group is done, ask them to share what they've learned.

## STEP 7 Dive In Activity

This activity offers a hands-on application of one of the lesson's main ideas: the problem with grumbling. Make sure everyone has something to write with. Go over the instructions carefully and answer students' questions.

**BIBLICAL CHARACTER VIDEO**

As before, ask students to put away phones, close laptops, and avoid other distractions so they can give their full attention to the video presentation. Ask them to pay special attention to what Tanner and Gideon teach us about saying yes to God.

**BIBLICAL CHARACTER PROFILE**

Read the text in the workbook about Gideon, one of the Israelite judges. You can select students to read different paragraphs aloud to increase class participation. Notice how, when God calls us to do something, he equips us to do it.

BIBLICAL CHARACTER VIDEO

**Gideon . . . . . . . . . . . . . . . . . . . . . . . . . . . . . . Tanner Kalina**

"And [Gideon] said to him, 'Please, Lord, how can I deliver Israel? Behold, my clan is the weakest in Manasseh, and I am the least in my family.'" —Judges 6:15

## BIBLICAL CHARACTER PROFILE

# Gideon

In high school, Tanner struggled with self-confidence. Then one day, the school counselors asked him to lead a small group on an upcoming retreat. At first, Tanner didn't want to do it because he didn't think he had what it took. Him? Talking about Jesus and being a role model? But the counselors persuaded him, and Tanner ended up leading the retreat group. To his surprise, it went so well that some of the other students named Tanner's leadership as a highlight of the whole retreat.

**Gideon** was also insecure and uncertain when God called him. Gideon also questioned his own ability. After all, he came from the lowest clan and was the least important member of his own family. But God called Gideon, instructing him to do bold things—like destroying a false temple and fighting the huge Midianite army with just three hundred men. Even though Gideon was afraid and unsure, he followed and obeyed God. And he triumphed.

God is calling you, too. Maybe you're thinking, "Why me? Doesn't God know that I'm not as smart or holy as my friends?" or "What if people think I'm weird?" or "What if God asks me to do something I'm afraid to do?"

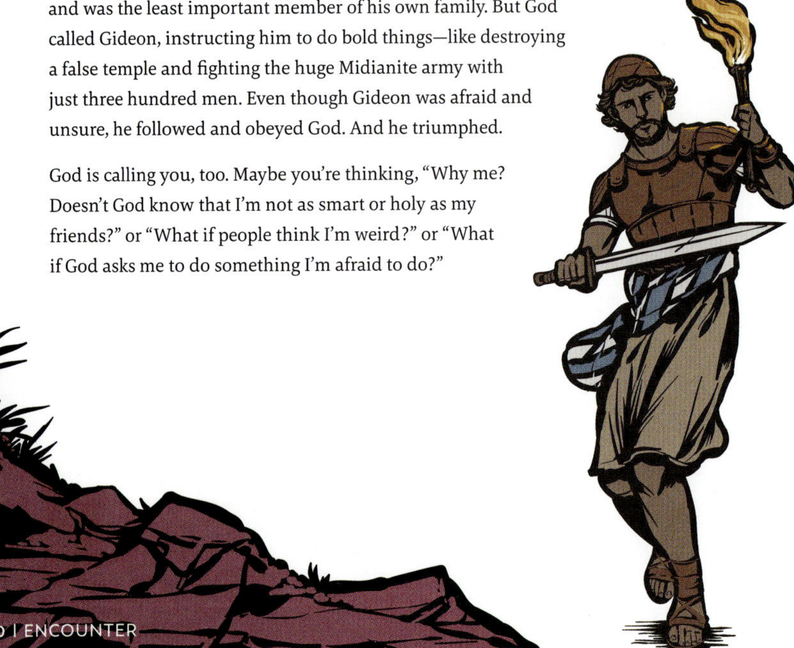

60 | ENCOUNTER

## STEP 8 Biblical Character Profile: GIDEON

This step features a short video by Tanner Kalina, the read-aloud profile of Gideon in the workbook, and an exercise for students to do during class or at home.

After you play the video, review the video notes on pages 76–77 of the Leader's Guide and ask students about specific points of interest. Then read the profile text aloud and give your students time to do the "I Will Be with You" exercise.

You—yes, you!—are called to be a saint. God wants to use you to show others more about him. Remember, God doesn't call the equipped; he equips the called. The Lord invites you to say yes to a mission that only you can do. God knows you even better than you know yourself, so you can trust him even if you're unsure or afraid.

God worked through Tanner and Gideon, and he will work through you! Go forward with confidence and strength.

## "I Will Be with You"

Find Gideon on your *Bible Timeline* chart. Which period is he in? Now read the beginning of his story in **Judges 6:11–16**.

Gideon was considered one of the mightiest judges of Israel. His story reminds us that when God asks us to do something, he gives us what we need to do it.

- Have you ever succeeded at something you didn't think you were good at? What was it?
- How did it turn out? How did you feel afterward?
- Is there anything in your life right now that you won't do because you think you won't be good at it? What is it? Do you think God might be nudging you to try?

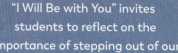

### BIBLICAL CHARACTER EXERCISE

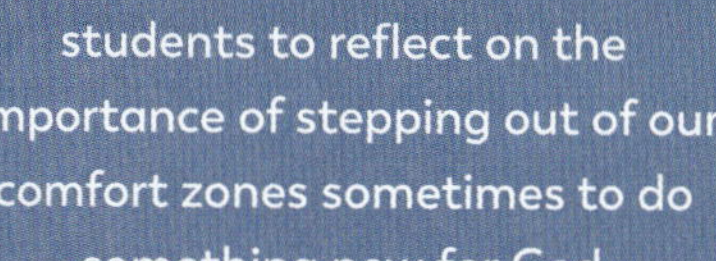

"I Will Be with You" invites students to reflect on the importance of stepping out of our comfort zones sometimes to do something new for God.

Make sure everyone has a *Bible Timeline* chart, paper to write on, and something to write with. Before starting the activity, invite students to find Gideon on the timeline chart. Then navigate to Judges 6:11–16 in the Bible and read it aloud as a class.

Go over the discussion prompts carefully. Answer students' questions and give them time to think about each prompt. Then, depending on the group and on how much time you have, use the prompts to lead a group discussion or invite students to use them for journaling. You can also assign the exercise as homework.

**Notes**

### LIVING IT OUT

Ask students how last week's activities went. Then read this lesson's "Living It Out" text in the workbook, which suggests some ways to put God first in their lives. Encourage them to turn the ideas into a personal action plan.

For this lesson, you may want to point students to the Morning Offering prayer in on page 131 of the workbook or make copies of another short morning prayer for them. Also consider sharing some Christian artists they can look up for music playlists.

### FAMILY CATECHESIS

Remind parents to use the "Living It Out" activities for family catechesis. Their help makes all the difference! Invite them to brainstorm with their child this week, thinking of new ways they can put God first as a family, and encourage them to put their ideas into practice.

## Find Out More

Manna in the Desert ....................... Exodus 16:14–21

The Israelites Build the Ark of the Covenant ....................... Exodus 25:10–22

Twelve Spies Sent to Survey Canaan ...... Numbers 13:1–14:9

Balaam and His Talking Donkey .......... Numbers 22:21–35

Joshua Leads the People into Canaan........ Joshua 3:14–17

The Fall of Jericho .......................... Joshua 6:12–17

**Exodus, Desert Wanderings, Conquest & Judges**

Here are stories you can read to learn more about what happened to the Israelites from the time they left Egypt until they settled in Canaan.

## Living It Out

Does your life show that God is number one? When others interact with you, can they see how important God is to you?

- Make an effort to practice your faith at all times. Go to Mass even when you're on vacation (check masstimes.org to find Masses wherever you are). Pray grace before every meal, including in public at school or in restaurants. This small choice shows that we recognize God's constant providence and that we place him first.
- Choose a short favorite prayer or Scripture verse to offer as soon as you wake up every morning. Consider putting your prayer or verse where you'll see it as soon as you open your eyes. No matter how briefly, pray first every day.
- Add some Christian music to your playlists. Have fun exploring all the different styles of Christian music. When these songs queue up, they will remind you to think about God and his goodness throughout the day.

62 I ENCOUNTER

## Find Out More & Living It Out

For students who are interested and like to read, mention the stories in "Find Out More," which they can read at home. You may also consider using one of these passages for *lectio divina*.

The "Living It Out" activities are specially designed to be done at home. Read the workbook text together to give your students ideas for putting what they have learned into practice. Remind them that you will check in with them the next time you meet.

## WORDPLAY

**Ark of the Covenant**: The wooden, gold-covered chest that held the two stone tablets of the Ten Commandments and other sacred objects of the Israelites.

**I AM WHO I AM**: The holy name of God, first spoken to Moses. "I AM" or "I AM WHO I AM" is the English translation of the four-letter Hebrew word YHWH (commonly pronounced "Yahweh").

**judges**: The twelve leaders of Israel who were chosen by God to help defend the Israelites from their enemies.

**manna**: The heavenly food that God gave the Israelites while they wandered in the desert. Manna was white and sweet and could be made into cakes.

**Passover**: The Jewish feast that commemorates the night when God "passed over" the Israelite homes in Egypt, protecting their children from death and freeing them from slavery.

**plagues**: A series of devastating catastrophes that fell upon the Egyptians after Pharaoh refused to let the Israelites go and worship God.

**Tabernacle**: The portable tent that the Israelites used for worship in the desert. It housed the Ark of the Covenant.

**Ten Commandments**: Ten laws that God gave to the Israelites to teach them how to live and worship as a free people.

## CLOSING PRAYER

"Lord God, we see ourselves in the Israelites who struggled to keep you first. We too get distracted and lazy about prayer and weak in our trust. We too put other things before you in our hearts. Give us the grace to see your goodness all around us, every day. When we are afraid to trust you, give us courage. Thank you for your patient love that always allows us to try again. In Jesus' name, we pray. Amen."

## Closing Prayer

Remind students of their homework assignments. Then lead them in the closing prayer. Begin and end the prayer with the Sign of the Cross.

**THIS WEEK'S HOMEWORK**

1. Memorize the memory verse: Exodus 20:2–3.
2. Do their "Living It Out" activity.

# Lesson Five

## ROYAL KINGDOM – DIVIDED KINGDOM

### LESSON OVERVIEW

This lesson dives into the stories of Israel's kings. It is a chance to lead students through central figures such as David and Solomon while also introducing them to a lesser-known king, Josiah. The big idea is that Israel had to learn that God was ultimately their king, because human kings turned out to be quite imperfect.

That said, we also see, especially in David, how God can call, choose, and anoint imperfect people to be part of the big story of salvation. These stories of Israel's kings are captivating, and this lesson will help students see how they can be inspired by a king like David and learn from the cautionary tale of a king like Saul.

This lesson also makes clear (and will become even clearer in later lessons) that all the stories told here foreshadow Jesus Christ, the true king of Israel. This stretch of history can help students see their own call away from vain pride to true, faithful leadership, the need to be cautious about trusting any earthly power too deeply, and the need to enthrone God as the true king of their hearts.

### LESSON OBJECTIVES

Students will

- **Learn** the basic narrative of the kings of Israel from Saul to the Exile.
- **Understand** why God cautioned against establishing a king in Israel.
- **Follow** the causes of Israel's decline into schism and ultimate exile.
- **Encounter** King David as a particularly relevant figure for young people.
- **Distinguish** between faithful leadership and the failures of Israelite kings.

### VIDEO LESSON NOTES

#### DIVE IN VIDEO – **ROYAL KINGDOM AND DIVIDED KINGDOM** – MARK HART

Mark will prompt you to pause the video to read these passages:

**1 Samuel 16:7, 10–13, Samuel Anoints David**
**2 Kings 23:2–3, King Josiah Renews the Covenant**

- We pick up with the Israelites finally at home in the Promised Land, but now they are complaining that they don't have a king while every other nation has a king.
- Their leader is a judge and prophet named Samuel. As a prophet, Samuel talks directly to God. The Israelites keep begging for a king. Samuel tells them (in effect) that having a king isn't all it's cracked up to be. And the people say (in effect) that they know what they want, and they want a king. So God finally tells Samuel to give them a king.

## King Saul

- Samuel anoints King Saul. Bam! Israel now has a king.
- Mark tells us that King Saul starts out strong, following God's will. He leads the people of Israel in battle and defeats almost all their enemies. BUT—he gets a big head.
- Samuel reminds Saul to follow God's will. Instead, Saul builds himself a cool monument. Eventually, God tells Samuel it's over with Saul. Time for a new king.

## King David

- God sends Samuel to a tiny little town called Bethlehem and to a man named Jesse. Jesse presents his sons to Samuel one by one, but none is the man God is seeking. God is seeking David, Jesse's youngest son, who is out tending sheep. Samuel anoints David, blessing him with oil for his special mission as king. (But David doesn't become king until later.)
- David shows us that God doesn't see from the outside in; he sees from the inside out. The Lord looks at the heart. David has a heart for the Lord. He kills the giant Goliath and goes on to become a popular war hero and musician. He rules Israel as king for about forty years.
- Mark reminds us that David isn't perfect, but he trusts God. He sets his heart on God and follows him. And if you follow God, you can accomplish more than you think you can.
- Mark emphasizes that God doesn't judge by appearances but by the heart. The most important thing about you is your heart.
- Mark says, "You need to know God loves you and keep your heart set on him. You too have a mission. And you either have been or will be anointed—depending on when you get confirmed—with oil, for a special mission as well. Not as a king or as a queen, but as a member of God's family, through the Sacrament of Confirmation."

## King Solomon

- King Solomon, David's son, follows God, builds the Temple in Jerusalem, and expands the kingdom. He is also known for being incredibly wise.
- But Solomon's heart changes. He is very powerful, and in his pride, he marries many wives. Many of his wives come from nations that worship false gods. Solomon's heart moves away from the Lord to the false gods of his wives. Solomon's bad choices affect all his people and everyone who follows him.
- Mark reminds us how important it is for us to set our hearts on God because bad things happen—to us and to the people who depend on us—when our hearts are divided.
- After Solomon dies, the kingdom of Israel splits in two, into the Northern Kingdom and the Southern Kingdom, and it gets messy. Some kings are good, but a lot are bad. God keeps sending prophets to say, "KEEP YOUR HEART SET ON THE LORD." Most of them don't.
- But a few kings do. The video highlights King Josiah, who has a pretty awful father and grandfather. Josiah becomes king when he is eight years old. At age sixteen, he goes to the Temple in Jerusalem, where he discovers the Law of God, which completely turns his heart.

- Even though he is a young man, Josiah gathers the entire kingdom together and reads them the Law. And the people renew the covenant with God.

### Hearts for God

- We see that God calls imperfect people. David wasn't perfect. Solomon wasn't perfect. Josiah wasn't perfect. People are messy. But at the end of the day, what matters is whether people are trying—whether their hearts are set on the Lord, or themselves, or the world, or false gods.

  Mark says, "Whenever a holy man or holy woman stands up and follows God with their whole heart, they can help communities, nations, kingdoms."

As this time period comes to a close, the Northern Kingdom gets completely destroyed. Soon after, the Southern Kingdom will be overtaken and the people will be forced into exile, as we will learn in the next lesson.

### BIBLICAL CHARACTER VIDEO – **DAVID** – FR. FRANKIE CICERO

When Fr. Frankie was 13, he went to Bible camp. While on the bus on the way there, one of the leaders asked him to share his testimony that night with all the other kids and grownups.

He was terrified. His fears were like the giant Goliath in his head.

Fr. Frankie tells the story of David and Goliath. David, a teenager, is taking food to his older brothers, who are soldiers. Everyone is quaking as Goliath, an enemy warrior, taunts them. Nobody wants to fight him. But David stands up and says, "I'll fight him! I'm not scared. Let's do this!" This courage arose in him because he remembered what the others had forgotten: it was him *and* God going against Goliath.

At Bible camp, Fr. Frankie was scared to give his testimony. But he asked God to be with him. And he was surprised by a gift of courage. He threw his notes away and talked to the other kids with confidence. Fr. Frankie's trust in God allowed God to use him to touch the hearts of other kids with his testimony.

We have the same God on our side! God wants to work powerfully through us. God is with us, and when we stay faithful to walking with him, we will slay giants! When you walk with God, you never walk alone.

## BEFORE- AND AFTER-CLASS REMINDERS

### Before students arrive:

Make sure you have all the supplies needed for the lesson, such as Student Workbooks, Bibles, copies of *The Bible Timeline* chart, materials for activities, paper, and pens or pencils.

If you are handing out Bibles, place one at each student's place.

Review the video notes for the lesson and take note of anything you would like to mention to the class before they watch the video presentations.

Set up the equipment for the video presentations and queue the first video so that it is ready to play.

## After class:

Follow up with students who missed the lesson.

If you would like someone from the parish or community to talk to your class for Lesson Seven (see "Living It Out" on page 152 in this guide), this week would be a good time to invite him or her.

### NOTES

WELCOME

Some suggested ice-breakers:

- What's the funniest joke you know?
- What do you and your family like to do in the summer?

# Lesson Five

## Royal Kingdom – Divided Kingdom

ROYAL KINGDOM 1 SAMUEL 9–31, 2 SAMUEL, 1 KINGS 1–11 

DIVIDED KINGDOM 1 KINGS 12–22, 2 KINGS 1–16

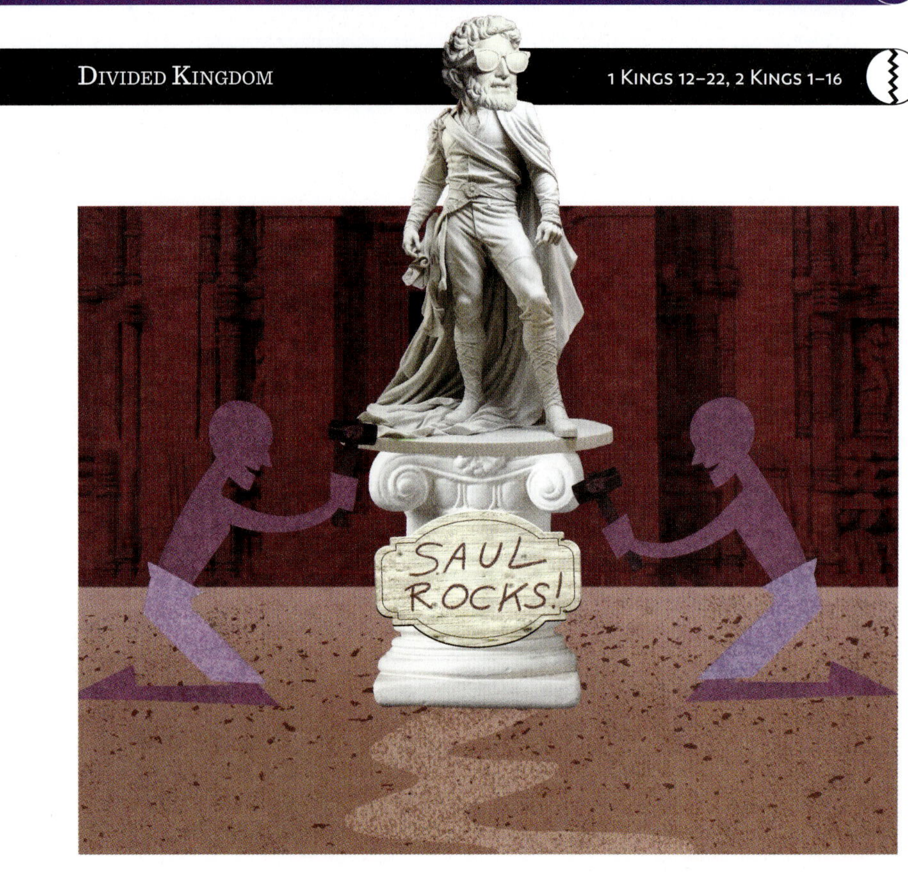

## STEP 1 Welcome – The Big Picture

Greet students by name as they arrive, and take attendance so that you can follow up later with students who are absent. Ask an ice-breaker question to put students at ease. Then read "The Big Picture" text together.

## The Big Picture

Who is the king of your heart? That's an important question. It can also be a tough question. In the previous lesson, we saw how the Israelites still clung to Egyptian idols and false gods in the desert, despite everything God had done to provide for them. Later, during the time of the judges, they began to clamor for an earthly king.

The Israelites' story teaches us that, just as we shouldn't rely on false idols, we shouldn't put all our trust in princes or kings. We will see how Israelites learned this reality the hard way. There can be good earthly leaders, of course, such as King David—but even King David was great only when he acted as a man after God's heart. God must be our ultimate king—or, like the kingdom of Israel, our hearts will be divided.

**THE BIG PICTURE**

This lesson's "Big Picture" prepares students for the major ideas of the lesson: the Royal Kingdom and Divided Kingdom, and bravery in the face of big challenges. For this lesson, it will be helpful for you and your students to bookmark Psalm 93, 1 Samuel 16, 1 Samuel 17, and 2 Kings 23.

### OPENING PRAYER

"God our King, we place our full trust in you. Thank you for the men and women who serve as leaders and who remind us of your kingship. Help them always to follow you as the ultimate king. Help us always to serve you first, to be dedicated to serving you, and to give you honor and obedience. Long live Christ, our Eternal King! In Jesus' name, we pray. Amen."

## Opening Prayer

When students have settled, invite them to share their prayer requests. Then pray the opening prayer in the Student Workbook, beginning with the Sign of the Cross. You may lead the prayer yourself, pray it aloud as a class, or ask a student to read it.

If you wish, end the prayer with a Hail Mary or Glory Be. (See "Further Resources," p. 129, at the back of their workbook.) End with the Sign of the Cross.

**MEMORY VERSE**

Read **Psalm 93:1** aloud. What does *majesty* mean? (Hint: supreme power, authority, dignity.)

***LECTIO DIVINA*** **(OPTIONAL)**

Invite your students to close their eyes and open their hearts and minds to the Holy Spirit. Read **Psalm 93:1** slowly and prayerfully out loud. Pause and then ask the students to read and reflect on the verse themselves. Encourage them to focus on a specific word or phrase that seems important.

After a minute or two, invite a willing student to share the word or phrase that stood out for them. Then ask whether it resonated with anyone else, and invite others to share.

If you want to use a longer passage for *lectio divina*, consider one listed in "Find Out More" on page 78 of the workbook. More information about *lectio divina* can be found in "Further Resources," on page 135 of the workbook.

REMEMBER THIS!

"The Lord reigns; he is robed in majesty!"

—Psalm 93:1

Salvation history is about God's relationship with his Chosen People and reveals his saving actions to deliver them from sin. Both in our own lives and across human history, we see a constant struggle to put God first. But when we pray and praise God, we proclaim that God is first, the King of the universe and of our hearts. Praise and prayer can be short, simple, and easy to remember, just like this verse. The Lord reigns!

66 | ENCOUNTER

## STEP 3 Remember This!

Ask "Who can recite the memory verse from the last class?" (It's Exodus 20:2–3.) Be ready to award small prizes to those who can recite it successfully!

This lesson's memory verse glorifies God. The verse is written in their workbooks, but you may want to ask students read it in their Bibles: Psalm 93:1. Ask them to memorize it, and remind them that you will ask them about it at the next class. You may also (optionally) use the verse for *lectio divina*.

## WARM UP

# Good to Be King

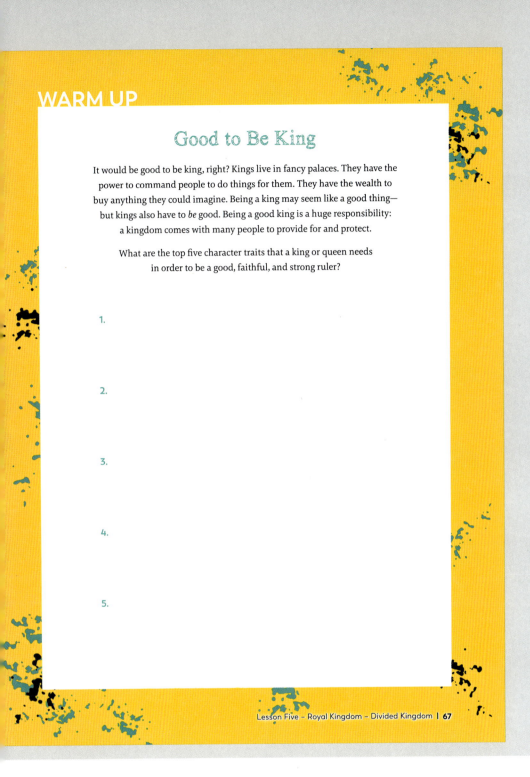

It would be good to be king, right? Kings live in fancy palaces. They have the power to command people to do things for them. They have the wealth to buy anything they could imagine. Being a king may seem like a good thing—but kings also have to *be* good. Being a good king is a huge responsibility: a kingdom comes with many people to provide for and protect.

What are the top five character traits that a king or queen needs in order to be a good, faithful, and strong ruler?

1.

2.

3.

4.

5.

## STEP 4 Warm Up: *Good to Be King*

This activity will help students reflect on the qualities of virtuous leadership, which they can apply in their own lives.

Make sure everyone has a workbook and something to write with. Go over the instructions carefully and answer questions. You may want to help students get started by coming up with examples together as a class. When everyone has finished, ask students to share the traits they think are important.

## TIME PERIOD OVERVIEW

# Royal Kingdom and Divided Kingdom

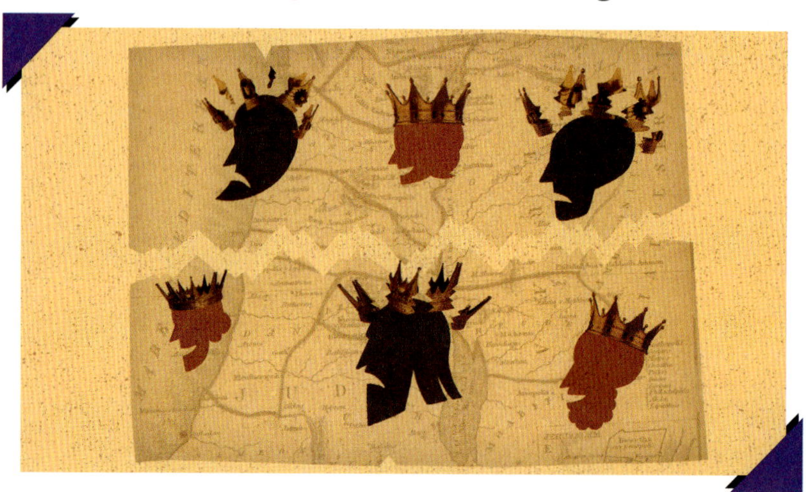

In the last lesson, the Israelites finally reached the Promised Land. They conquered their enemies, and each tribe settled into its own region. The people were led by their judges, but they wanted a human king.

On your *Bible Timeline* chart, find the **Royal Kingdom** (purple) and **Divided Kingdom** (black) panels. Notice which books tell these stories—1 and 2 Samuel and 1 and 2 Kings. Also, notice the names with crowns along the red bar at the bottom of those panels. Those are some of the Israelite kings.

The Israelites were a vast people now, a nation formed from the twelve ever-growing tribes. But they were not like other nations, and they were not meant to live like other nations. God called them

## Time Period Overview: Royal Kingdom and Divided Kingdom

Invite students to take out their *Bible Timeline* charts and open them to the purple and black time period panels. Review the key events and people, the covenant with David, and the approximate dates in history to give additional context to the lesson. Notice that the world power changes from Egypt to Assyria.

Review the key word and then read the "Time Period Overview" text. You can select students to read different paragraphs aloud to increase class participation.

specifically to be his people, set apart. But they wanted to be like everyone else. They wanted to be led by an earthly king, just like most other nations at that time.

What they didn't realize was how the kings of other nations sent people's sons to war, heavily taxed the people, and often oppressed them. Samuel, Israel's last judge, warned the people that having a king would lead to trouble, but they insisted on having their own way. So, Israel received its first king.

In this lesson, we will look at four of Israel's kings:

- Saul (1 Samuel 9–31)
- David (1 and 2 Samuel)
- Solomon (1 Kings 1–11 and 2 Chronicles 1–9)
- Josiah (2 Kings 22–23 and 2 Chronicles 34–35)

After Solomon, the kingdom split into two parts: the Northern Kingdom (Israel) and the Southern Kingdom (Judah). Other kings followed; most of them were bad, and the two kingdoms grew weaker and weaker.

But God never wastes anything, not even our mistakes. He used these kings to foreshadow our salvation. The flashes of greatness in King David and King Solomon gave the people a glimpse of God's ultimate plan. In time, the Father would give his Son, the promised **MESSIAH**, to reign as King over all creation and conquer death itself.

## If You Ask Me

- Why do you think the Israelites struggled so much with wanting to be like everyone else? How does this same problem affect our own lives?
- Jesus is not the ruler of a government or nation, but he is the King of the kingdom of heaven. How is he different from earthly kings? How does he use his power and authority?



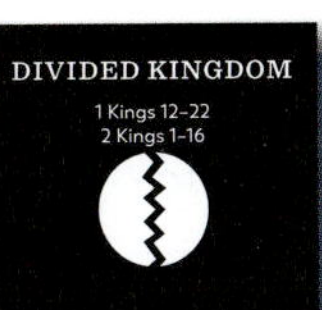

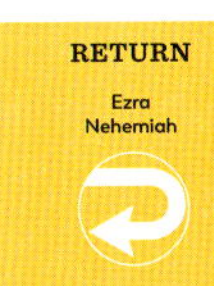

### IF YOU ASK ME

These questions are about kingship—having a king or being a king. To ease students into a whole-class conversation, consider starting them off in pairs or small groups and then transition to a large group discussion.

The key takeaway for this lesson is how the Israelites were chosen by God to be a people set apart, but he still listened to their request for a king—and he even used David's kingly line to prepare for the promised Messiah.

**DIVE IN VIDEO**

Make sure the video and sound system are set up. Mark will ask your students to read **1 Samuel 16:7, 10–13** and **2 Kings 23:2–3** during the presentation, so invite them to find and bookmark those passages in their Bibles before they watch the video. Also consider reviewing the "Got It?" questions together (see p. 74 of the workbook) so they can listen for the answers.

Finally, ask students to put away their phones, close laptops, and avoid other distractions so they can give the video their full attention. Be prepared to pause the presentation for Bible reading when prompted.

**DIVE IN TEXT**

Review the key word, and then read the "Dive In" text in the workbook, which covers the first three kings of Israel—Saul, David, and Solomon—and a later king, Josiah, who was crowned when he was only eight years old. The text can be read aloud in class or assigned for quiet reading.

DIVE IN VIDEO

**Royal Kingdom and Divided Kingdom . . . . . . . . . . . Mark Hart**

"God doesn't see from the outside in. He sees from the inside out. The Lord looks at your heart." —Mark H.

*During the video, Mark will ask you to pause and read two Bible stories. Find and mark them in your Bibles now so that you can open to them quickly when you need to:*

- *1 Samuel 16:7, 10–13, Samuel Anoints David*
- *2 Kings 23:2–3, King Josiah Renews the Covenant*

King Saul united the kingdom, and King David made it larger and stronger. King Solomon enriched it and built the glorious Temple in the city of Jerusalem (the kingdom's capital). Later, King Josiah renewed the people's commitment to God.

Samuel **ANOINTED** Saul to be Israel's first king. The king was meant to rule by obeying the commandments and listening to leaders like Samuel who spoke for God. Saul began well; he united the kingdom and defeated its enemies. But then he grew resentful, vain, and jealous. He lost his trust in God and was no longer fit to lead God's people.

The next king was David, a handsome shepherd and brave warrior. David's heart delighted in God, and he became a sign to the people of God's own kingship. Best of all, God promised David that the Messiah would come from his family and establish a kingdom that would last forever.

**A Man After God's Own Heart**

"[God] raised up David to be their king; of whom he testified and said, 'I have found in David, the Son of Jesse, a man after my heart, who will do all my will.' Of this man's posterity God has brought to Israel a Savior, Jesus, as he promised."

—Acts 13:22–23

70 | ENCOUNTER

## Main Content Teaching

After you watch Mark's teaching video, you will read the "Dive In" text in the Student Workbook together. Three more "If You Ask Me" questions follow the text along with a quick "Got It?" quiz. Detailed notes on the video content start on page 94 of this Leader's Guide.

> "Then Solomon said ... 'I have built you an exalted house, a place for you to dwell in for ever.'"
>
> —I Kings 8:12–13

After David came King Solomon, David's son, who built the magnificent Temple in Jerusalem. It became the center of worship for the whole nation of Israel. Inside was the Ark of the Covenant, the precious vessel that supported the mercy seat, where God's presence dwelt, and contained the Israelites' most sacred objects. (Remember the desert? Back then, the people had carried the Ark of the Covenant wherever they went.)

**SOLOMON'S TEMPLE**

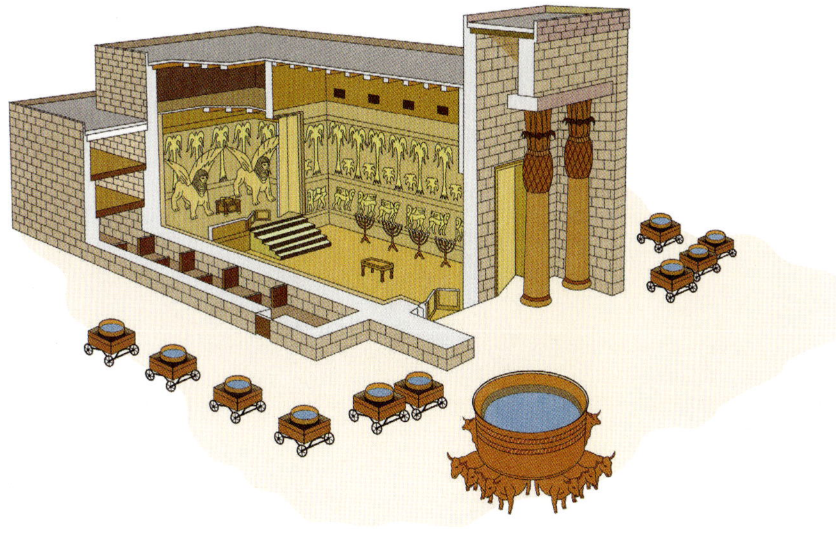



## Notes

Under the reign of Solomon's son Rehoboam, the kingdom split into two hostile kingdoms—which made them easy prey for conquering armies. But one of the good kings after the split was young King Josiah of Judah, who was crowned when he was only eight. When he was older, he restored Temple worship and renewed the people's commitment to God's commandments.

Look at the graphics on this page and the next page to keep track of who's who. See what you can learn from each.

**King:** Saul

**Strengths:** Started strong by leading God's people into battle

**Weaknesses:** Grew prideful and vain and lost his way. Followed his own will, not God's.

**Known for:** Being Israel's first king but failing to trust God and obey him.

**King-size truth:** Don't forget who you really are, what your mission is, and that God is God. You can be happy and successful only if you put God's will first.

**King:** David

**Strengths:** "A man after God's heart." Deep personal faith. Repented with his whole heart after major sins.

**Weaknesses:** Fell into sin and temptation.

**Known for:** Slaying a huge giant, loving God, being a great king, writing many psalms, singing.

**King-sized truth:** Trust in the Lord and turn your heart to him constantly.

72 | ENCOUNTER

## Notes

**King:** Solomon

**Strengths:** A wise and understanding heart. He built and dedicated the Temple in Jerusalem.

**Weaknesses:** His heart grew away from God. He taxed the people too heavily.

**Known for:** His wisdom, composing the Song of Songs, expanding and enriching the kingdom.

**King-sized truth:** Ask God for the grace and heart that you need to finish strong (Solomon didn't).

**King:** Josiah

**Strengths:** Being a good king even though his father and grandfather were awful kings. Initiating many religious reforms.

**Weaknesses:** He received a warning from God against fighting the king of Egypt, but he fought him anyway and was killed.

**Known for:** Recommitting to the covenant, reforming Judah.

**King-sized truth:** Turn your heart to God and his law, even if those around you don't.

## If You Ask Me

- Of the four kings we've talked about, who is your favorite? What do you like about this person?
- How did God's warning about the Israelites having a king come true?
- Why do you think so many kings started well but ended up turning away from God?



**IF YOU ASK ME**

These questions are about kings and kingship. Consider talking about them in small groups, with class discussion to follow.

**Notes**

**GOT IT?**

Ask students to complete the quiz in the workbook, and review their answers together. After you've gone over the answers, consider checking in to see if your students have any other questions about the lesson so far.

# Got It

Each line below describes one of these kings. Use each king twice.

a. Saul b. David c. Solomon d. Josiah

1. The first king of Israel ___A___
2. A shepherd ___B___
3. Built the Temple ___C___
4. Had a father and grandfather who were bad kings ___D___
5. Rediscovered the Law and committed his heart ___D___
6. Sinned big time, but then repented ___B___
7. Asked God for wisdom ___C___
8. Was rejected by God for following his own will, not God's. ___A___



**Notes**

DIVE IN ACTIVITY

## Songs for the Lord

King David wrote the psalms as songs. The psalms were sung to music that was played on the harp or lyre.

Think of a line or a couple of lines from one of your favorite songs. Choose lines that remind you of God's goodness, his love, or something related to your faith.

What about these lines reminds you of God? Share your reflections with the group if you like.

______________________________

______________________________

______________________________

______________________________

______________________________

______________________________

______________________________



**SONGS FOR THE LORD**

Go over the instructions and answer questions. As an example, consider playing a praise song you like or choose a psalm from the Bible. Then talk about a line or a verse that speaks to you about God's beauty, goodness, truth, or love.

Invite students to share the songs they thought about and their reflections on the lyrics that resonate with them.

### Dive In Activity

This activity offers students an opportunity to praise God in song as David did. Students can work independently, as partners, or as teams.

BIBLICAL CHARACTER VIDEO

**David** . . . . . . . . . . . . . . . . . . . . . . . . . **Fr. Frankie Cicero**

"Then David said to the Philistine, 'You come to me with a sword and with a spear and with a javelin; but I come to you in the name of the Lord of hosts, the God of the armies of Israel, whom you have defied.'" —1 Samuel 17:45

**BIBLICAL CHARACTER VIDEO**

As before, ask students to put away phones, close laptops, and avoid other distractions so they can give their full attention to the video presentation. Ask them to pay special attention to what Fr. Frankie and David teach us about doing things that seem impossible.

**BIBLICAL CHARACTER PROFILE**

Read the text in the workbook about David. You can select students to read different paragraphs aloud to increase class participation. Pay special attention to what it means to walk with God, trusting him to fight for you.

## BIBLICAL CHARACTER PROFILE

# David

When Fr. Frankie was 13 years old, he went to Bible camp. As he got on the bus to depart, one of the leaders invited him to share his testimony to the group later. Fr. Frankie was terrified! What would he say? What if people laughed at him? What if he sounded stupid? These fears were like the giant Goliath in his head. As he faced his fears, Fr. Frankie was like **David**.

David's brothers were all warriors, but David was a shepherd. While his brothers were off fighting the Philistines, David was at home, caring for his aging father, Jesse, and tending the family's sheep. One day Jesse asked David to deliver food to his brothers in the army camp.

When he arrived at their camp, David found the Israelite army being terrorized by Goliath, the giant. No soldier had the courage to fight Goliath, so the giant continued to taunt and threaten them. David had no military training, no armor, no heavy sword, and no weapons other than a sling. But he had complete confidence that God was with him, and he volunteered to fight Goliath himself. David's trust in God allowed God's power to work through him. The shepherd defeated the giant.

Fr. Frankie was scared to give his testimony, but he prayed and asked God to be with him. God provided: Fr. Frankie

76 | ENCOUNTER

## STEP 8 Biblical Character Profile: DAVID

This step features a short video by Fr. Frankie, the read-aloud profile of David in the workbook, and an exercise for students to do during class or at home.

After you play the video, review the video notes on page 96 of the Leader's Guide and ask students about specific points of interest. Then read the profile text aloud and give your students time to do the "Slaying Goliath" exercise.

went from clinging to his notes to tearing them up and throwing them away. His fears vanished and he delivered his testimony with confidence. Fr. Frankie's trust in God allowed God to touch others through his testimony.

You have the same God on your side! God wants to work powerfully through you. God is with you, and when you stay faithful in walking with him, you will slay giants. When you walk with God, you never walk alone.

## Slaying Goliath

Find David on your *Bible Timeline* chart. What period did he live in? Now read the story of David and Goliath in **1 Samuel 17:1–50**.

In your own life, what "Goliath" do you need to slay? Your giant is probably not a literal enemy soldier, but it may be fear, insecurity, self-doubt, anxiety, or even a bad habit. A Goliath can be any problem that seems impossible to solve. Fr. Frankie shared how, with God's help, he faced his Goliath of fear and self-doubt and rose to the occasion.

Write a short reflection about a Goliath in your life. How does this Goliath affect your life negatively? What do you wish was different? Ask God to help you conquer your Goliath. Share your reflection with the group.

___

___

___

___

___

___

77

### BIBLICAL CHARACTER EXERCISE

"Slaying Goliath" invites students to reflect on the Goliaths in their own lives.

Make sure everyone has a *Bible Timeline* chart, their workbook, and something to write with. Before starting the activity, invite students to find David on the chart. Then navigate to 1 Samuel 17:1–50 in the Bible and read it as a class.

Go over the instructions for the exercise carefully, answer questions, and give students time to write. When they have finished, invite them to share their reflections with the group.

Depending on time, you can use the prompts to lead a group discussion or assign the exercise as homework.

**Notes**

___

___

___

___

___

___

___

Ask students how last week's "Living It Out" activities went. Then read the text in the workbook, which suggests some ways to honor Jesus as our King as well as ways to honor the human dignity we all share. Encourage students to turn the ideas into a personal action plan.

For this lesson, you may want to share a prayer to Jesus that is special to you.

**FAMILY CATECHESIS**

Remind parents to use the "Living It Out" activities for family catechesis. (They are available on Thinkific, as are the videos and other resources.) Parents' help makes all the difference! Invite them to brainstorm with their child this week, thinking of ways to serve other people and honor their God-given dignity.

## Find Out More

**Royal Kingdom and Divided Kingdom**

Here are some stories you can read about the times when the Israelites had a king.

David Moves the Ark to Jerusalem ............ 2 Samuel 6:1–5

Solomon Builds the Temple ......1 Kings 6:1, 7, 11–13, 21–28, 38

Elijah on Mount Carmel .................... 1 Kings 18:20–39

The Prophet Jonah and the Big Fish................Jonah 1–2

## Living It Out

Is Jesus the true king of your heart? Did you know that by your **BAPTISM**, you also share in Jesus' royalty? You are a son or daughter of the King of Kings! Here are some ideas to help you begin living up to your royal calling:

- Write a brief prayer to Jesus as the king of your heart. Display it where you will see it and pray it often. Consider inviting your family to join you in this daily prayer.
- Jesus shows us that a true king reigns by serving others. This week, commit to doing one act of service each day. It may be something you do directly for your family or friends, like volunteering for extra chores or helpful tasks. It may be something small or even unknown by others, like saving someone a seat or saying a prayer for someone's intentions. It may even be something you do for a stranger or for the community, like picking up trash on the sidewalk when you pass by.
- The Church's teaching on **MORALITY** in the *Catechism of the Catholic Church* begins with St. Leo's words: "Christian, recognize your dignity" (CCC 1691). Understanding your own dignity as God's son or daughter is essential to your life in the Church.

  This week, try to build up your dignity and the dignity of others. Maybe you can be extra polite and courteous to others and avoid humor that makes fun of others. Maybe you can limit negative thoughts and statements about yourself and your body. Maybe you can respond to your parents the first time they ask you to do something instead of dragging your feet. You could dress nicely for Mass. You could pay more attention when someone is talking to you. If you look closely, you will find many ways to build up dignity in your ordinary day.

78 | ENCOUNTER

## Find Out More & Living It Out

For students who are interested and like to read, mention the stories in "Find Out More," which they can read at home. You may also consider using one of these passages for *lectio divina*.

The "Living It Out" activities are specially designed to be done at home. Read the workbook text together to give your students ideas for putting what they have learned into practice. Remind them that you will check in with them the next time you meet to see how they are doing.

## WORDPLAY

**anoint**: From a Latin word meaning "to smear with oil." Anointing is a ceremonial practice in which holy oil is smeared on someone as a sign that they are set apart for a special purpose.

**Baptism**: From a Greek word meaning "to immerse." Through Baptism, we become a new creation, an adopted son or daughter of God, and an official member of the Church.

**Messiah**: From the Hebrew word that means "anointed one." The Messiah was prophesied to be the one who would deliver the Jewish people from oppression.

**morality**: The principles that determine whether something is right or wrong, good or evil.

## CLOSING PRAYER

"Lord our God, we commit ourselves to serving you as our King. We also commit to serving those around us as we share in your reign. May we open our hearts to others instead of remaining distant. Help us to seek you in all that we do. In Jesus' name, we pray. Amen."

### Closing Prayer

Remind students of their homework assignments. Then lead them in the closing prayer. Begin and end the prayer with the Sign of the Cross.

**THIS WEEK'S HOMEWORK**

1. Memorize the memory verse: Psalm 93:1.
2. Do their "Living It Out" activity.

# EXILE – RETURN – MACCABEAN REVOLT

## LESSON OVERVIEW

In this lesson, students journey with the people of God through some really dark times. The lesson explores the Exile in Babylon, the return of the Jews to Jerusalem under Persian rule, and the brutal time of the Maccabees under Greek occupation.

The focus is on the lights that shine in darkness—particularly the prophet Daniel. His story figures heavily into the narrative of the lesson and points students to their own call to be faithful in tough times. This lesson also shows students a path to rededication and commitment through Ezra's leadership in Israel during the return after the Exile.

Middle school students can learn about how to endure in times of trial. This lesson is deeply relevant for each of them and the challenges they may face. This lesson also reaches forward to the coming of Christ and sets the stage for the time and place into which Christ was born.

## LESSON OBJECTIVES

Students will

- **Learn** the narrative of the tough times that Israel faced in captivity and under the domination of several empires.
- **Encounter** the prophet Daniel as a model of faithfulness in tough times.
- **Explore** ways to recommit and restore after chaotic trials such as those Israel faced in captivity.
- **Trust** in the larger plan that God has even when we find ourselves in captivity and times of ruin.
- **Anticipate** how these events pave the way for God to enter history in the person of Jesus and address all humanity through Israel's ongoing drama.

## VIDEO LESSON NOTES

### DIVE IN VIDEO – **EXILE, RETURN, MACCABEAN REVOLT** – MARK HART

Mark will prompt you to pause the video to read these passages:

> **Daniel 6:16–23, Daniel in the Lion's Den** (Note: Students using a Bible that is not RSV-2CE may find these verses from Daniel numbered differently.)
>
> **Ezra 3:10–11, Worship Restored in Jerusalem**

We start with the reality that the kingdom is divided. Both the Northern and the Southern Kingdoms have had bad kings who snatched the people's hearts away from God. At the end of the last lesson, the whole Northern Kingdom has been conquered and destroyed.

## Daniel: A Light in the Darkness of Exile

- The Southern Kingdom also falls. God tries to warn the people and rescue them, but they won't follow him. The Temple is destroyed, families are separated, and the people are exiled to a foreign land. Everything seems hopeless.
- Daniel is a Jew who follows God, even in the darkness of exile. (The Jews are the Israelites who lived in Judah, the Southern Kingdom.) Even though Daniel is a foreigner in Babylon, the king trusts him and depends on him for guidance (just as Pharaoh depended on Joseph back in Egypt).
- But Daniel's enemies persuade the king to pass a law that makes it a crime to pray to any god except the king. They know that Daniel prays to the true God and will not pray to the king.
- So Daniel is arrested and thrown into a den of lions. But Daniel trusts in God, and miraculously, the lions do not hurt him. Mark connects this to the students' lives: "No matter how scary it is around you, how scary the enemy is, even in times of suffering, God is never going to abandon you."

## Returning Home

- God releases the Jews from captivity by changing the heart of the Persian king Cyrus, who lets them return to their homeland. But the land they go back to is in ruins. They need to rebuild the Temple, their houses, their government, and most of all their relationship with God. They have lived for many years among people who worship false gods, and they have forgotten God's Word and his promises.
- God uses the prophets and leaders like Haggai and Ezra to remind them who he is. Ezra leads them as they rebuild the Temple and restore worship. And the people rejoice!
- When worship comes first, everything else works itself out.

## Maccabean Revolt

- The Book of Maccabees tells another dark and violent story. This one is about how, many years later, the Jews fight the most powerful army in the world: the Greeks.
- The Greeks have invaded Jerusalem and now control it. They demand that the Jewish people burn incense to false gods.
- One man refuses: Mattathias. Mattathias destroys the altar of the false god and kills a Greek officer and a Jew who were there to burn incense.
- With his sons and brothers, Mattathias starts a revolution. They become known as the Maccabees ("the Hammers"). They fight for many years, refusing to give up—and finally, they win. They defeat the Greeks. They reclaim the Temple and restore worship there.

## Put God First

- What can we learn from this?

  Mark says, "If you're ever in a period of darkness, if you're ever challenged by bullies who want to pressure you into doing the wrong thing, if you're in your own lion's den, put God first. His love can carry you through the darkest days. Bullying isn't new. Suffering isn't new. ... If you can kneel before God, you can stand before anyone."

After the Greeks, it will be the Romans who occupy the land. Jesus is about to be born, and he's going to do things no one has ever done before. As we learn in the next lesson, God's light will soon be fully revealed, and the darkness will be defeated forever.

### BIBLICAL CHARACTER VIDEO – **ESTHER** – CHIKA ANYANWU

Chika says she is a really good runner. She's especially good at running away from tough, awkward, and uncomfortable situations. But over time she has learned to live out the words of St. Paul to St. Timothy, that God has given us "a spirit of power and love and self-control" (2 Timothy 1:7).

Chika and others were having dinner one night when a man in the group made angry and racist comments. Nobody said anything. After dinner, despite the urge to run, Chika decided to ask her friends to pray for her for wisdom, charity, and fortitude. She also fasted. Finally, she was ready to talk to the man. He was surprisingly receptive, and he repented for what he had said.

Chika's story reminds us of Esther. Esther was a Jew who became a queen of Persia when she married the pagan king Ahasuerus. Haman, one of the king's powerful advisors, gave an order that all the Jews would be killed the following month. As queen, Esther was safe from Haman's order. But she fasted and prayed, and all the Jews fasted and prayed. Then, on the third day, Esther did something very dangerous: she approached King Ahasuerus without being invited. (This could have cost her her life.) But she was strengthened by her prayers and the prayers of her people. She persuaded the king to revoke Haman's order. He did, and Haman was hanged.

Chika shares some lines from Esther's prayer: "Remember, O Lord; make yourself known in this time of our affliction, and give me courage. ... Save me from my fear" (Esther 14:12, 19).

Chika encourages students to run toward God and to not be afraid to ask for prayers. Chika's and Esther's stories remind us that prayer and fasting—both our own and others'—can give us great courage.

## LEADER-GUIDED DISCUSSION (OPTIONAL)

If you have time, talk to your students about fasting and prayer, which play a large part in the story of Esther, in Chika's story, and in our lives today.

### Fasting and Prayer

Esther and her friends fasted and prayed for three days before Esther asked the king to deliver her people.

What is fasting? *Fasting* usually means doing without food or drink—having less than usual or none at all for a certain period of time. But it can also mean sacrificing other comforts or activities we enjoy, like video games. The point of fasting is to pray better and become closer to God. We let ourselves get hungry, and our hunger helps us pay better attention to God and turn our hearts to him. In our hunger, we ask him for the help we need for ourselves and for other people. We prepare ourselves to do his will.

People fast throughout the Bible. The Israelites fasted before they went into battle (Judges 20:26–28; 1 Samuel 7:5–11; 1 Maccabees 3:47), when they were in mourning (2 Samuel 1:12; 1 Chronicles 10:12), when asking for deliverance or protection (2 Samuel 12:16; Esther; Ezra 8:23, Judith 4:13), and when they were sorry for their sins (1 Kings 21:27). Most importantly, Jesus fasts and prays for forty days before he begins his public ministry, as we will learn in Lesson Seven. In Matthew 6:16–18, Jesus shows his followers that he expects them to fast when he teaches them how to fast. The early Church fasts and prays for Paul and Barnabas when they are sent out (Acts 13:2–3) and for newly appointed elders (Acts 14:23).

Catholics between the ages of 18 and 59 are required to fast on Ash Wednesday and Good Friday. On those days, we may have just one full meal and two smaller meals that do not equal a full meal. We also abstain from meat on Fridays during Lent.

Have you ever fasted? What are some things you can fast from? In your opinion, what is worth fasting *for*? Could you fast for someone you love or for something that is important to you? Could you fast to better know God's will?

## BEFORE- AND AFTER-CLASS REMINDERS

### Before students arrive:

Make sure you have all the supplies needed for the lesson, such as Student Workbooks, Bibles, copies of *The Bible Timeline* chart, materials for activities, paper, and pens or pencils.

If you are handing out Bibles, place one at each student's place.

Review the video notes for the lesson and take note of anything you would like to mention to the class before they watch the video presentations.

Set up the equipment for the video presentations and queue the first video so that it is ready to play.

### After class:

Follow up with students who missed the lesson.

**NOTES**

**WELCOME**

Some suggested ice-breakers:

- Would you rather be a dolphin or an eagle?
- What is your favorite season? Why?

# Lesson Six

## Exile – Return – Maccabean Revolt

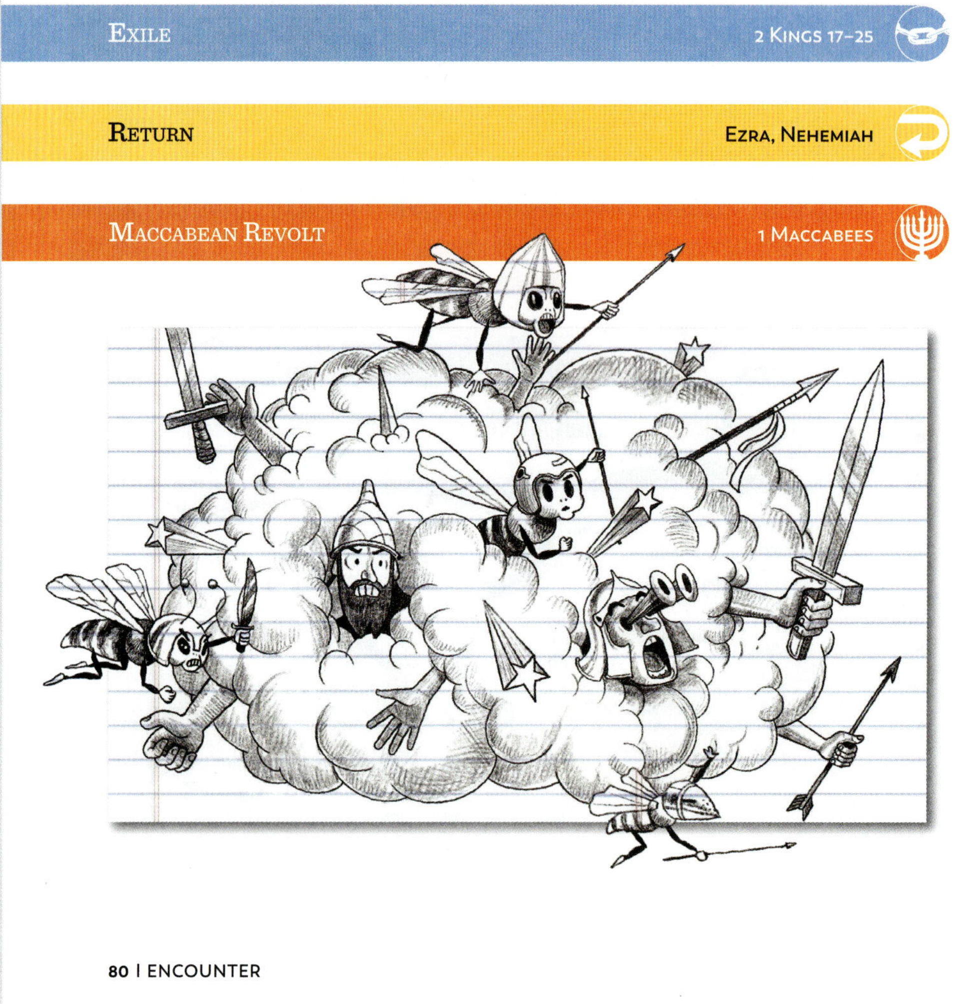

Exile — 2 Kings 17–25

Return — Ezra, Nehemiah

Maccabean Revolt — 1 Maccabees

80 | ENCOUNTER

## STEP 1 Welcome – The Big Picture

Greet students by name as they arrive, and take attendance so that you can follow up later with students who are absent. Ask an ice-breaker question to put students at ease. Then read "The Big Picture" text together.

## The Big Picture

God's light shines even in the darkest moments. This lesson is about a dark time in Israel's history. God's Chosen People had become a kingdom—the kingdom of Israel—but the kingdom had split. Foreign powers conquered them, and the Israelites now faced exile and the destruction of Solomon's Temple.

Still, God's light shone through those who were faithful. The prophet Daniel is a great example. He was faithful to God even in the most extreme circumstances—even when he was face to face with lions.

**THE BIG PICTURE**

This lesson's "Big Picture" prepares students to see light in the dark time of Israel's Exile, with Daniel and Esther as powerful examples of being faithful in hard times. For this lesson, it will be helpful for you and your students to bookmark Isaiah 43, Daniel 6, Ezra 3, and Esther 14.

### OPENING PRAYER

"Lord God, you are faithful to us always. In tough times, you are close. Help our hearts to know and trust you every day, in every situation. Give us the grace to be faithful and have confidence in you. May we learn from the faithful men and women of Scripture and imitate their trust in you. In Jesus' name, we pray. Amen."

## Opening Prayer

When students have settled, invite them to share their prayer requests, and then pray the opening prayer in the Student Workbook, beginning with the Sign of the Cross. You may lead the prayer yourself, pray it aloud as a class, or ask a student to read it.

If you wish to end the prayer with a Hail Mary or Glory Be, remind students that they can find the words in "Further Resources," on page 129 of their workbook. End the prayer with the Sign of the Cross.

**MEMORY VERSE**

Read **Isaiah 43:2** aloud. What is God saying to us? What does this verse tell us about him?

***LECTIO DIVINA* (OPTIONAL)**

Invite your students to close their eyes and open their hearts and minds to the Holy Spirit. Read **Isaiah 43:2** slowly and prayerfully out loud. Pause and then ask your students to read and reflect on the verse themselves. Encourage them to focus on a specific word or phrase that seems important.

To encourage conversation, you can invite a willing student to share the word or phrase that stood out for them. Then ask whether it resonated with anyone else, and invite others to share.

If you want to use a longer passage for *lectio divina*, consider one listed in "Find Out More" on page 92 of the workbook.

## REMEMBER THIS!

"When you pass through the
waters I will be with you;
and through the rivers,
they shall not overwhelm you;
when you walk through fire
you shall not be burned,
and the flame shall
not consume you."

—Isaiah 43:2

God is faithful. The Bible shows us in this lesson how true that is—in tough times, exile, and even a lion's den. Through the prophet Isaiah, God speaks to us about his faithfulness. He doesn't promise that things will be easy, fun, or comfortable. But God does promise that he will be with us and that he will bring us through whatever happens.

What a powerful promise! Keep this verse close to your heart for tough times. Hard math test? Your team is losing by fifty points? Someone has hurt your heart? In all these situations, remember: "The flame shall not consume you!"

82 | ENCOUNTER

## Remember This!

Ask "Who can recite the memory verse from the last class?" (It's Psalm 93:1.) Be ready to award small prizes to those who can recite it successfully!

This lesson's memory verse reminds us that God is always close, especially during hard times. The verse is written in the workbook, but you may want to ask students to find Isaiah 43:2 in their Bibles. Ask them to memorize it, and remind them that you will ask them about it at the next class. You may also use the verse for *lectio divina*.

WARM UP

## Prophets

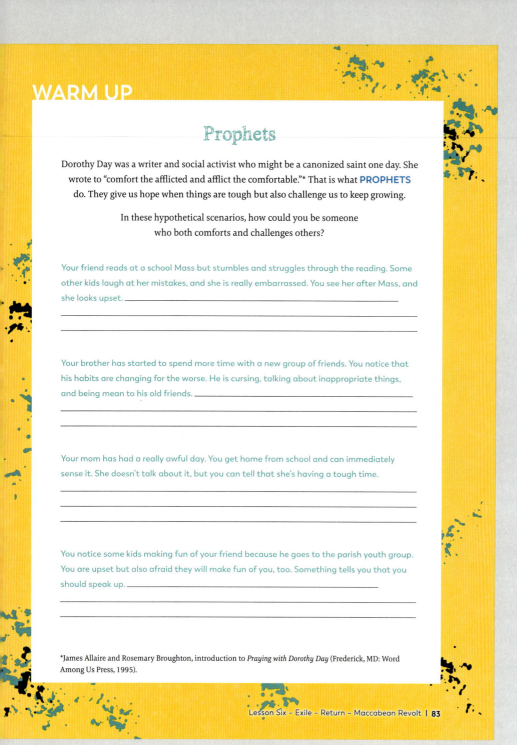

Dorothy Day was a writer and social activist who might be a canonized saint one day. She wrote to "comfort the afflicted and afflict the comfortable."* That is what **PROPHETS** do. They give us hope when things are tough but also challenge us to keep growing.

In these hypothetical scenarios, how could you be someone who both comforts and challenges others?

Your friend reads at a school Mass but stumbles and struggles through the reading. Some other kids laugh at her mistakes, and she is really embarrassed. You see her after Mass, and she looks upset. ____________________

____________________

____________________

Your brother has started to spend more time with a new group of friends. You notice that his habits are changing for the worse. He is cursing, talking about inappropriate things, and being mean to his old friends. ____________________

____________________

____________________

Your mom has had a really awful day. You get home from school and can immediately sense it. She doesn't talk about it, but you can tell that she's having a tough time.

____________________

____________________

____________________

You notice some kids making fun of your friend because he goes to the parish youth group. You are upset but also afraid they will make fun of you, too. Something tells you that you should speak up. ____________________

____________________

____________________

*James Allaire and Rosemary Broughton, introduction to *Praying with Dorothy Day* (Frederick, MD: Word Among Us Press, 1995).

Lesson Six – Exile – Return – Maccabean Revolt | 83

### Warm Up: *Prophets*

This activity will help students reflect on ways they can bring hope to others.

Make sure everyone has a workbook and something to write with. Go over the instructions carefully and answer questions. For this activity, you may want to have students write down their thoughts individually or work through each scenario in pairs or small groups. When they have finished, invite them to share what they came up with.

## TIME PERIOD OVERVIEW

### Exile, Return, and Maccabean Revolt

On your *Bible Timeline* chart, look for the Exile (baby blue), Return (yellow), and Maccabean Revolt (orange) panels. You'll find the stories of this period in 2 Kings, Ezra, Nehemiah, and 1 Maccabees.

In our last lesson, we saw that most of Israel's kings were disasters. They were unfaithful to God, and some even worshiped the idols of false gods. Even the better kings, like Solomon and David, committed serious sins. The kings' selfishness and sin always brought trouble to the people.

After Solomon came his son Rehoboam, who greedily taxed the people and caused great suffering. The people rebelled, and Israel split into two weak kingdoms. The northern kingdom was conquered by the Assyrians and eventually disappeared. The southern kingdom of Judah lasted a little longer but was conquered by the Babylonians, who took the people captive and made them slaves.

## STEP 5 Time Period Overview: Exile, Return, and Maccabean Revolt

Invite students to take out their *Bible Timeline* charts and open them to the baby blue, yellow, and orange panels. Review the key events and people and the approximate dates in history to give additional context to the lesson. Notice the changes in world power—from Assyria to Babylon, Persia, Greece, and then Rome.

Review the key word in the "Time Period Overview" text in the workbook, and then read the text together. You can ask students to read different paragraphs aloud to increase class participation.

## HANUKKAH

After the Maccabeans defeated the Greeks, they returned to Jerusalem to find the Temple in ruins. The people went to work immediately. They repaired the Temple, purified it, and made new holy vessels. Finally, they rededicated the Temple to God, celebrating with songs and thanksgiving for eight days (2 Maccabees 10:1–8).

Jewish tradition tells us that a miracle occurred at the rededication, for the people could find only a small jar of oil to burn in the Temple menorah—enough oil for one day. But the oil lasted miraculously through all eight days!

If you have Jewish friends, you know that Jews still celebrate the rededication of the Temple and the miracle of the oil every year during the eight days of Hanukkah.

But God's light shone in the darkness of the **EXILE**, especially in the lives of people like Daniel, who remained loyal to God even when it meant risking his life.

After the Exile, the people returned from Babylon in stages. They were now called Jews because their homeland was Judah. Their beautiful Temple had been destroyed, and Jerusalem lay in ruins—so they got to work. They rebuilt the Temple, renewed the covenant, and rebuilt Jerusalem's walls.

Even though they were still ruled by different conquering empires, the Jews lived in relative peace for many years. But when they were living under Greek rule, they could not worship God freely, and the people rebelled. Judas Maccabeus and his brothers led an uprising that Jews still celebrate now, every Hanukkah.

## If You Ask Me

- Have you ever felt betrayed by someone who was supposed to be a friend? What was the experience like? How hard was it for you to forgive them?
- Why do you think God remained faithful to the Israelites even though they repeatedly failed to stay faithful to him?

### IF YOU ASK ME

These questions are about faithfulness. To ease students into a whole-class conversation, consider starting them off in pairs or small groups and then transition to a large group discussion.



DIVIDED KINGDOM
1 Kings 12–22
2 Kings 1–16

EXILE
2 Kings 17–25

RETURN
Ezra
Nehemiah

MACCABEAN REVOLT
1 Maccabees

MESSIANIC FULFILLMENT
Luke

THE CHURCH
Acts

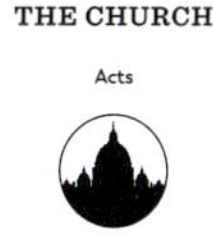

The key takeaway here is that the Exile was a direct consequence of the sins and unfaithfulness of the leaders of Israel, and yet even in these dark times, God remained faithful to his people.

## DIVE IN VIDEO

Make sure the video and sound system are set up. Mark will ask your students to read **Daniel 6:16-23** and **Ezra 3:10-11** during the presentation, so invite them to find and bookmark those passages in their Bibles before watching the video. Also consider reviewing the "Got It?" questions together on page 88 of the workbook so they can be alert for the answers as they watch.

Finally, ask students to put away phones, close laptops, and avoid other distractions so they can give the video their full attention. Be prepared to pause the presentation when prompted for Bible reading.

## DIVE IN TEXT

Read the "Dive In" text in the workbook, which tells the stories of Daniel in the lion's den and the rebuilding of Jerusalem after the Exile. The text can be read aloud in class or assigned for quiet reading.

DIVE IN VIDEO

**Exile, Return, Maccabean Revolt . . . . . . . . . . . . . .Mark Hart**

"Sometimes the light of God is clearest in the darkest moments." —Mark H.

*During the video, Mark will ask you to pause and read two Bible stories. Find and mark them in your Bibles now so that you can open to them quickly when you need to:*

- *Daniel 6:16–23, Daniel in the Lion's Den*
- *Ezra 3:10–11, Worship Restored in Jerusalem*

In the dark period of exile, Daniel stands out as a light. Daniel was one of the Jews enslaved in Babylon. He was a holy and prayerful man; though he was a captive, he even impressed the Babylonian king, Nebuchadnezzar. Like Joseph in Genesis, Daniel became an important advisor to Nebuchadnezzar and the kings who came after him.

Other advisors became jealous of Daniel's special favor and hatched a plan to destroy him. They convinced the king that he was a god, so anyone who prayed to another god must be a threat. The king agreed and issued new laws that made praying to another god punishable by death. Meanwhile, Daniel remained faithful and prayed to God as he always had—so Daniel's enemies pounced, accusing him of breaking the king's new laws.

The king faced a dilemma. He had to enforce his own laws so he would not appear weak, but he also really liked Daniel and did not wish to kill him. But his pride won. The king sent Daniel to certain death in the lion's den, telling him, "May your God, whom you serve continually, deliver you" (Daniel 6:16). To everyone's astonishment, God did just that! The hungry lions refused to touch Daniel, and he survived miraculously.

Daniel's story shows God's faithfulness even in dark, terrible times. The Israelites were once again enslaved. They had been unfaithful to God, but God remained faithful to them. Eventually, God worked through Cyrus, the king of Persia, to bring them out of slavery in Babylon.

86 I ENCOUNTER

## Main Content Teaching

After you watch Mark's teaching video, read the "Dive In" text in the Student Workbook together. Three more "If You Ask Me" questions follow the text along with a quick "Got It?" quiz. Detailed notes on the video content start on page 114 of this Leader's Guide.

When Jews returned to the Promised Land, their hearts were still far from the Lord. In Babylon, they had adopted many false gods, just as they had when they were slaves in Egypt. Now, again, they needed God to cleanse their hearts. They had forgotten God's law, the Temple had been destroyed, and they had fallen into idolatry.

But God continued to be faithful. Upon their return, God sent prophets and great leaders like Haggai, Ezra, and Nehemiah. Haggai and Nehemiah led them to rebuild the Temple and the city of Jerusalem. Ezra encouraged them, teaching them about God's law and leading them to renew the covenant with God.

"Do not be grieved, for the joy of the LORD is your strength."
—Nehemiah 8:10

## If You Ask Me

- Is there anyone in your life or in our world today who reminds you of Daniel because of his or her faithfulness, even during difficulty? How does this person show faithfulness?
- Who are some "prophets" that God sends to our modern society to remind us of our faith?



**IF YOU ASK ME**

These questions are about faithfulness and hope. Consider talking about them in small groups, with class discussion to follow.

### Notes

### GOT IT?

Ask students to complete the quiz in the workbook, and review their answers together. After you've gone over the answers, see if your students have any other questions about the lesson so far.

# Got It?

1. **The story of the prophet Daniel is similar in some ways to the story of ________ in the book of Genesis.**

   a. Adam

   b. Joseph (circled)

   c. Abraham

   d. Noah

2. **God miraculously saved Daniel from execution by ________.**

   a. lions (circled)

   b. a firing squad

   c. drowning

   d. burning

3. **Which of these was the pagan king God used to send the Jews home from exile?**

   a. Daniel

   b. Cyrus (circled)

   c. Ezra

   d. Nehemiah



## Notes

DIVE IN ACTIVITY

## Prophets of Hope

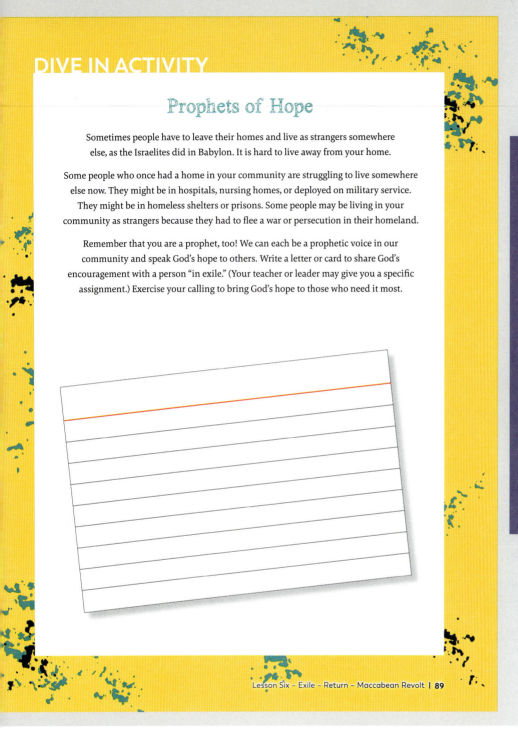

Sometimes people have to leave their homes and live as strangers somewhere else, as the Israelites did in Babylon. It is hard to live away from your home.

Some people who once had a home in your community are struggling to live somewhere else now. They might be in hospitals, nursing homes, or deployed on military service. They might be in homeless shelters or prisons. Some people may be living in your community as strangers because they had to flee a war or persecution in their homeland.

Remember that you are a prophet, too! We can each be a prophetic voice in our community and speak God's hope to others. Write a letter or card to share God's encouragement with a person "in exile." (Your teacher or leader may give you a specific assignment.) Exercise your calling to bring God's hope to those who need it most.

Lesson Six – Exile – Return – Maccabean Revolt | 89

**PROPHETS OF HOPE**

Make sure everyone has paper and a pen. To prepare in advance for this activity, you may wish to research local nursing homes and shelters and check on the requirements for letters to service members, prisoners, or other possible recipients of students' letters.

Go over the activity instructions carefully and answer students' questions. When they have finished writing their letters, collect them to send to the appropriate recipients. For safety and security reasons, make sure students sign their letters only with their first name.

### Dive In Activity

This activity offers students an opportunity to think about what modern-day exile could be like and what it means to be a prophet. Students can work independently, as partners, or in teams.

BIBLICAL CHARACTER VIDEO

**Esther . . . . . . . . . . . . . . . . . . . . . . . . . . . . Chika Anyanwu**

"'O God, whose might is over all, hear the voice of the despairing, and save us from the hands of evildoers. And save me from my fear!'" —Esther 14:19

## BIBLICAL CHARACTER PROFILE

# Esther

Chika says she is a good runner. But she isn't talking about racing or marathons—she's talking about running away from tough or awkward situations. She used to distract herself, run away from apologizing, and avoid situations that made her uncomfortable. But as she grew, she learned to live out the words of St. Paul to St. Timothy: God has given us a spirit of "power and love and self-control" (2 Timothy 1:7).

Chika found herself in an extremely uncomfortable situation after a dinner where someone had used racist stereotypes. Chika realized that nobody else was going to say anything. Despite her urge to run and avoid it, she made a different choice. She decided to speak to the man who had made the comments. Chika asked her friends to pray for her to have wisdom, charity, and fortitude. She fasted. Finally, she was ready to have a conversation with him. He was surprisingly receptive and repented for what he had said.

Chika's story reminds us of Esther. Esther was a Jew who became the queen of Persia when she married Cyrus, the pagan king. Haman, a powerful advisor to the king, gave an order for all the Jews in the kingdom to be killed on the thirteenth of the month.

Safe in the palace, Esther could have avoided getting involved. Instead, Esther sent a message to her cousin Mordecai

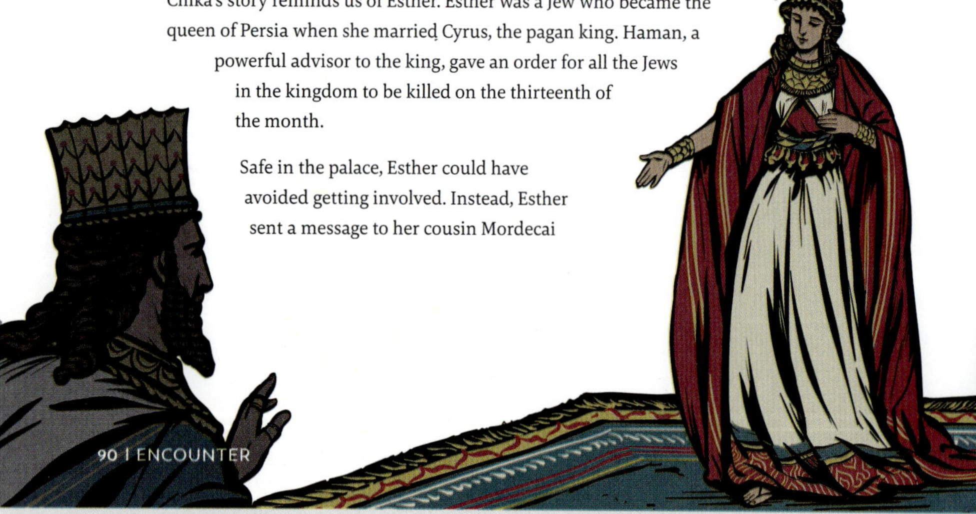

90 | ENCOUNTER

**BIBLICAL CHARACTER VIDEO**

As before, ask students to put away phones, close laptops, and avoid other distractions so they can give their full attention to the video presentation. Ask them to pay special attention to what Chika and Esther teach us about praying and fasting to gain courage and build spiritual strength.

**BIBLICAL CHARACTER PROFILE**

Read the text in the workbook. You can select students to read different paragraphs aloud to increase class participation. Notice how both Chika and Esther fast for the courage to do what's right. If you have time, share "Fasting and Prayer," the leader-guided discussion on pages 116–117 of this guide.

## STEP 8 Biblical Character Profile: ESTHER

This step features a short video by Chika Anyanwu, the read-aloud profile of Esther in the workbook, and an exercise for students to do during class or at home.

After you play the video, review the video notes on page 116 of the Leader's Guide and ask students about specific points of interest. Then read the profile text aloud and give your students time to do the "Fast and Pray" exercise.

to gather all the Jews for a three-day fast. She too fasted and prayed. On the third day, Esther did something extremely dangerous: she approached King Cyrus without an invitation. (This was not allowed and could have cost her life.) But Esther was strengthened by the prayers and the fasting of her community. She didn't run but went forward courageously, empowered by prayer. She asked the king to spare the Jews, and he did. She spoke up for her people and saved them.

Chika's and Esther's stories remind us that prayer and fasting—both our own and that of others—can give us great courage.

## Fast and Pray

Find Esther on your *Bible Timeline* chart. What period is her story in? Now read Esther's prayer in **Esther 14:1–19**.

Think about opportunities to fast and pray in your own life. Fasting can help us build strength and discipline. It is also a way for us to pray. Fasting, even in small ways, helps focus our hearts on hearing God more clearly. Think about the concrete ways you can offer more fasting and prayer.

I can fast from food and also from ______________________________

______________________________.

Like Esther, I can fast and pray when I witness injustice and want to stand up for what is right; I can also fast and pray when/for ______________________________

______________________________.



**BIBLICAL CHARACTER EXERCISE**

"Fast and Pray" invites students to think about fasting and prayer. It can be done in class or assigned as homework.

Make sure everyone has a *Bible Timeline* chart, their workbook, and something to write with. Invite students to find Esther on the chart. Then navigate to Esther's prayer in Esther 14:1–19 in the Bible and read it as a class. You may read it yourself out loud, select students to read it, or ask the group to read it silently.

Next, go over the instructions for the exercise carefully, answer questions, and brainstorm ideas for (1) what to fast *from* and (2) what to fast *for*. Give students time to write. When they have finished, invite them to share their reflections with the group. Consider sharing your own experiences with fasting.

**Notes**

**LIVING IT OUT**

Ask students how last week's "Living It Out" activities went. Then read this lesson's text in the workbook, which suggests some ways to stay faithful to God during difficult times.

Encourage students to turn the ideas into a personal action plan. (This might be a good time to put their plan of fasting into practice!)

**FAMILY CATECHESIS**

Remind parents to use "Living It Out" (and "Fast and Pray") for family catechesis. It is available on Thinkific, as are the videos and other resources. Their help makes all the difference!

Invite parents to work with their child to find ways to deepen their prayer. Encourage them to join their students in a fast of their own this week!

### Find Out More

Assyria Conquers the Northern Kingdom ....... 2 Kings 17:6–8
Babylon Conquers Jerusalem ............... 2 Kings 24:10–17
Zerubbabel Rebuilds the Temple .................... Ezra 5:2
Ezra Reads the Book of the Law ........ Nehemiah 8:1–3, 9–10
Judas Maccabeus Leads the Revolt ........ 1 Maccabees 3:1–9
The Maccabees Purify the Temple........ 1 Maccabees 4:36–58

**Exile, Return, and Maccabean Revolt**

Here are more stories you can read from the times of Exile and Return, along with two stories about Judas Maccabeus and his brothers.

### Living It Out

This lesson has addressed some dark times. How can we live out what we have learned through the stories of God's faithful prophets?

- Be consistent in prayer like Daniel. Keep talking to God no matter how well or how badly things are going. Prayer is not only for times we feel close to God but for *all* times. God wants to hear from you no matter what you are experiencing. Even in the toughest times, God will not leave you alone or abandon you.
- Be patient. God's deliverance and plan often follow a different timeline than what we want. Sometimes we go through hard things and wonder if God is still with us. Yes, he is! Always! A tough time is never a sign that God has abandoned us, but it may be a time for us to grow in trust when we aren't sure how things will work out.
- Be prophetic. God wants to speak through you. Listen for God's voice. Listen as he comforts and challenges you to do better and change accordingly. Ask God to show you when to offer others comfort or a challenge.

## Find Out More & Living It Out

For students who are interested and like to read, mention the stories in "Find Out More," which they can read at home. You may also use one of these passages for *lectio divina.*

The "Living It Out" activities are specially designed to be done at home. Read the workbook text together to give your students ideas for putting what they have learned into practice. Remind them that you will check in with them the next time you meet to see how they are doing.

## WORDPLAY

**exile**: To be forced from your native home and have to live somewhere else. During the Exile period, God's people were conquered by their enemies and led away from the Promised Land.

**prophets:** Individuals chosen by God to proclaim God's will to the people and call everyone to live according to the covenant.

## CLOSING PRAYER

"Lord God, we can imagine what it was like for the Israelites who lived in exile. The world around us tempts us too to turn away from you, and sometimes we struggle. Give us the courage to be faithful to you, just as Daniel and Esther were. Help us to trust you everywhere we go and in everything we do. When we are afraid, teach us to fast and pray so that we may grow strong in you. In Jesus' name, we pray. Amen."

## Closing Prayer

Remind students of their homework assignments. Then lead them in the closing prayer. Begin and end the prayer with the Sign of the Cross.

### THIS WEEK'S HOMEWORK

1. Memorize the memory verse: Isaiah 43:2.
2. Do the "Fast and Pray" activity if not done in class.
3. Do their "Living It Out" activity.

# Lesson Seven

## MESSIANIC FULFILLMENT: JESUS AND THE GOSPELS

## LESSON OVERVIEW

Now we arrive at "the Main Event." This lesson is about the Incarnation, the life of Christ, and the Paschal Mystery—Jesus' Passion and death, his Resurrection, and his Ascension. Students will see that God's plan came to fulfillment in Jesus. The lesson seeks to draw students into the narrative of the Gospels with some specific stories at the forefront. While we survey the life of Christ, we take time to focus on Jesus' temptation, the healing of the paralyzed man, and the disciples' encounter with the resurrected Jesus on the road to Emmaus.

This lesson—with the whole program—aims to put students not only in contact with Jesus but "in communion, in intimacy with Jesus Christ [because] only he can lead us to the love of the Father in the Spirit and make us share in the divine life of the Holy Trinity."* Exploring the Gospel as an encounter with Christ—not only in the past but now—will be a powerful experience for your students. Lessons One through Six will have prepared them well for this.

## LESSON OBJECTIVES

Students will

- **Learn** the story of Jesus' life.
- **Encounter** Jesus as the revelation of God the Father's love for us and the source of all salvation.
- **Imagine and engage** specific Gospel stories as they reveal who Jesus is.
- **Connect** specific moments in the Gospel to their own experiences.
- **Grow** in their familiarity with the Gospels and with Jesus himself.

## VIDEO LESSON NOTES

### DIVE IN VIDEO – **MESSIANIC FULFILLMENT** – MARK HART

Mark will prompt you to pause the video to read these passages:

**Luke 4:1–13, The Temptation of Jesus**

**Luke 5:17–26, The Paralyzed Man and His Friends**

**Luke 24:13–31, The Walk to Emmaus**

The Israelites have been through a lot. Mark recaps salvation history and points out the need for an ultimate king.

*John Paul II, *Catechesi Tradendae* (October 16, 1979), 5, vatican.va.

## Jesus Christ

- "This is the most important part of the story," Mark says. "The stories we've covered so far are all leading up to this. The ultimate hero shows up to save the day. I'm sure you know his name: Jesus Christ."
- The Israelites have been through a lot. Mark recaps salvation history and points out the need for an ultimate king.
- Mark shares the core message of the Gospel: God sent us his only Son, who slipped quietly into the world, conceived by the Holy Spirit and born of the Virgin Mary in a dingy little stable.

## Jesus' Forty Days in the Desert

- Mark tells us about the quiet life of Jesus, his baptism, and the forty days in the desert. Notice the first thing that Jesus does as his ministry begins: "Before anything else, he turns his heart to his Father."
- What happens during Jesus' temptation in the desert? The devil (Satan, the evil one, the ultimate bad guy) is determined to take Jesus out. Mark points out that the devil "was the serpent in the garden, the one who turned the Israelites' hearts to false gods, and he doesn't play fair. He attacks people when their defenses are down."
- That's what Satan does with Jesus. Jesus is fasting, and he's alone, and the devil tries to make him doubt who he is: "If you really are the Son of God, do this. Do that." But the devil fails. Jesus knows who he is. He stays calm and answers each of the devil's lies with Scripture! His heart is totally united to the Father, and the devil flees.

## Jesus' Public Ministry

- No one knows who Jesus is when he begins his public ministry. But he quickly gains followers by doing things that no one has ever done before:
  - » He calms a storm with his words.
  - » He casts out demons with his words.
  - » He multiplies loaves and fish to feed thousands.
  - » He heals the deaf and the blind with just spit from his mouth.
  - » He walks on water.
  - » He even raises the dead.
- Jesus' teachings and miracles make the religious leaders uncomfortable, but the poor and the outcasts come to him in huge crowds.

## Jesus Heals the Paralyzed Man

- Mark explains the story of the paralyzed man. The paralyzed man is at the mercy of everyone. But he has some really good friends who will stop at nothing to bring him to Jesus. The house where Jesus is preaching is packed with people, and they can't get anywhere near Jesus. So they break through the roof of the house and let him down with ropes to where Jesus is standing.

- Jesus shows his authority over sin and sickness. He forgives his sins and heals him. The paralyzed man gets up and walks.
- We all need friends like that! We need friends who will do anything to bring us to Jesus.

## Jesus Gives Us the Eucharist

- Jesus grows in fame and popularity. He says challenging things and claims to be the only Way to the Father. He forgives peoples' sins and says that his flesh is true food and his blood is true drink.
- His followers often don't understand and fail to understand when he predicts his Passion and death.
- In Jerusalem, Jesus and his closest followers celebrate the Passover, the feast that commemorates Moses leading the people of Israel out of slavery. He takes bread in his hands and says, "This is my Body, broken for you"—that he will die as a sacrifice for them.

## Jesus' Passion, Death, and Resurrection

- That night, Jesus is betrayed and arrested, and all his friends run away scared. Like us, Jesus knows what it means to feel abandoned and alone. Jesus is falsely accused, sentenced to death, and crucified.
- Jesus' death on the Cross is what God had been planning the whole time. Jesus' perfect sacrifice destroys the power of death forever and ends the rule of evil. The love of God enters into death, and death cannot hold him.
- On the third day after his crucifixion, Jesus rises from the dead so that we all can do the same one day. Mary Magdalene is the first witness of Jesus' Resurrection. Over the next forty days, Jesus appears again and again to his Apostles and to hundreds of witnesses.

## The Road to Emmaus

- The story of the road to Emmaus captures the sadness of his followers at losing him and the wonder they experience as they grasp that he has risen from the dead.
- Cleopas and another disciple are walking from Jerusalem to the village of Emmaus. A man joins them and speaks to them about salvation history, connecting the dots throughout Scripture to show how God promised a Savior from the beginning and how Jesus won our redemption on the Cross.
- As the man speaks, the disciples' hearts are burning within them, but they don't recognize him. It is only when he shares a meal with them and breaks the bread that they know it is Jesus.
- Jesus is made known to them in the breaking of the bread. We too know him in the breaking of the bread: at Mass, in the Eucharist.
- Mark says, "Remember this: Jesus is not just a teacher, he's not just a healer, he's not someone who just says nice things. Jesus is your Savior, and he loves you more than you can ever comprehend."

This all sets the stage for our last lesson, which introduces the adventures of the early Church.

## BIBLICAL CHARACTER VIDEO – **THE BOY WITH THE LOAVES AND FISH** – ASHLEY HINOJOSA

Ashley tells a story about being called to study theology. She faced many obstacles on the way—she had to find money for university, she had to move to a new state, and she was on her own in a new place. She became discouraged and prayed one morning for a sign that she was doing what God wanted her to do.

After Mass that day, she found out she'd been chosen for a big scholarship. It would cover all her tuition! This was an amazing sign. It showed her that she was doing the right thing. Even more, it showed her that God always provides what we need when we need it.

Ashley tells the story of the multiplication of loaves in John 6. Jesus has been preaching to a huge crowd. How will they feed everyone? He asks the Apostles, and they don't know. Then a boy comes up to them with five barley loaves and two fish and offers them to Jesus. The Apostles say it will never be enough. But Jesus blesses the food, breaks the bread, and feeds everyone. They have as much as they want.

God took what the boy offered. It was enough. What the boy offered was all he needed to provide for the crowd.

Like the boy's five loaves and two fish, Ashley's yes was all she had to offer. But it was enough for God to use. What may seem impossible to us is not impossible for God.

## LEADER-GUIDED DISCUSSION (OPTIONAL)

There is so much to talk about in the life of Christ. If you have extra time during the lesson, consider talking to your students about these topics:

### The Beatitudes

Jesus gives us the Beatitudes in his most famous sermon, the Sermon on the Mount (Matthew 5:1–12). The Beatitudes are eight blessings that describe true happiness, which is very different from what the world offers. The world encourages those who seek riches; Jesus blesses the poor in spirit. The world praises the powerful; Jesus blesses the meek. The world often scorns the pure in heart, but Jesus blesses them.

Taken together, the Beatitudes describe what the Christian life looks like when lived truly. They are listed and described more fully in "Further Resources," on page 185 of this guide.

**Questions to ask your students:**

- What do you think it means to be poor in spirit?
- What does it mean to be meek, to hunger and thirst for righteousness, or to be pure in heart?
- Can you think of someone who has been persecuted for righteousness' sake?

### Prophet, Priest, and King

A discussion prompt after the "Time Period Overview" on page 143 asks students to consider the roles of prophet, priest, and king in Jesus' mission and in their own missions. Consider reminding them of the ways God spoke to his people through the prophets, priests, and kings of the Old Testament. As God's Son, Jesus is the fulfillment of these Old Testament offices—the perfect priest, prophet, and king. Today, we share in his mission through our Baptism and Confirmation:

> "Jesus Christ is the one whom the Father anointed with the Holy Spirit and established as priest, prophet, and king. The whole People of God participates in these three offices of Christ and bears the responsibilities for mission and service that flow from them." (CCC 783)

## The Crucifixion

During the "Dive In" discussion or before the closing prayer, consider inviting your students to take a few minutes to think about Jesus' crucifixion in a personal way. Alternatively, print copies of the following meditation for them to take home:

### Thinking About the Crucifixion

If you think you know the story of Jesus' crucifixion or you've heard it all before, pause now and think about what it means that Jesus died for us.

Do you know anyone who would die for you? Even if they did, how much time would their sacrifice add to your life? Even if you live to an old age, death still looms. No other person, even one willing to lay down his or her life for you, has the power to save you from death forever.

But Someone does have that power, Someone who loves you more than you could ever hope—Someone with the power to save you not just for a day or a decade or a lifetime, but for all eternity.

When Jesus Christ died on the Cross, he opened the door to eternal life for us.

# BEFORE- AND AFTER-CLASS REMINDERS

## Before students arrive:

Make sure you have all the supplies needed for the lesson, such as Student Workbooks, Bibles, copies of *The Bible Timeline* chart, materials for activities, paper, and pens or pencils.

If you are handing out Bibles, place one at each student's place.

Review the video notes for the lesson and take note of anything you would like to mention to the class before they watch the video presentations.

Set up the equipment for the video presentations and queue the first video so that it is ready to play.

## After class:

Follow up with students who missed the lesson.

**NOTES**

**WELCOME**

Some suggested ice-breakers:

- What is the latest you have ever stayed up at night?
- If you could travel anywhere, where would you go?

# Lesson Seven

## Messianic Fulfillment: Jesus and the Gospels

MESSIANIC FULFILLMENT LUKE 

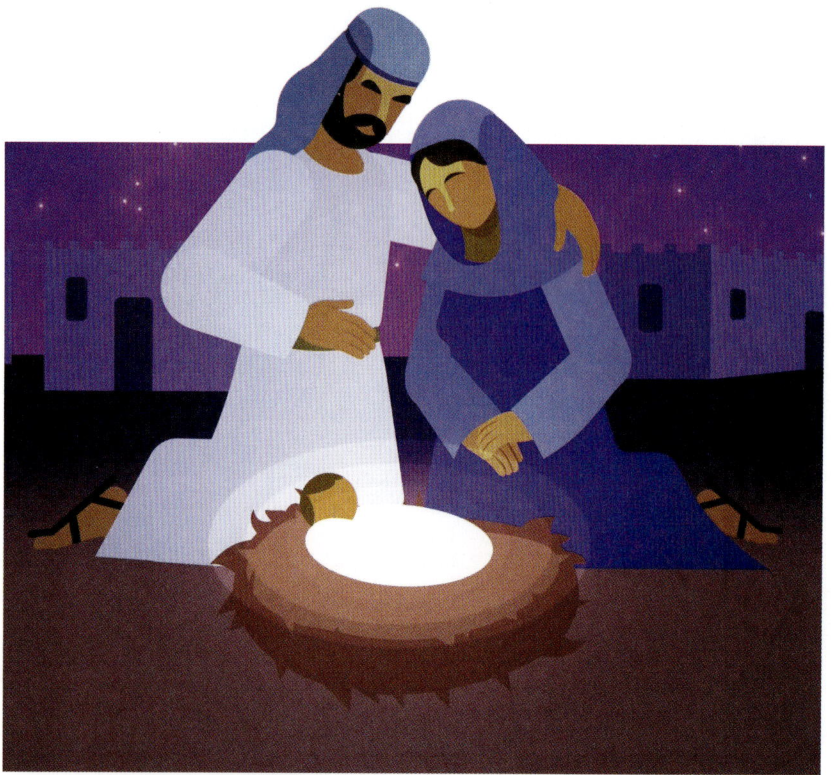

### STEP 1 Welcome – The Big Picture

Greet the students by name as they arrive. Take attendance so that you can follow up later with students who are absent.

Depending on how you ended class last week, invite them to share whether they undertook a personal fast and how it went, or ask an ice-breaker question to put students at ease. Then read "The Big Picture" text together.

## The Big Picture

The center of history. The world's most important event. The greatest thing that ever happened: God became one of us.

God the Son became man and was born in Bethlehem. He is the Messiah, the Savior whom the prophets foretold. Jesus is the one who restores our friendship with God. In his life and ministry, Jesus made clear everything about who God is and who we are. Then by his **Passion**, death, and Resurrection, he proved to be the ultimate hero who won the greatest victory—saving not just the moment or the day, but life itself. Jesus suffered, died, and rose from the dead so that you and I could have eternal life.

**THE BIG PICTURE**

This lesson's "Big Picture" prepares students for this central lesson: to know Jesus, God-with-us, who came to earth to free us from sin and bring us eternal life. You may wish to bookmark John 3 and 6 and Luke 4, 5, and 24. Invite students to bookmark their Bibles, too.

**OPENING PRAYER**

"Lord Jesus, you are the Word made flesh. You are the ultimate hero who came to set me free. Today I am yours. I am sorry for my sins, and I offer you my heart. You are the Savior of the world and my Savior. Open my mind to learn more about your love today. In your name, we pray. Amen."

## Opening Prayer

When students have settled and shared their prayer requests, pray the opening prayer in the Student Workbook, beginning with the Sign of the Cross. You may lead the prayer yourself, pray it aloud as a class, or ask a student to read it. Follow the prayer with a Hail Mary or Glory Be if you wish, and end with the Sign of the Cross.

**MEMORY VERSE**

Read **John 3:16** aloud. Why did God send us his Son? What does this verse tell us about God?

***LECTIO DIVINA* (OPTIONAL)**

Invite your students to close their eyes and open their hearts and minds to the Holy Spirit. Read **John 3:16** slowly and prayerfully out loud. Pause and then ask your students to read and reflect on the verse themselves. Encourage them to focus on a specific word or phrase that seems important.

To encourage conversation, you can invite a willing student to share the word or phrase that stood out for them. Then ask whether it resonated with anyone else, and invite others to share.

If you want to use a longer passage for *lectio divina*, consider one listed in "Find Out More" on page 108 of the workbook.

REMEMBER THIS!

"For God so loved the world that he gave his only-begotten Son, that whoever believes in him should not perish but have eternal life."

—John 3:16

Jesus spoke these words to a Jewish rabbi named Nicodemus. Nicodemus was interested in Jesus and his work, but he was nervous about what others would think of his curiosity—so he met with Jesus in secret. He had many questions for Jesus. In his answers, Jesus shared the heart of his mission. (You can read the story of Nicodemus' secret meeting with Jesus in John 3:1–21.)

The reason Jesus came into the world is summed up in this verse. Jesus is the perfect image of the Father's love, sent for our salvation. Keep this verse in your heart and hold on to this important truth. Use the verse as a prayer, and don't be afraid to share it and proclaim it to others.

96 | ENCOUNTER

## Remember This!

Ask "Who can recite the memory verse from the last class?" (It's Isaiah 43:2.) Be ready to award small prizes to those who can recite it successfully!

This lesson's memory verse may already be familiar to your students. The verse is written in the workbook, but you may want to ask them to find John 3:16 in their Bibles. Ask them to memorize it, and remind them that you will ask them about it at the next class. You may also use the verse for *lectio divina*.

WARM UP

## Who Is Jesus?

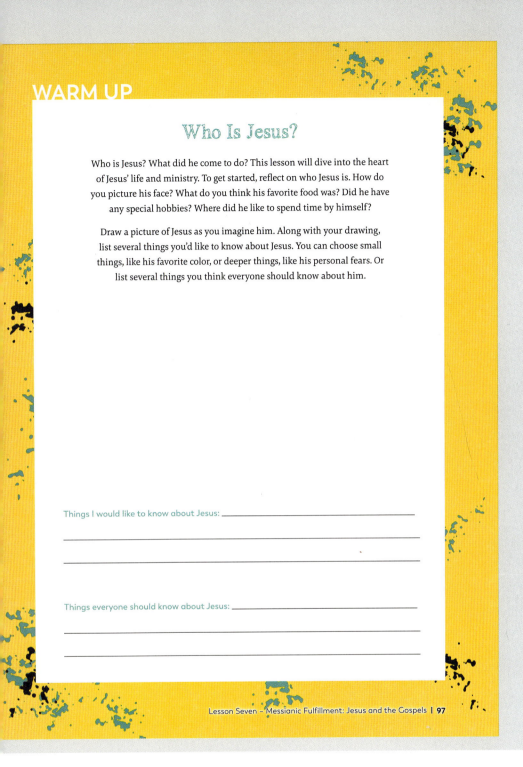

Who is Jesus? What did he come to do? This lesson will dive into the heart of Jesus' life and ministry. To get started, reflect on who Jesus is. How do you picture his face? What do you think his favorite food was? Did he have any special hobbies? Where did he like to spend time by himself?

Draw a picture of Jesus as you imagine him. Along with your drawing, list several things you'd like to know about Jesus. You can choose small things, like his favorite color, or deeper things, like his personal fears. Or list several things you think everyone should know about him.

Things I would like to know about Jesus: ______________________

______________________

______________________

Things everyone should know about Jesus: ______________________

______________________

______________________

Lesson Seven – Messianic Fulfillment: Jesus and the Gospels | 97

### Warm Up: *Who Is Jesus?*

This activity will help students to image what Jesus was like.

Make sure everyone has their workbook, something to write with, and colored pencils or markers for drawing. Go over the instructions carefully and answer questions.

When your students have finished, ask them to share what they drew and wrote. Remind them that the point of this activity is not about how well they draw. It's about using their imagination to reflect on Jesus in a new way.

## TIME PERIOD OVERVIEW

### Messianic Fulfillment

On your *Bible Timeline* chart, look for the **Messianic Fulfillment** panel (gold). This is the period of Jesus' life on earth, the heart of history. It is when all the Old Testament covenants, all God's promises, and all humanity's hopes are fulfilled. We will follow the story in the **GOSPEL** of Luke, and it is also found in the Gospels of Matthew, Mark, and John.

The Old Testament gave us a glimpse of God's ultimate plan. Every single thing so far has led to the ultimate hero of that plan: Jesus.

No matter how much his Chosen People messed up, God never stopped loving them and never abandoned his covenant. Nor will God ever stop loving us. What he wants most from each of us is our heart. He proved this once and for all in Jesus. God didn't send another prophet, priest, or king to deliver his people. He sent his only Son—the highest prophet, priest, and king of all.

When he arrived on earth, God's Son didn't descend from the clouds. He didn't ride in with an army of angels. He quietly slipped into the world like any other child. This is called **THE INCARNATION**—

## STEP 5 Time Period Overview: Messianic Fulfillment

Invite students to take out their Bible Timeline charts and open them to the gold panel. This period, when Jesus Christ became man, is the fulfillment of salvation history.

To give additional context to the lesson, review together the key events of the time period, especially the New Covenant in Christ and the world power (Rome). Notice how dates change with the birth of Jesus: from BC ("before Christ") to AD (*anno Domini*, "the year of Our Lord").

when God took on a human body and became one of us. Conceived by the Holy Spirit, born of the Virgin Mary, Jesus was known for most of his life only by his family and close neighbors. As he grew up, it's possible that nobody saw him as anyone special. He spent most of his life working as a carpenter, quietly praying and turning his heart to the Father as he waited for his public ministry to begin.

When that time came, Jesus was baptized in the Jordan River by John the Baptist, and then he went into the desert to pray and fast for forty days. Satan tried to tempt him there with promises of worldly power, but Jesus resisted him (Luke 4:1–15).

Jesus relied wholly on God, often going off by himself to be with the Father and pray. The *Catechism* tells us that his prayer was "humble and trusting" (CCC 2600). Jesus prayed at his baptism (Luke 3:21–22), and he prayed all night before choosing his twelve Apostles (Luke 6:12–13). Jesus was praying when Peter confessed that he was the Christ (which is the Greek word for the Messiah, the "anointed one"), and he was praying as he was **TRANSFIGURED**, appearing in all his glory in front of Peter, James, and John (Luke 9:18–20, 29). Jesus was also praying when one of his followers asked him to teach them to pray; that's when Jesus taught them the **OUR FATHER** (Luke 11:1–4).

Jesus also taught his followers to pray for their enemies (Luke 6:28), to persevere in prayer (Luke 11:5–13), and to pray simply and humbly (Luke 18:9–14).

On the night before he died, Jesus prayed so earnestly in the Garden of Gethsemane that he sweated blood (Luke 22:39–46). The following day, his final words on the **CROSS** were to the Father: "Into your hands I commit my spirit!" (Luke 23:46).

Jesus is our **REDEEMER**, our Savior, and our Lord. Being made perfect through prayer, suffering, and obedience, he became "the source of eternal salvation to all who obey him" (Hebrews 5:9).

## If You Ask Me

- What stories from the Old Testament remind you of Jesus' life?
- Why do we (and the Israelites) need a divine Savior? Why weren't the prophets, priests, and kings of the Old Testament enough?
- What do prophets, priests, and kings do? How can you participate in Jesus' mission as a prophet? A priest? A king?



DIVIDED KINGDOM
1 Kings 12–22
2 Kings 1–16

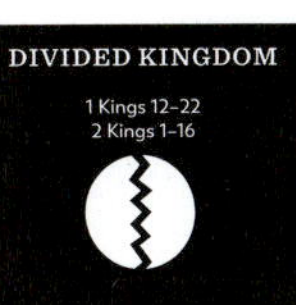

EXILE
2 Kings 17–25

RETURN
Ezra
Nehemiah

MACCABEAN REVOLT
1 Maccabees

MESSIANIC FULFILLMENT
Luke

THE CHURCH
Acts

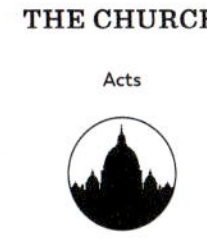

**IF YOU ASK ME**

These questions are about our need for a savior and our participation in Jesus' mission. To ease students into a whole-class conversation, consider starting them off in pairs or small groups and then transition to a large group discussion. If you have time, review and discuss "Prophet, Priest, and King," the leader-guided discussion on pages 135–136 of this guide.

In the workbook, review the key words in the "Time Period Overview," and then read the text together, asking students to read different paragraphs aloud.

The key takeaways here are that Jesus is the crux of God's ultimate plan for our salvation, and as his disciples, we are called to be like him.

**DIVE IN VIDEO**

Make sure the video and sound system are set up. Mark will ask your students to read three passages—**Luke 4:1-13**, **Luke 5:17-26**, and **Luke 24:13-31**—during the presentation, so invite them to find and bookmark these passages in their Bibles before watching the video. Also consider reviewing the "Got It?" questions together on page 104 of the workbook so they can be alert for the answers as they watch.

Finally, ask students to put away phones, close laptops, and avoid other distractions so they can give the video their full attention. Be prepared to pause the presentation when prompted for Bible reading.

**DIVE IN TEXT**

Review the key words, and then read the "Dive In" section, which complements the video presentation and explores Jesus' life, sacrifice, and victory over death. Invite students to take turns reading paragraphs out loud, or ask them to read the text quietly to themselves.

DIVE IN VIDEO

**Messianic Fulfillment . . . . . . . . . . . . . . . . . . . . Mark Hart**

"The paralyzed guy couldn't help himself. The four friends understood that Jesus *could* help him. We need friends like that. We need to *be* friends like that." —Mark H.

*During the video, Mark will ask you to pause and read three Bible stories. Find and mark them in your Bibles now so that you can open to them quickly when you need to:*

- *Luke 4:1–13, The Temptation of Jesus*
- *Luke 5:17–26, The Paralyzed Man and His Friends*
- *Luke 24:13–31, The Walk to Emmaus*

In a desert outside Jerusalem, Satan watched as Jesus prayed and fasted. Satan didn't yet know exactly who Jesus was. Son of God? What did that mean? Satan did know one thing: Jesus was different. This time, God wasn't coming after Pharaoh, the Amalekites, Goliath, or the Babylonians. This time, death itself was the target. Satan knew that something had to be done to stop this Jesus.

Satan got to work, using his standard strategy of fear and lies. As Jesus fasted and prayed in the desert, Satan whispered, "If you're really the Son of God…" and tempted Jesus with a series of dares (Luke 4:3–11). But he couldn't trick Jesus, not even when Jesus was tired, hungry, and alone. True God and true man, Jesus was like us in all things, including temptation—but never sin.

Jesus challenged everything that humanity expected and everything that was possible. He preached with authority, forgave sins, and gave us the Beatitudes, blessing the poor and those who mourn. He calmed a storm with his words, multiplied loaves and fish, walked on water, healed the deaf and the blind, cured **LEPERS**, cast out demons, and raised the dead—all in front of many witnesses. Even people who didn't care much for faith or religion wanted to see this carpenter from Galilee perform miracles. Meanwhile, Jesus' mission made the religious leaders suspicious. They saw Jesus as a threat. Yet massive crowds of the poor and needy kept coming to see him. Jesus offered them something more than physical healing, something nobody else had ever offered before.

You can find an example of this in Luke 5:17–26. The friends of a paralyzed man had heard of Jesus and were determined to bring their friend before him. But the house where Jesus was teaching was too crowded to enter, so they took off part of the roof and lowered their paralyzed friend down to Jesus from there. What determined and faithful friends! Jesus did indeed heal the man's body—but more importantly, he satisfied the needs of his heart and soul.

100 | ENCOUNTER

## Main Content Teaching

After you watch Mark's teaching video, read the "Dive In" text in the Student Workbook together. Three more "If You Ask Me" questions follow the text along with a quick "Got It?" quiz. Detailed notes on the video content start on page 132 of this Leader's Guide.

The Paralyzed Man

"Finding no way to bring him in, because of the crowd, they went up on the roof and let him down with his bed through the tiles into their midst before Jesus. And when he saw their faith he said, 'Man, your sins are forgiven you. ... Rise, take up your bed and go home.'"

—Luke 5:19-20, 24

Jesus grew in fame but not necessarily in popularity. People from all over Judea wanted to see his amazing works, but Jesus also had difficult teachings that some people resisted. For example, Jesus said that his flesh would be real food and his blood would be real drink (John 6:55). Even his own disciples didn't fully understand what this meant.

Three years into his ministry, as he celebrated the Passover meal with his friends, Jesus knew what suffering awaited him. That night he took bread in his hands and gave it to them, saying, "This is my body which is given for you" (Luke 22:19). Then he took a cup of wine and gave it to them, saying, "This chalice which is poured out for you is the new covenant in my blood" (Luke 22:20). This event is called the **LAST SUPPER**. It was Jesus' last meal with his friends and the first Eucharist, the sign of the **NEW AND EVERLASTING COVENANT**.

*The Last Supper* by Juan de Juanes

## Notes

Up to this point, the people had offered ritual sacrifices in the Temple. But in Jesus, God himself became the sacrifice—the final one. Only Jesus, true God and true Man, could offer the perfect and unrepeatable sacrifice for all time and for all people in his **PASSION** and death. The Temple sacrifices were no longer needed.

Jesus had predicted his own death several times, which made everyone uncomfortable. The jealous leaders had continued to plot against him, trying to find an opportunity to execute him—and they finally found it during Passover. Judas, one of Jesus' closest followers, betrayed him that night. Judas led the authorities to Jesus, they arrested him on false charges, and his friends deserted him in fear. Jesus was accused, abandoned, beaten, mocked, and finally condemned to death.

When Jesus was nailed to the Cross and died, his enemies thought they had won. But how wrong they were! God had been planning this offering all along. From the moment of the Fall, God had been gathering his people so that they could know him and serve him in holiness. He had chosen the Israelites and called them to himself through the covenants, teaching them and preparing their hearts for the Savior.

But, over and over again, people turned away from God, breaking their promises and committing horrible sins. They deserved the punishment and desperately needed a Savior.

We are the same.

Jesus took our punishment and died in agony. Why? Because he loves us. And he won't ever stop loving us. Jesus offered the perfect sacrifice—himself—which broke the power of sin and death forever. And he rose again so that we could, too.

Jesus isn't just a teacher or a healer or someone who says wise things. He is Emmanuel, "God with us." He's the Savior—*your* Savior. Only Jesus and no one else conquered death so that your sins could be forgiven and you could live with him forever in heaven.

## If You Ask Me

- How would you answer the question, "Who is Jesus?"
- How would you answer the question, "What did Jesus come to do?"
- What stories about Jesus do you like most? Why are these stories meaningful to you?



**IF YOU ASK ME**

These questions are about who Jesus is and what he came to earth to do. Use them to lead a class discussion, and answer students' spontaneous questions. If you have time, consider adding the optional leader-guided discussion of the Beatitudes on page 135 of this guide.

**Notes**

## THE EVENT THAT CHANGED THE WORLD

Jesus rose from the dead. We call this extraordinary event the Resurrection.

Jesus truly died on the Cross. The Gospel of John tells us that to make sure he was dead, a soldier used his spear to pierce Jesus' side, and blood and water poured from the wound. Jesus' "death was a real death, ... [the] end of his earthly human existence" (CCC 627).

His followers anointed his body with spices and wrapped it in linen cloths, as was the Jewish custom back then. Then they laid his body in a cave-like tomb sealed with a huge stone.

Early in the morning on the third day following his crucifixion, Mary Magdalene and other holy women came to the tomb to finish anointing his body. What they saw frightened them: the stone at the entrance had been rolled away. Inside, the linen cloths were lying where Jesus' body had been—but his body was gone. The tomb was empty!

What had happened? Had someone stolen the body? Soon the women understood. The Risen Christ appeared to them and spoke to them. Then he appeared to Peter and the other Apostles. Jesus had risen from the dead! Over the next forty days, Jesus spoke with the Apostles many times and even ate with them. On one occasion, he appeared to more than five hundred people.

Jesus' glorified body was different from our earthly bodies. We aren't sure exactly what it was like, but we know from Scripture that some people didn't recognize him at first, though they knew him when he spoke to them or broke bread with them. We know that his skin showed the wounds of his crucifixion. We also know that he could appear and disappear without warning, yet he was not a ghost. He ate with the Apostles, spoke to them, and walked with them.

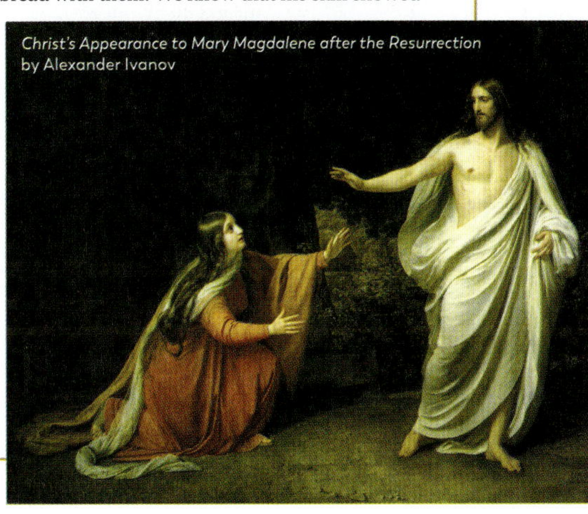

*Christ's Appearance to Mary Magdalene after the Resurrection* by Alexander Ivanov

The Resurrection changed human history. By it, Jesus opened a path to new life, eternal life, for us. The Resurrection is proof that Jesus is God's Son, the confirmation of his teachings and miracles, and the promise of our future resurrection.



**Notes**

**GOT IT?**

Ask students to complete the quiz in the workbook, and review their answers together. After you've gone over the answers, see if your students have any other questions about the lesson so far.

# Got It?

1. **Jesus successfully resisted the devil's attacks when Jesus was ________.**
   a. healing people in the Temple
   b. sleeping and dreaming
   c. eating a meal with his friends
   d. praying and fasting in the desert

2. **In the video, Mark focused on the healing of a ________ man whose friends helped him get to Jesus.**
   a. blind
   b. deaf
   c. paralyzed
   d. left-handed

3. **Jesus is ________.**
   a. the Savior
   b. a Gentile
   c. a prince
   d. a wise guru

104 | ENCOUNTER

**Notes**

DIVE IN ACTIVITY

## *Visio Divina*

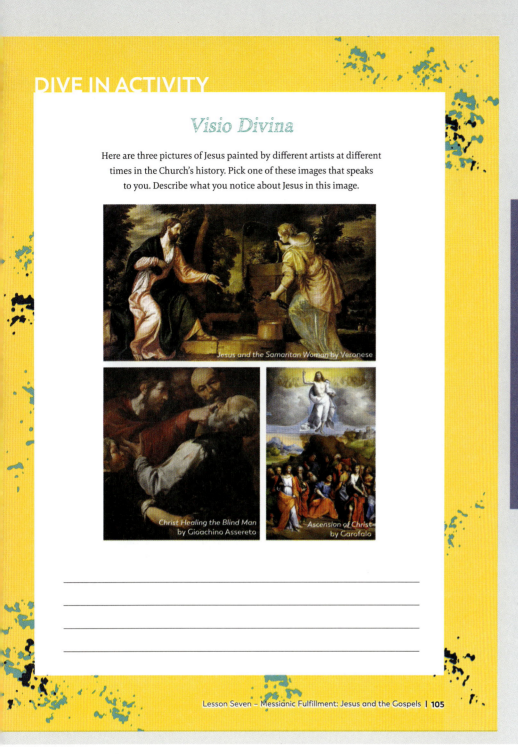

Here are three pictures of Jesus painted by different artists at different times in the Church's history. Pick one of these images that speaks to you. Describe what you notice about Jesus in this image.

*Jesus and the Samaritan Woman* by Veronese

*Christ Healing the Blind Man* by Gioachino Assereto

*Ascension of Christ* by Garofalo

Lesson Seven – Messianic Fulfillment: Jesus and the Gospels | 105

**VISIO DIVINA**

Before you begin this activity, you may want to explain how *visio divina* is similar to *lectio divina*—but instead of using Scripture passages to inspire prayer, *visio divina* uses images.

For the activity, direct students to the paintings in the workbook, and mention the title and artist of each one. Then go over the activity instructions carefully and answer questions. When everyone has finished, ask them to share what they learned.

## Dive In Activity

This activity offers students an opportunity to pray with a visual image of Jesus. As a prayer activity, it works best if each student does it independently.

**BIBLICAL CHARACTER VIDEO**

As before, ask students to put away phones, close laptops, and avoid other distractions so they can give their full attention to the video presentation. Ask them to pay special attention to what Ashley and the story of the boy teach us about how Jesus sees us, accepts our gifts, and provides for us.

**BIBLICAL CHARACTER PROFILE**

Read the text in the workbook, paying special attention to what the story teaches us about trusting God to provide for us. You can select students to read different paragraphs aloud to increase class participation.

BIBLICAL CHARACTER VIDEO

**The Boy with the Loaves and Fish . . . . . . . . . Ashley Hinojosa**

"Andrew, Simon Peter's brother, said to [Jesus], 'There is a lad here who has five barley loaves and two fish; but what are they among so many?'" —John 6:8–9

BIBLICAL CHARACTER PROFILE

## The Boy with the Loaves and Fish

Ashley shared her story about being called to study theology. She knew there would be challenges. She would have to move, make new friends, adapt, and somehow come up with money for tuition. She had no idea how she would do it, but she still felt called by God to go.

Deciding to follow God's call brought her joy and peace at first, but later she had many questions and fears. One day at Mass, she prayed about everything. She told God that she had been confident at first but now felt afraid. She asked for his strength.

After Mass, she returned a missed call as she walked to her car. She had been chosen for a big scholarship that would cover all her tuition! This was an amazing sign for her about how God will provide what we need when we need it.

This story reminds us of the multiplication of loaves in John 6. More than five thousand hungry people had gathered to hear Jesus. A boy offered to share his five loaves and two fish, even though that was nowhere near enough food to feed the huge crowd. But Jesus took the boy's offering and miraculously multiplied it—so much so that after everyone ate, there were twelve baskets of leftovers! The boy had been willing to give even what little he had, and God used it to feed thousands.

We can have faith that Jesus always sees us and never leaves us wanting. Like the boy with the loaves and fish, Ashley trusted God and stepped out in faith; God did the rest. What may seem impossible to us is not impossible for God.

106 | ENCOUNTER

## STEP 8 Biblical Character Profile: THE BOY WITH THE LOAVES AND FISH

This step features a short video by Ashley Hinojosa, the read-aloud profile in the workbook, and an exercise for students to do during class or at home.

After you play the video, review the video notes on page 135 of the Leader's Guide and ask students about specific points of interest. Then read the profile text aloud and give your students time to do the "My Loaves and Fish" exercise.

## My Loaves and Fish

Find "The Miracles of Jesus" on your *Bible Timeline* chart. Now read the story of the loaves and fish in **John 6:3–13**.

You have something to offer. Don't ever doubt this or compare yourself to others. God has given you something special to share with others. If you let him, he can and will multiply it.

Complete the following exercise to identify what you can offer to Jesus.

- What are some things people say you're good at?
- What are some things you like doing?
- What are some ways you like to help others?
- What is a need that you see in your community?
- Who do you feel called to serve?

107

**BIBLICAL CHARACTER EXERCISE**

"My Loaves and Fish" invites students to think about what they have to offer the Lord. It can be done in class or assigned as homework.

Make sure everyone has a *Bible Timeline* chart, their workbook, and something to write with. Notice "The Miracles of Jesus" on the chart, and then navigate to the story of the loaves and fish at John 6:3–13.

Go over the instructions and prompts for the exercise, and answer students' questions. Invite students to respond to the prompts and then share their responses. If time is limited, consider assigning this activity as homework.

**Notes**

**LIVING IT OUT**

Ask students how last week's "Living It Out" activities went. Then read this week's text in the workbook, which asks students to talk to someone they think of as a follower of Jesus and ask them questions.

Consider having someone from your parish or local community talk to your class about what it's like to follow Jesus. Alternatively, students can ask their parents or a family friend, or they can find out about a young saint or saint-to-be and answer the questions as they think the saint might answer them. Examples are Bl. Carlo Acutis, Bl. Pier Giorgio Frassati, St. José Sánchez del Río, and Bl. Chiara Badano.

**FAMILY CATECHESIS**

Remind parents to use "Living It Out" (and "Fast and Pray") for family catechesis. It is available on Thinkific, as are the videos and other resources.

Invite parents to answer their child's questions about following Jesus. Parents might suggest other friends or family members who would also like to talk about this with their child, or they can help their child find out about young saints who loved Jesus and followed him.

### Find Out More

An Angel Announces Jesus' Birth to Mary........Luke 1:26–38
Jesus Is Born in Bethlehem........Luke 2:1–7
Jesus Is Baptized........Luke 3:21–22
Jesus Fasts and Is Tempted in the Desert........Luke 4:1–13
Jesus Changes Water to Wine at a Wedding......John 2:1–12
Jesus Preaches the Sermon on the Mount.......Luke 6:17–49
Jesus Gives Peter the Keys to the Kingdom Matthew 16:13–20
Jesus Is Transfigured in Glory........Luke 9:28–36
Jesus Institutes the Eucharist........Luke 22:14–20
Jesus Is Crucified........Luke 23:32–49
Jesus Rises from the Dead........Luke 24:1–12
Jesus Ascends into Heaven........Luke 24:49–53

**Major Events of Jesus' Life**

Jesus is the Son of God, the Word made flesh. Everything he said and did when he lived on earth shows us who God is.

A good way to learn more about Jesus is to read the Gospels: Matthew, Mark, Luke, and John. A good Gospel to start with is the Gospel of Luke.

### Living It Out

How should a follower of Jesus live? Think of someone you know whom you would consider a present-day follower of Jesus. It might be someone in your parish or even someone in your family. Talk to that person this week about following Jesus. What would you like to ask him or her about Jesus? Here are some questions to get you started:

- How did he or she come to know Jesus?
- What is the most important thing he or she does every day to stay close to him?

108 | ENCOUNTER

## Find Out More & Living It Out

"Find Out More" lists some of the major events of Jesus' life, which students can read at home. You may also use one of these passages for *lectio divina*.

The "Living It Out" activities are specially designed to be done at home. Read the workbook text together to give your students ideas for putting what they have learned into practice. Remind them that you will check in with them the next time you meet to see how they are doing.

## WORDPLAY

**Cross**: In the Roman Empire, crucifixion was a form of execution carried out by nailing or binding a person to a wooden cross. Jesus' Cross has since become a universal Christian symbol of Christ's sacrifice and victory over sin and death.

**Gospel**: From the Old English words meaning "good news." In the New Testament, the four Gospels detail the life, teachings, miracles, death, and Resurrection of Jesus.

**Incarnation, the**: From the word "incarnate," which means to take on flesh or human form. Through the Incarnation, God the Son assumed a human body, was born of Mary, and became man.

**Last Supper**: The Passover meal that Jesus ate with his Apostles on the same night as his betrayal and arrest. It was during this meal that he instituted the Eucharist.

**lepers**: People who contracted the disease of leprosy. According to the Law of Moses, lepers were unclean and had to live away from other people.

**New and Everlasting Covenant**: The final, perpetual covenant that God made with the entire human family through Jesus, making it possible for us to dwell with him in heaven for eternity.

**Our Father**: Also called the "Lord's Prayer." This prayer that Jesus taught his disciples is considered a summary of the whole Gospel.

**Passion, the**: The time of Jesus' suffering, from his agony in the Garden of Gethsemane through his arrest, trial, and crucifixion.

**Redeemer, Redemption**: From a Latin word meaning "to buy back." Jesus is our Redeemer because he paid the price for us with his own blood and saved us from sin and death.

**transfigured**: Transformed into something better or more beautiful.

## CLOSING PRAYER

"Lord Jesus, you gave everything to your Father. You loved perfectly and triumphantly. Help me now to do the same. I claim you as my Lord and Savior. I reject and repent of my sins. I am yours, Jesus. In your name, we pray. Amen."

## Closing Prayer

Remind students of their homework assignments. Then, before reciting the prayer, consider leading them in a short meditation on the Crucifixion. (See the leader-guided discussion on p. 136 of this guide.)

Finally, lead them in the closing prayer, beginning and ending with the Sign of the Cross.

### THIS WEEK'S HOMEWORK

1. Memorize the memory verse: John 3:16.
2. Do the "Living It Out" activity.

# Lesson Eight

## THE CHURCH (AND YOUR ROLE IN IT)

## LESSON OVERVIEW

This final lesson begins by connecting everything that students have learned so far, and it continues by painting a picture of the early Church, beginning with the election of St. Matthias. We emphasize the role of the Holy Spirit in all things and consider how Pentecost launched a tremendous outpouring of growth, faith, miracles, and fortitude—perseverance amidst persecution.

The lesson introduces students to the adventures of Saints Peter and Paul and to Priscilla and Aquila, a married couple who played a small but vital role in the early community of the Church. The goal of the lesson is not only to introduce students to the narrative facts but also to help them enter the narrative of the Book of Acts and see their own lives as part of the same adventure that unfolds there.

This lesson marks the completion of the *Encounter* journey, but it's not the end of your students' encounter with Christ in Scripture. Our hope is to equip them to keep exploring God's plan in history and his plan for them here and now.

## LESSON OBJECTIVES

Students will

- **Journey** with the early Church from the Ascension through the Acts of the Apostles.
- **Recognize** the power of the Holy Spirit in the life of the Church through history.
- **Learn** about the risks the Apostles took to share the Gospel.
- **Be equipped** to put Christ's teachings into action today.
- **Embrace** their identity and mission as followers of Christ and members of his Church.

## VIDEO LESSON NOTES

### DIVE IN VIDEO – **THE CHURCH** – MARK HART

Mark will prompt you to pause the video to read these passages:

**Acts 1:21–26, The Apostles Choose Matthias to Replace Judas**
**Acts 12:1–11, Herod Imprisons Peter; Peter Escapes**
**2 Corinthians 11:23–30, Paul's Sufferings as an Apostle**

Mark begins with a recap of the program through Lesson Seven, which marks the beginning of the New Testament—the New Covenant established in Jesus, God's Son, by his life, death, and Resurrection.

Lesson Eight, this final lesson, describes the first years of the Church as the early Christians began to put the New Covenant into practice. But it isn't just a history lesson, because putting Christ's teachings into action is exactly what Christians here and now are also called to do.

## Jesus' Ascension into Heaven

- The story is told mostly in the Acts of the Apostles, which was written by St. Luke as the sequel to his Gospel. Acts 1 picks up right where the Gospel of Luke left off.
- Jesus has spent the forty days after his Resurrection with his Apostles, and now it's time for him to return to the Father. He tells them that he will send the Holy Spirit and commands them to preach to all people and to build his Church. Then he ascends into heaven as the Apostles look on.

## Being an Apostle

- The Apostles are Jesus' closest followers. One of the first things they do is choose Matthias to succeed Judas as an Apostle. Mark reminds students that this episode is a testimony to how God chooses and equips each of us for mission. What were the Apostles looking for in a new apostle? They had only two requirements: Did the new apostle follow Christ? Did he truly believe in him? The requirements are the same for us today.
- Don't compare yourself to others. Remember David? God looks at us from the inside out. He wants you to be so close to him that when people look at you, they see him.
- Next, we look at some regular, everyday believers and how they shared their faith, the "people in the pews" who did great things in the early Church—people like Priscilla and Aquila, a married couple who became great evangelists and preachers in their city.
- It isn't always easy. Mark talks about the great persecutions that the early Church faced and breaks for a story about Peter's boldness and persecution.

## St. Peter's Jailbreak

- Peter is in jail for preaching the Gospel when an angel appears, and—boom!—the door opens, Peter's chains fall off, and he sneaks past the guard and off into the night.
- Peter makes his way to the house of Mark's mother in Jerusalem, the location of the Last Supper and the descent of the Holy Spirit at Pentecost. This is home base for Mother Church—for the Christian community.

## Saul Becomes Paul

- St. Paul first appears in the book of Acts as a bad guy. His name was Saul, and he was a Jewish leader who hated Christians and persecuted them for proclaiming Jesus as the Messiah—something he considered blasphemy, the worst thing that could come out of a person's mouth as far as the Jewish leaders were concerned.
- But after an encounter with the risen Christ, Paul converted and became one of the greatest missionaries in Church history. He traveled thousands of miles on missionary journeys in the Mediterranean region, establishing church communities. As he traveled, he wrote letters to these communities—letters we often hear during the readings at Mass.
- Paul's journeys were full of hardship and difficulty. Through them, he teaches us how to endure suffering for the sake of the Gospel. Paul kept going because of *his relationship with a person*: Jesus Christ. We too can have that relationship with Jesus through the sacraments and the teachings of the Church. This is why Paul established a church community in each place he went.

## Our Role in the Church

- We are to bring others to Jesus as Peter and Paul did and as Christians have done since the beginning of the Church. That's why we talk about the power of the Holy Spirit in the Church from Pentecost all the way to now.
- Students are reminded of what St. Paul told the people in Ephesus: you are God's handiwork (see Ephesians 2:10). God created you; he crafted you. You were created for greatness, and you were created to be a saint.
- The closer you stay to God's Word in the Bible—and the closer you stay to Jesus in the sacraments of the Church, especially the Eucharist—the more you will fulfill your mission on earth. And someday you will become a saint.

Thanks for joining us for *Encounter*. We love you. We're praying for you. God bless you.

### BIBLICAL CHARACTER VIDEO – **PRISCILLA** – CHIKA ANYANWU

Chika has always been told to live her life in a way that inspires others to ask questions. The question she wants people to ask is "What is it about you?" For Chika, the answer is Jesus.

St. Paul said he had been crucified with Christ. He no longer lived his own life, but Christ lives through him (see Galatians 2:20). When people looked at St. Paul, they saw Jesus in him.

When Paul met a couple named Priscilla and Aquila, they saw Christ in him. They became followers of Jesus and close collaborators with Paul.

Priscilla was one of the first female preachers in the Church and one of the most influential. She and Aquila traveled with Paul and worked with him wherever they went. As they listened to a man named Apollos preaching one day, they saw that he needed more training. They didn't criticize him but instead shared their faith with him, teaching and encouraging him until he was ready to tell others that Jesus was the Christ.

We are called to be like Priscilla and Aquila: to live out our faith in a way that points directly to Jesus. When people meet us, our lives should make them ask, "What is it about you?" And our lives should also show them the answer: "It's Jesus."

# LEADER-GUIDED DISCUSSION (OPTIONAL)

If you have time, use the following prompts to explore the meaning of the number forty in the Bible.

## The Number Forty

After the Resurrection, Jesus spends forty days with his disciples before he ascends to heaven. The number forty keeps showing up in our lessons. What does it mean?

- In Noah's time, it rained for forty days and nights as the earth was flooded (Genesis 7:12).
- Moses fasted for forty days and nights before he received the Law (Exodus 34:28).
- The Israelites wandered in the desert for forty years (Numbers 14:34).
- The prophet Elijah walked for forty days and nights to reach Mount Horeb, God's mountain (1 Kings 19:8).

- Goliath taunted the Israelites for forty days (1 Samuel 17:16).
- The baby Jesus is presented in the Temple forty days after his birth (Luke 2:22, which mentions the time for purification, which was forty days after the birth of a boy).
- Jesus fasted for forty days and nights in the desert (Luke 4:1–2).
- Jesus remained with the Apostles for forty days, from the Resurrection to the Ascension (Acts 1:3).

It's interesting too that a human pregnancy lasts about forty weeks—the time it takes a new life to form in the womb.

Ask your students what all these events suggest about the meaning of the number forty in the Bible. Answers may include growth, an important change, testing, transformation, and new life.

In almost all cases, the number forty indicates a time of preparation before something extraordinary happens. In Jesus' life, it represents the time just before his public ministry began and the time leading up to his Ascension.

## BEFORE- AND AFTER-CLASS REMINDERS

### Before students arrive:

Make sure you have all the supplies needed for the lesson, such as Student Workbooks, Bibles, copies of *The Bible Timeline* chart, materials for activities, paper, and pens or pencils.

If you are handing out Bibles, place one at each student's place.

Review the video notes for the lesson and take note of anything you would like to mention to the class before they watch the video presentations.

Set up the equipment for the video presentations and queue the first video so that it is ready to play.

### After class:

Follow up with students who missed the lesson.

**WELCOME**

Some suggested ice-breakers:

- What is your favorite *Bible Timeline* period?
- Do you have a favorite Bible story? A favorite character? What attracts you to that story or that person?
- What did you like best about the *Encounter* program?

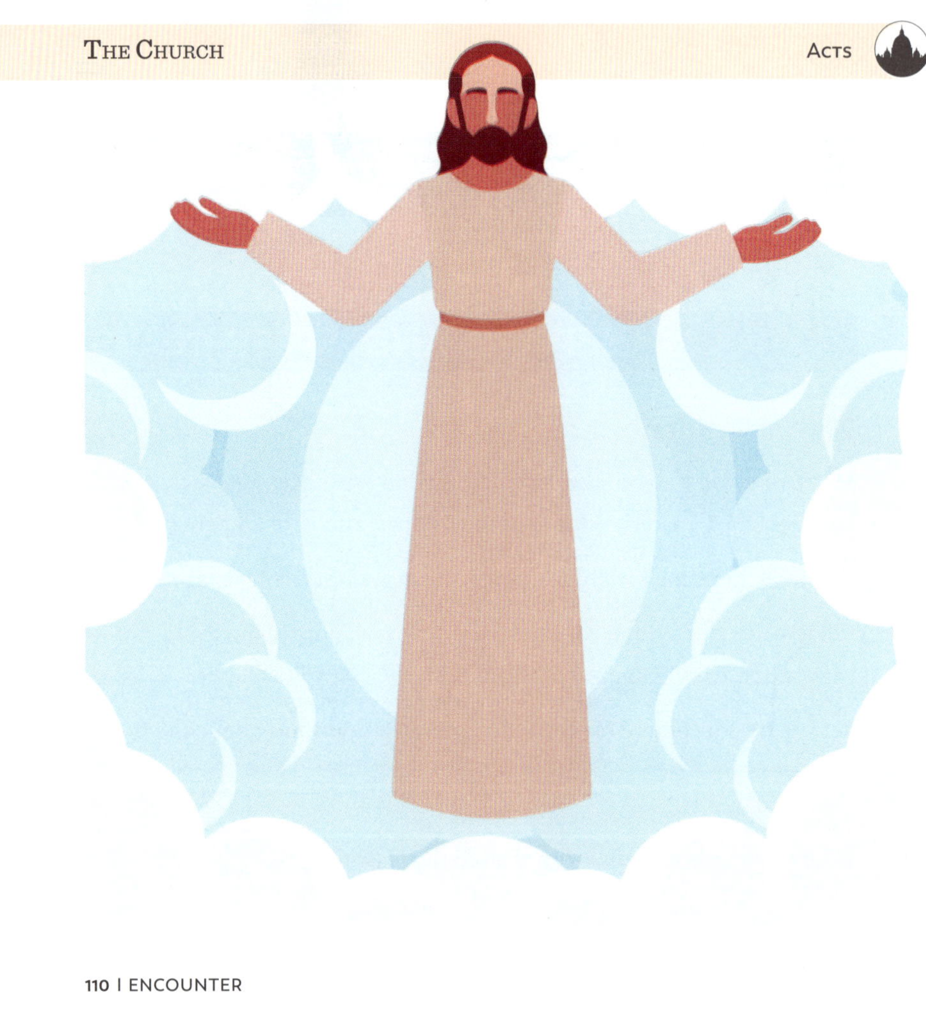

# Lesson Eight

## The Church (and Your Role in It)

## Welcome – The Big Picture

Greet the students as they arrive. As you welcome them, you may want to congratulate them on all the good work they have done up to now. Take attendance one last time so you can follow up with any students who are absent.

As an ice-breaker for this final lesson, invite students to talk about a favorite moment or takeaway from the class. Then read "The Big Picture" text together.

## The Big Picture

This lesson covers the early Church, but it isn't just a history lesson: it is about how Christians live. The New Testament shows us how the first Christians learned to live out the Faith in their own time and spread the word about Jesus. They were entrusted with sharing the Good News (Gospel)—and they shared it far and wide. They shared the Gospel even when they knew they could be killed because of it, just as Jesus was.

With the help of the Holy Spirit, we are called to do the same. The words of St. Luke, St. Paul, and other sacred authors are real and relevant to you **today**. The lessons of the early Church can apply to the adventure of your life at school, on your team, in your family, at your parish, and even in your personal prayer life.

**THE BIG PICTURE**

Read "The Big Picture" to prepare students for the major ideas of this lesson: the early Church and their call to be modern-day disciples. You and your students may want to bookmark the following chapters from Scripture: Luke 24; Acts 1, 12, and 18; Romans 16; 1 Corinthians 16; and 2 Corinthians 11.

**OPENING PRAYER**

"God the Holy Spirit, you came upon the disciples at Pentecost and empowered the early Church in its mission. Come upon us again today. Capture our minds, hearts, and imaginations with the same mission to share the Good News with the world. Help us continue the mission of Jesus wherever we are. Inspire us and empower us. In Jesus' name, we pray. Amen."

## Opening Prayer

When students have settled and shared their prayer requests, pray the opening prayer in the Student Workbook, beginning with the Sign of the Cross. You may lead the prayer yourself, pray it aloud as a class, or ask a student to read it. Follow the prayer with a Hail Mary or Glory Be if you wish, and end with the Sign of the Cross.

**MEMORY VERSE**

Read **Luke 24:49** aloud. What is "the promise of the Father"?

***LECTIO DIVINA* (OPTIONAL)**

Invite your students to close their eyes and open their hearts and minds to the Holy Spirit. Read **Luke 24:49** slowly and prayerfully out loud. Pause and then ask your students to read and reflect on the verse themselves. Encourage them to focus on a specific word or phrase that seems important.

To encourage conversation, you can invite a willing student to share the word or phrase that stood out for them. Ask whether it resonated with anyone else, and invite others to share.

If you want to use a longer passage for *lectio divina*, consider one listed in "Find Out More" on page 122 of the workbook.

**REMEMBER THIS!**

"And behold, I send the promise of my Father upon you; but stay in the city, until you are clothed with power from on high."

—Luke 24:49

Jesus promised his closest followers, the Apostles, that when he returned to the Father, he would send them an **ADVOCATE**: the Holy Spirit. This promise was fulfilled at Pentecost when the Apostles were filled with the Spirit and were able to courageously proclaim the Gospel.

Through your Baptism and Confirmation, the same Holy Spirit is poured out and unleashed in your soul.

The Father's promise is for the Church both in the time of the Apostles and now! When the Holy Spirit moves in your heart, don't be afraid to be a witness for Jesus wherever you are.

112 | ENCOUNTER

## Remember This!

Ask "Who can recite the memory verse from the last class?" (It's John 3:16.) Be ready with small prizes for those who can recite it successfully! Since this is the last lesson, you may want to challenge them further by inviting them to recite any of the memory verses from the previous lessons.

This lesson's memory verse, Luke 24:49, is written in the workbook, but you can also ask them to find it in their Bibles. Ask them to memorize it, and use it for *lectio divina* if you wish.

## WARM UP

# Empowered!

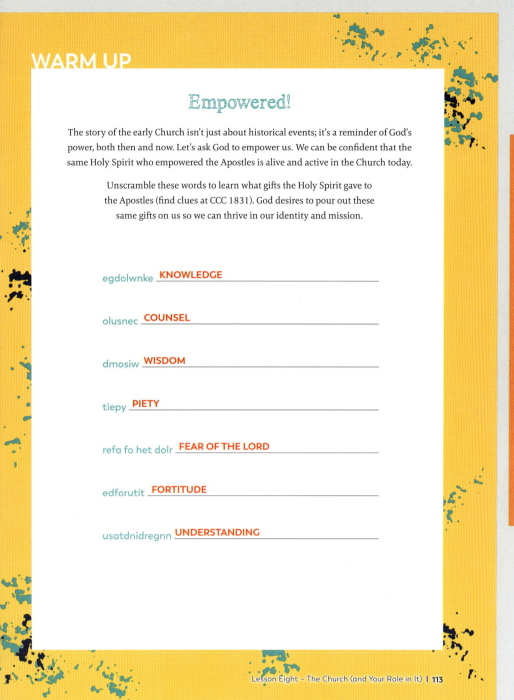

The story of the early Church isn't just about historical events; it's a reminder of God's power, both then and now. Let's ask God to empower us. We can be confident that the same Holy Spirit who empowered the Apostles is alive and active in the Church today.

Unscramble these words to learn what gifts the Holy Spirit gave to the Apostles (find clues at CCC 1831). God desires to pour out these same gifts on us so we can thrive in our identity and mission.

egdolwnke **KNOWLEDGE**

olusnec **COUNSEL**

dmosiw **WISDOM**

tiepy **PIETY**

refa fo het dolr **FEAR OF THE LORD**

edforutit **FORTITUDE**

usatdnidregnn **UNDERSTANDING**

Lesson Eight – The Church (and Your Role in It) | 113

### THE SEVEN GIFTS OF THE HOLY SPIRIT

The *Catechism of the Catholic Church* describes the importance of the gifts of the Holy Spirit and names them:

"The moral life of Christians is sustained by the gifts of the Holy Spirit. These are permanent dispositions which make man docile in following the promptings of the Holy Spirit." (CCC 1830)

"The seven *gifts* of the Holy Spirit are wisdom, understanding, counsel, fortitude, knowledge, piety, and fear of the Lord. They belong in their fullness to Christ, Son of David (see Isaiah 11:1–2)." (CCC 1831)

## Warm Up: *Empowered!*

This activity will familiarize students with the gifts of the Holy Spirit.

Make sure everyone has their workbook and something to write with. Go over the instructions and answer questions. To prepare students for the activity, you may wish to read and talk about the *Catechism*'s description of the gifts (see the side margin above). Be prepared to explain the unfamiliar terms.

When everyone has finished, review the answers.

## TIME PERIOD OVERVIEW

### The Church

Pentecost by Jean Restout

What a journey we have taken! Now we have arrived at the final lesson. The first six lessons told the story of God's Chosen People, the Israelites. The seventh lesson covered the coming of God's Son, Jesus, and the mystery of his life, his death, and the Resurrection. This final lesson describes the early Church as Christians began to live out the New Covenant. This history is told mostly in the Acts of the Apostles, which was written by St. Luke. Acts picks up where the Gospel of Luke ends. On your *Bible Timeline* chart, look for the Church panel (white).

After the Resurrection, Jesus spent forty days with his Apostles. He commanded them to preach to all people and to build his Church. He promised that he would send the Holy Spirit to empower them. That same day, as the Apostles looked on, Jesus ascended into heaven. Trusting his promise, the Apostles prayed and waited for him to send the Holy Spirit.

114 | ENCOUNTER

## Time Period Overview: The Church

Invite students to open their *Bible Timeline* charts to the white panel. Notice that the dates continue to the present. (If anyone asks, Rome ceased to be a world power by the year 476.)

In the workbook, review the key words in the overview, and then read the text together, asking students to read different paragraphs aloud.

Nine days passed. (Fun fact: those nine days of prayer were the first novena!) Then, at Pentecost, the Holy Spirit came upon them like tongues of fire, and the Church was born. Suddenly the Apostles—the same ones who had run away when Jesus was arrested—became brave and joyful preachers, sharing the Gospel with everyone they met.

What did the early Church, empowered by the Holy Spirit, look like? Immediately after Pentecost, the Apostles began preaching the Gospel wherever they went. Through the power of the Holy Spirit, they healed and worked miracles, like Jesus had. Believers gathered in people's homes to read Scripture, share Jesus' message, and receive the Eucharist. The Gospel began to spread from town to town and from country to country.

As the Church formed and grew after Jesus' **ASCENSION**, miracles and wonders—along with **PERSECUTION** and even **MARTYRDOM**—were all part of the story.

The Holy Spirit, the third Person of the Trinity, is often pictured as a dove. Other symbols for him include fire, wind, water, and anointing with oil.

## If You Ask Me

- How do you imagine the Holy Spirit? How do you think the Holy Spirit could empower you in your own life?
- How do you feel about yourself as a modern disciple? How can you share the Good News where you are?
- How connected do you feel to the Church?



DIVIDED KINGDOM 1 Kings 12–22 2 Kings 1–16

EXILE 2 Kings 17–25

RETURN Ezra Nehemiah

MACCABEAN REVOLT 1 Maccabees

MESSIANIC FULFILLMENT Luke

THE CHURCH Acts

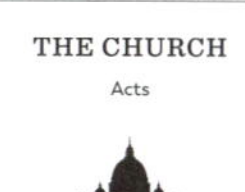

### IF YOU ASK ME

Use the prompts to lead a discussion. To ease students into a whole-class conversation, consider breaking the group into pairs or small groups first and gather as a class afterward.

Depending on the age of the group, you may wish to invite students to share about the day they received the Sacrament of Confirmation and how the graces of that sacrament relate to being a modern disciple.

The key takeaway is that Jesus sent us the Holy Spirit, empowering the Apostles to fulfill his command to preach the Gospel to all people. And we are their direct descendants! The Holy Spirit guides and empowers us to carry out Christ's mission, too!

**DIVE IN VIDEO**

Make sure the video and sound system are set up. Mark will ask students to read three passages during the presentation—**Acts 1:21-26**, **Acts 12:1-11**, and **2 Corinthians 11:23-30**—so invite them to bookmark these passages before you start the video. Also consider reviewing the "Got It?" questions together on page 118 of the workbook so they can be alert for the answers as they watch.

Finally, ask them to put away phones, close laptops, and avoid other distractions so they can give the video their full attention. Be prepared to pause the presentation when prompted for Bible reading.

**DIVE IN TEXT**

Review the key word, and then read the "Dive In" section, which looks at the mission of the early Church and our mission today. Invite students to take turns reading paragraphs out loud, or ask them to read the text quietly to themselves.

DIVE IN VIDEO

**The Church . . . . . . . . . . . . . . . . . . . . . . . . . .Mark Hart**

"Faith is about a relationship: your relationship with Jesus." —Mark H.

*During the video, Mark will ask you to pause and read three Bible stories. Find and mark them in your Bibles now so that you can open to them quickly when you need to:*

- *Acts 1:21–26, The Apostles Choose Matthias to Replace Judas*
- *Acts 12:1–11, Herod Imprisons Peter; Peter Escapes*
- *2 Corinthians 11:23–30, Paul's Sufferings as an Apostle*

## DIVE IN

The Acts of the Apostles introduces us to many people in the early Church: Priscilla and Aquila, the married evangelists; Stephen, the first deacon and martyr; Paul, the Pharisee (Jewish leader) who became an Apostle; Lydia, an early believer; and others. Life for these early Christians wasn't easy. They were resisted and mocked, and they risked their lives to follow Jesus.

"If you continue in my word, you are truly my disciples, and you will know the truth, and the truth will make you free."

—John 8:31-32

St. Paul was an unlikely Apostle, a fierce enemy of Jesus who became one of the greatest missionaries in Church history. After the Resurrection, Paul was on his way one day to arrest believers in Damascus—and Jesus appeared to him in a miraculous vision. Paul fell to the ground, blinded; Jesus told him to go to Damascus and wait. When Paul went there, the Christians in Damascus—the same ones Paul had planned to persecute—took him in, healed his blindness, and baptized him.

Paul became the Apostle to the Gentiles (non-Jews), traveling thousands of miles on missionary journeys to establish new Church communities across the Mediterranean region. As he traveled, Paul also wrote letters of advice to the new communities—letters that are preserved in the New Testament and which are read aloud at Mass.

Both St. Peter and St. Paul had dramatic adventures as they followed God's call, and both were eventually martyred (killed) for their Christian faith.

What would you do for your faith? Would you risk your life so that others could know how and why Jesus came to save them?

116 | ENCOUNTER

## Main Content Teaching

After you watch Mark's teaching video, read the "Dive In" text in the Student Workbook together. Three more "If You Ask Me" questions follow the text along with a quick "Got It?" quiz. Detailed notes on the video content start on page 154 of this Leader's Guide.

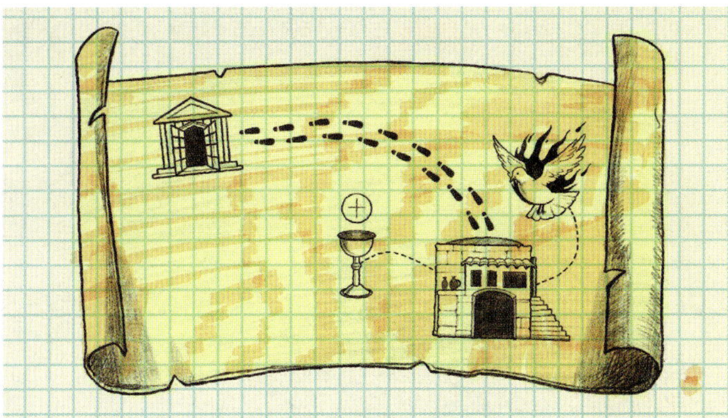

Our mission is the same mission that God gave to Peter and Paul: to bring others to Christ. We have the Holy Spirit to empower us and remain with us, so we know we are not alone. We have the Church to teach us and bring us the sacraments (outward signs of inner grace, instituted by God). We have the saints to pray for us. And we have our priests, our parents, and our teachers and leaders to guide us, like the people who are leading your *Encounter* program.

We stay close to Jesus through his **GRACE**, his life in our souls. Grace is his free gift to help us love him and grow in holiness. We receive grace especially through the sacraments and through prayer. Grace gives us the power to love as God loves and to know (and obey) God's will.

As you concentrate on staying close to Jesus, your mission will become clear. It will become the desire of your heart, as well as his.

Always remember who you are: an unrepeatable individual who is wanted and loved by God. He created you for greatness. He made you to be a saint.

> "I am sure that neither death, nor life, nor angels, nor principalities, nor things present, nor things to come, nor powers, nor height, nor depth, nor anything else in all creation, will be able to separate us from the love of God in Christ Jesus our Lord."
>
> —Romans 8:38–39

## If You Ask Me

- What do you think it takes to be a disciple today?
- Why do you think the Holy Spirit is often depicted as a dove? As fire? As water?
- How do you feel about the idea that you were created to be a saint? What do you think that means?

Lesson Eight – The Church (and Your Role in It) | 117

### IF YOU ASK ME

These questions are about the Holy Spirit and discipleship. Use them to lead a class discussion, and answer students' spontaneous questions.

In the video, Mark mentions the forty days between Jesus' Resurrection and the Ascension. If you have time, consider talking to students about what is special about the number forty in the Bible (see "Leader-Guided Discussion" starting on page 156).

### Notes

**GOT IT?**

Ask students to complete the quiz in the workbook, and review their answers together. After you've gone over the answers, see if your students have other questions about the lesson.

# Got It?

1. **Who was chosen to fill Judas' position as an Apostle?**
   a. Barnabas
   b. Aquila
   c. Matthias
   d. Ralph

2. **Many of the early Christians faced __________ for practicing their faith.**
   a. resistance
   b. mockery
   c. martyrdom
   d. all of the above

3. **Which Apostle was formerly a Pharisee and an enemy of Christianity?**
   a. Matthias
   b. Barnabas
   c. Paul
   d. Andrew



## Notes

## DIVE IN ACTIVITY

### Letters

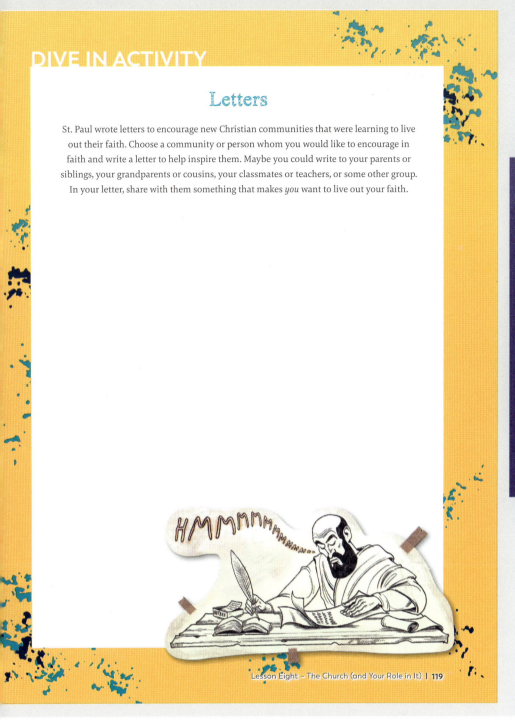

St. Paul wrote letters to encourage new Christian communities that were learning to live out their faith. Choose a community or person whom you would like to encourage in faith and write a letter to help inspire them. Maybe you could write to your parents or siblings, your grandparents or cousins, your classmates or teachers, or some other group. In your letter, share with them something that makes *you* want to live out your faith.



**LETTERS**

Make sure everyone has paper and something to write with. Go over the instructions carefully and answer questions. Brainstorm together to think of people who would appreciate encouragement in their faith—such as people in RCIA, missionaries, prisoners, and aid workers. When students have finished, review their letters and encourage them to give or send them to the persons addressed. (For safety and security reasons, remind students to sign letters to strangers with their first name only.)

## Dive In Activity

This activity offers students an opportunity to encourage others in letters just as St. Paul did.

**BIBLICAL CHARACTER VIDEO**

As before, ask students to put away phones, close laptops, and avoid other distractions so they can give their full attention to the video presentation. Play the video, asking students to pay special attention to Chika's experience and what Priscilla's story tells us about teaching and encouraging one another as Christians.

**BIBLICAL CHARACTER PROFILE**

Read the text in the workbook, paying special attention to what it tells us about the importance of keeping Jesus at the center of our lives. You can select students to read different paragraphs aloud to increase class participation.

BIBLICAL CHARACTER VIDEO

**Priscilla and Aquila . . . . . . . . . . . . . . . . . . . . Chika Anyanwu**

"Greet Prisca and Aquila, my fellow workers in Christ Jesus, who risked their necks for my life, to whom not only I but also all the churches of the Gentiles give thanks." —Romans 16:3–4

### BIBLICAL CHARACTER PROFILE

## Priscilla and Aquila

Chika has always been told to live her life in a way that makes others ask questions. The main question she wants her life to inspire is "What is it about you?" For Chika, the answer is Jesus. Chika is still growing, but Jesus has taught her how to be kind and inviting, steadfast and charitable, courageous and forgiving, and sensitive and attentive to the needs of others.

St. Paul said he had been crucified with Christ. He no longer lived his own life; rather, Christ lived through him (Galatians 2:20). When people looked at Paul, he wanted them to see Jesus. That is exactly what happened when two tentmakers, a married couple named Priscilla and Aquila, met Paul: they saw Christ in him and became ardent followers of the Lord.

Priscilla and Aquila traveled with Paul and worked closely with him wherever they went. Once, as Priscilla and Aquila were listening to the preaching of a man named Apollos, they realized that Apollos didn't know many things about "the Way" that he needed to know. ("The Way" was what early Christianity was called.) Apollos needed more training. Instead of criticizing him for what he didn't know, Priscilla and Aquila taught him gently and encouraged him, and Apollos became a helpful and powerful preacher in the early Church.

120 | ENCOUNTER

## STEP 8 Biblical Character Profile: PRISCILLA AND AQUILA

This step features a short video by Chika Anyanwu, the read-aloud profile in the workbook, and an exercise for students to do during class or at home.

After you play the video, review the video notes on page 156 of the Leader's Guide and ask students about specific points of interest. Then read the profile text aloud and give your students time to do the "There's Something Different About You" exercise.

Priscilla and Aquila made their home in whatever community they visited and even offered their own home in Rome as a church.

We are called to be like them—to live out our faith in a way that points directly to Jesus. When people meet us, our lives should make them ask, "What is it about you?" And our lives should also give the answer: "It's Jesus."

"Now there are varieties of gifts, but the same Spirit; and there are varieties of service, but the same Lord; and there are varieties of working, but it is the same God who inspires them all in every one. To each is given the manifestation of the Spirit for the common good."

—1 Corinthians 12:4–7

## "There's Something Different About You"

Find the Holy Spirit on your *Bible Timeline* chart. Now read about Priscilla and Aquila in **Acts 18:1–3, 18, 24–28; Romans 16:3–4;** and **1 Corinthians 16:19**.

Chika's teaching about Priscilla and Aquila is an invitation to us. How can we live in a way that makes people ask, "What is different about you?" How can we live in a way that shows the answer is Jesus?

Priscilla and Aquila were ordinary people who were open to life in Christ. What would life in Christ look like for you? Use the prompts below to help you reflect on that.

I really enjoy ____________________. How can I do it in a way that glorifies God and helps others?

Sometimes I become too attached to something. (It might be a person, an activity, or a possession.) I think I'm too attached to ____________________. How can I let go of it to live more fully for Jesus?

Other people tell me I'm good at ____________________. How can I use this gift to build up his kingdom on earth?

I sometimes wish I could help other people. Who are they? What is something I could help them with? ____________________

What can I do every day to live for God and put him first?

____________________

121

**BIBLICAL CHARACTER EXERCISE**

"There's Something Different About You" invites students to think about what their life in Christ might look like. Make sure that everyone has a *Bible Timeline* chart, their workbooks, and something to write with. Notice "Peter and Paul Spread the Gospel" on the chart. Then navigate to the verses about Priscilla and Aquila in Acts 18:1–3, 18, 24–28; Romans 16:3–4; and 1 Corinthians 16:19.

Go over the instructions and prompts in the workbook and answer students' questions. You may want to come up with an example for each prompt to help students get started. Briefly talk about the second prompt, "Sometimes I become too attached to something," to make sure students understand what "too attached" can mean.

Invite students to write their responses to the prompts in the workbook and then share what they wrote. If time is limited, consider assigning this activity as homework.

**Notes**

## LIVING IT OUT

Ask students how their "Living It Out" activity from the last lesson went. Then read the final "Living It Out" text together as a class to give them ideas for seeing their lives in the light of salvation history—specifically, under the arc of God's love for them and for all people.

You may wish to lead them in a final large group discussion to remind them of the key points of *Encounter* and help them identify the key events of their own timelines, especially the times when God has shown up and blessed their lives. Encourage them to imagine where their lives might go next as they live out their Catholic Faith and make it their own.

## FAMILY CATECHESIS

Remind parents to use "Living It Out" for family catechesis. Invite them to talk to their child about their family's timeline, especially how God has blessed them and how they have experienced Jesus' presence in their lives.

### Find Out More

The Apostles Receive the Gift of the Holy Spirit ........ Acts 2
Peter Heals a Lame Beggar .................... Acts 3:1–10
An Angel Frees the Apostles from Prison......... Acts 5:17–21
Stephen Is Martyred.......................... Acts 7:54–60
Paul (Saul) Is Converted on the Road to Damascus......................... Acts 9:1–19
Paul Escapes His Enemies in a Basket.......... Acts 9:23–25
Peter Escapes Prison Miraculously ............. Acts 12:4–11
Paul and Silas Baptize a Prison Guard and His Family ................. Acts 16:25–34
Priscilla and Aquila Mentor Apollos............ Acts 18:24–28
Eutychus Falls from a Window as Paul Preaches ..................... Acts 20:7–12
Paul Is Shipwrecked............................... Acts 27
Paul Survives a Poisonous Snake Bite ........... Acts 28:1–6

**Important Events in the Acts of the Apostles**

The events listed here are not necessarily the *most* important ones in the life of the early Church, but they will give you a taste of the power and joy that carried the Church forward.

### Living It Out

Along this journey through Scripture, we have seen God's master plan at work. Now it's time to look for God's plan in your own life. In what ways do you see God at work? How is your story connected to the story of salvation? Your story is still being written, so there are many things in God's plan for you that have yet to unfold. But there is no doubt that he is already working in your life.

Just as we considered a timeline of salvation history and the story of God's people, consider the timeline of your life so far. What are the key events? Where has God already shown up? What blessings has God already given you? Where have you already met or felt Jesus in your life?

Consider where the timeline of your story might go next. What do you think is in the future? The closer we grow to Jesus, the more beautiful and meaningful life becomes.

Whatever else happens and wherever else your story takes you, remember that Jesus is the center. He is your best friend and companion in the epic story of your life—a story that leads all the way to heaven.

122 | ENCOUNTER

## Find Out More & Living It Out

For the interested readers, "Find Out More" lists some major events in the early Church. You may also use one of these passages for *lectio divina*. Students have done the "Living It Out" activities at home. Review what they've learned. Then remind them that this is the last lesson, and brainstorm ideas for putting what they've learned into practice.

"Having gifts that differ according to the grace given to us, let us use them: if prophecy, in proportion to our faith; if service, in our serving; he who teaches, in his teaching; he who exhorts, in his exhortation; he who contributes, in liberality; he who gives aid, with zeal; he who does acts of mercy, with cheerfulness."

—Romans 12:6–8

## WORDPLAY

**Advocate**: From a Latin word meaning "to call to one's aid"; another name for the Holy Spirit.

**Ascension, the**: From a Latin word meaning "to go up." The Ascension occurred forty days after the Resurrection when the Apostles witnessed Jesus go up into heaven.

**grace**: The divine assistance freely given to us by God, which we did not need to earn. Grace allows us to respond to God's call to become his children.

**martyrdom**: From a Greek word meaning "witness." A martyr gives up his or her life in defense of the Faith.

**persecution**: The intentional harassment or abuse of a person or group by another person or group, often because of religious differences.

## CLOSING PRAYER

"Lord God, thank you for every heart that has been on this journey. Thank you for everything we have learned about you and your love for us. Help us to see how your love and your plan change the world. Help us to live out our part of your story of salvation. Help us to see your constant action, your calling for us, and the destiny of heaven that lies ahead. In Jesus' name, we pray. Amen."

## STEP 10 Closing Prayer

Lead the class in the closing prayer, beginning and ending with the Sign of the Cross.

As you finish the prayer, it would be a good time to thank students for journeying through Scripture with you and invite them to continue to study Scripture on their own, using their knowledge of *The Bible Timeline* to help them!

## Glossary

**ADVOCATE** – From a Latin word meaning "to call to one's aid"; another name for the Holy Spirit.

**ANOINT** – From a Latin word meaning "to smear with oil." Anointing is a sacred ceremonial practice in which holy oil is smeared on someone as a sign that they are set apart for a special purpose.

**APOSTLE** – From a Greek word meaning "one who is sent." The original twelve Apostles were chosen by Jesus to preach the Gospel and make disciples of all nations.

**ARK OF THE COVENANT** – The wooden, gold-covered chest that held the two stone tablets of the Ten Commandments and other sacred objects of the Israelites.

**ASCENSION, THE** – From a Latin word meaning "to go up." The Ascension occurred forty days after the Resurrection when the Apostles witnessed Jesus go up into heaven.

**BAPTISM** – From a Greek word meaning "to immerse." Through Baptism, we become a new creation, an adopted son or daughter of God, and an official member of the Church. The graces of Baptism help us to live and share in God's love.

**BIBLE** – From the Greek word *biblia,* which means "collection of books." The Bible contains seventy-three books of many different types.

**CATHOLIC** – A word meaning "universal"; the name for the Church instituted by Jesus and passed down through the successors of the Apostles.

**CHRISTIAN** – A follower of Christ who has been baptized in his name.

**CHURCH** – The whole assembly of baptized Christians throughout the world who profess the same faith in Jesus Christ.

**CONCUPISCENCE** – The desire or inclination to commit sin.

**COVENANT** – From a Latin word meaning "to agree on." More than a contract, a covenant is an exchange of persons that helps establish an ongoing relationship.

**CROSS** – In the Roman Empire, crucifixion was a form of execution carried out by nailing or binding a person to a wooden cross. Jesus' Cross has become a universal Christian symbol of his sacrifice and victory over sin and death.

**EXILE** – To be forced from your native home and have to live somewhere else. During the Exile period, God's people were conquered by their enemies and led away from the Promised Land by their captors, and they lived in exile for many years.

**FALL, THE** – The event in Genesis when Adam and Eve disobeyed God and "fell" from grace.

**GARDEN OF EDEN** – Also called "Paradise." God made this special place for Adam and Eve to live in before the Fall.

**GOSPEL** – From the Old English words meaning "good news." In the New Testament, the four Gospels are the four books that detail the life, teachings, miracles, death, and Resurrection of Jesus.

**GRACE** – The divine assistance freely given to us by God, which we did not need to earn. Grace allows us to respond to God's call to become his children.

**"I AM WHO I AM"** – The holy name of God, first spoken to Moses. "I AM" or "I AM WHO I AM" is the English translation of the four-letter Hebrew word YHWH (commonly pronounced "Yahweh").

**INCARNATION, THE** – From the word "incarnate," which means to take on flesh or human form. Through the Incarnation, God the Son assumed a human body, was born of Mary, and became man.

**INSPIRED** – From a Latin word meaning "to breathe into." The Holy Spirit guided the human authors of the Bible as they wrote the truth God wants us to know for our salvation.

**ISRAELITES** – The descendants of the Patriarch Jacob (whose other name was Israel). Jacob's twelve sons were the ancestors of the twelve tribes of Israel.

**JEWS** – Another name for the Israelite people, or "men of Judah," used in the period of the Exile and after.

**JUDGES** – The twelve leaders of Israel who were chosen by God to help defend the Israelites from their enemies.

**LAST SUPPER** – The Passover meal that Jesus ate with his Apostles on the same night as his betrayal and arrest. It was during this meal that he instituted the Eucharist.

**LEPERS** – People who contracted the disease of leprosy. According to the Law of Moses, lepers were unclean and had to live away from other people.

**MANNA** – The heavenly food that God provided to sustain the Israelites while they wandered in the desert. Manna was white and sweet and could be made into cakes.

**MARTYRDOM** – From a Greek word meaning "witness." A martyr gives up his or her life in defense of the Faith.

**MESSIAH** – From the Hebrew word that means "anointed one." The Messiah was prophesied to be as the one who would deliver the Jewish people from oppression.

**MORALITY** – The principles that determine whether something is right or wrong, good or evil.

**NEW AND EVERLASTING COVENANT** – The final, perpetual covenant that God made with the entire human family through Jesus Christ, making it possible for us to dwell with him in heaven for eternity.

**NEW TESTAMENT** – The latter part of the Bible that details the life, death, and Resurrection of Jesus Christ, along with the early history of his Church.

**OLD TESTAMENT** – The first part of the Bible, which details Creation, the Fall, and God's ongoing attempts to repair his relationship with humanity.

**ORIGINAL SIN** – The "stain" of sin that we inherited from Adam and Eve, which means we are born in a "state of sin" and require redemption.

**OUR FATHER** – Also called the "Lord's Prayer." This prayer that Jesus taught his disciples is considered a summary of the whole Gospel.

**PASSION, THE** – The time of Jesus' suffering, from his agony in the Garden of Gethsemane through his arrest, trial, and crucifixion.

**PASSOVER** – The Jewish feast that commemorates the night when God "passed over" the Israelite homes in Egypt, protecting their children from death and freeing them from slavery.

**PATRIARCH** – The male head of a family or tribe, often the eldest or most respected man in the family. A matriarch is the female head of a family or tribe. The Patriarchs of the Israelites are Abraham, Isaac, and Jacob.

**PERSECUTION** – The intentional harassment or abuse of a person or group by another person or group, often because of religious differences.

**PLAGUES** – A series of devastating catastrophes that fell upon the Egyptians after Pharaoh refused to let the Israelites go and worship God.

**PROMISED LAND** – The region that God promised to give to Abraham and his descendants as an inheritance. Other terms for this area are "Israel," "the Levant," "Palestine," and "Canaan."

**PROPHETS** – Individuals chosen by God to proclaim God's will to the people and call everyone to live according to the covenant. In biblical times, they often played an important role as inspired advisors to kings.

**REDEEMER, REDEMPTION** – From a Latin word meaning "to buy back." Jesus is our Redeemer because he paid the price for us with his own blood and saved us from sin and death.

**REVELATION** – Divine truth that God communicates to us through his Word (Scripture) and the teachings handed down to us (Tradition).

**SACRED SCRIPTURE** – The collection of ancient biblical texts that are inspired by God and reveal his nature and presence to his people.

**SALVATION** – Our deliverance through Jesus Christ from the powers of sin and death.

**SALVATION HISTORY** – The events that reveal God's redemptive plan in human history, culminating in Jesus Christ, who completely reveals the Father to us.

**SAVIOR** – Jesus Christ, the one who delivers us from the consequences of sin and death.

**TABERNACLE** – The portable tent that the Israelites used for worship in the desert. It housed the Ark of the Covenant.

**TEN COMMANDMENTS** – Ten laws that God gave the Israelites to teach them how to live and worship as a free people.

**TRINITY** – The three distinct Persons who make up the single divine nature of God: the Father, the Son, and the Holy Spirit.

**TRANSFIGURED** – Transformed into something better or more beautiful.

**WORSHIP** – To honor and show reverence to God alone.

# FURTHER RESOURCES

Catholic Prayers .......... 129

The Rosary .......... 132

The Divine Mercy Chaplet .......... 134

*Lectio Divina* .......... 135

The Ten Commandments .......... 136

The Beatitudes .......... 137

An Examination of Conscience for Middle School .......... 138

Verses to Help on Hard Days .......... 141

## Catholic Prayers

You may already know some of these prayers. Practice one or two every day. When you've memorized them, you'll be able to pray them anytime—at Mass, when you say the Rosary, when you or a friend needs help, or whenever you want to say thank you to God.

### THE OUR FATHER

Our Father, who art in heaven, hallowed be thy name; thy kingdom come, thy will be done, on earth as it is in heaven. Give us this day our daily bread, and forgive us our trespasses as we forgive those who trespass against us; and lead us not into temptation, but deliver us from evil. Amen.

### THE HAIL MARY

Hail Mary, full of grace, the Lord is with thee. Blessed art thou among women, and blessed is the fruit of thy womb, Jesus. Holy Mary, Mother of God, pray for us sinners, now and at the hour of our death. Amen.

### THE GLORY BE

Glory be to the Father, and to the Son, and to the Holy Spirit, as it was in the beginning, is now, and ever shall be, world without end. Amen.

### THE APOSTLES' CREED

I believe in God, the Father almighty, Creator of heaven and earth, and in Jesus Christ, his only Son, our Lord, who was conceived by the Holy Spirit, born of the Virgin Mary, suffered under Pontius Pilate, was crucified, died, and was buried; he descended into hell; on the third day he rose again from the dead; he ascended into heaven, and is seated at the right hand of God the Father almighty; from there he will come to judge the living and the dead. I believe in the Holy Spirit, the holy catholic Church, the communion of saints, the forgiveness of sins, the resurrection of the body, and life everlasting. Amen.

### FATIMA PRAYER

O my Jesus, forgive us our sins, save us from the fires of hell, and lead all souls to heaven, especially those in most need of thy mercy.

## ROSARY PRAYER

God, whose only begotten Son, by his life, death, and Resurrection, has purchased for us the rewards of eternal life, grant, we beseech thee, that meditating upon these mysteries of the Most Holy Rosary of the Blessed Virgin Mary, we may imitate what they contain and obtain what they promise, through the same Christ our Lord. Amen.

## HAIL, HOLY QUEEN

Hail, Holy Queen, Mother of mercy, our life, our sweetness, and our hope. To thee do we cry, poor banished children of Eve; to thee do we send up our sighs, mourning and weeping in this valley of tears. Turn, then, most gracious advocate, thine eyes of mercy toward us, and after this, our exile, show unto us the blessed fruit of thy womb, Jesus. O clement, O loving, O sweet Virgin Mary.

**V.** Pray for us, O Holy Mother of God.
**R.** That we may be made worthy of the promises of Christ.
Amen.

## THE *MEMORARE*

Remember, O most gracious Virgin Mary, that never was it known that anyone who fled to thy protection, implored thy help, or sought thine intercession was left unaided. Inspired with this confidence, I fly unto thee, O Virgin of virgins, my Mother; to thee do I come, before thee I stand, sinful and sorrowful. O Mother of the Word Incarnate, despise not my petitions, but in thy mercy, hear and answer me. Amen.

## THE *ANGELUS*

**V.** The angel of the Lord declared unto Mary,
**R.** And she conceived by the Holy Spirit.
Hail Mary ...

**V.** Behold the handmaid of the Lord.
**R.** Be it done unto me according to thy Word.
Hail Mary ...

**V.** And the Word was made flesh,
**R.** And dwelt among us.
Hail Mary ...

**V.** Pray for us, O Holy Mother of God,
**R.** That we may be made worthy of the promises of Christ.

Let us pray: Pour forth, we beseech thee, O Lord, thy grace into our hearts, that we, to whom the Incarnation of Christ, thy Son, was made known by the message of an angel, may by his passion and cross be brought to the glory of his Resurrection, through the same Christ our Lord. Amen.

## PRAYER TO ST. MICHAEL

St. Michael the Archangel, defend us in battle. Be our protection against the wickedness and snares of the devil. May God rebuke him, we humbly pray, and do thou, O Prince of the Heavenly Host, by the power of God, cast into hell Satan and all the evil spirits, who prowl throughout the world seeking the ruin of souls. Amen.

## PRAYER TO YOUR GUARDIAN ANGEL

Angel of God, my guardian dear, to whom God's love commits me here, ever this day (night) be at my side, to light and guard, to rule and guide. Amen.

## MORNING OFFERING

O Jesus, through the Immaculate Heart of Mary,
I offer you my prayers, works, joys, and sufferings of this day
for all the intentions of your Sacred Heart
in union with the Holy Sacrifice of the Mass throughout the world,
for the salvation of souls, the reparation of sins, the reunion of all Christians,
and in particular for the intentions of the Holy Father this month.
Amen.

## The Rosary

The Rosary gives us a chance to spend time with Our Lady and think about the events of Jesus' life, death, and Resurrection. For each mystery, put yourself into the scene, asking Mary to help you see it through her eyes. The Rosary is a beautiful way to pray with Mary—whether you pray by yourself, with your family, or with friends.

Rosary beads are special. They are often blessed by a priest or deacon, and so we should always treat the beads with respect and affection. (That's why, while the beads may look like a necklace, we don't wear them.) We hold the beads in our hands and keep count of the Rosary prayers with our fingers.

Our Lady gave the first Rosary to St. Dominic in 1208! For the text of the individual prayers, see pages 129–130.

### THE MYSTERIES OF THE ROSARY

**The Joyful Mysteries**

1. The Annunciation
2. The Visitation
3. The Nativity
4. The Presentation
5. The Finding of Jesus in the Temple

**The Luminous Mysteries**

1. The Baptism of Christ in the Jordan
2. The Manifestation of Christ at the Wedding of Cana
3. The Proclamation of the Kingdom of God, with His Call to Conversion
4. The Transfiguration
5. The Institution of the Eucharist

**The Sorrowful Mysteries**

1. The Agony in the Garden
2. The Scourging at the Pillar
3. The Crowning with Thorns
4. The Carrying of the Cross
5. The Crucifixion

**The Glorious Mysteries**

1. The Resurrection
2. The Ascension
3. The Descent of the Holy Spirit
4. The Assumption
5. The Coronation of the Blessed Virgin Mary

## HOW TO PRAY THE ROSARY

*For the text of the individual prayers listed here, see "Catholic Prayers" above.*

1. Holding the rosary beads, make the Sign of the Cross.
2. Pray the Apostles' Creed (on the crucifix).
3. Pray an Our Father (first bead).
4. Pray three Hail Marys (second through fourth beads).
5. Pray the Glory Be and the (optional) Fatima Prayer (fifth bead).
6. Announce the first mystery, and then pray the Our Father.
7. Pray ten Hail Marys on the next decade (ten beads), meditating on the mystery.
8. On the next single bead, pray the Glory Be and the (optional) Fatima Prayer.
9. On the same bead, announce the next mystery and pray the Our Father.
10. Repeat steps 7 to 9 for each of the four remaining mysteries.
11. After the fifth mystery, pray the Hail, Holy Queen (on the rosary centerpiece).
12. Conclude with the Rosary Prayer, and make the Sign of the Cross.

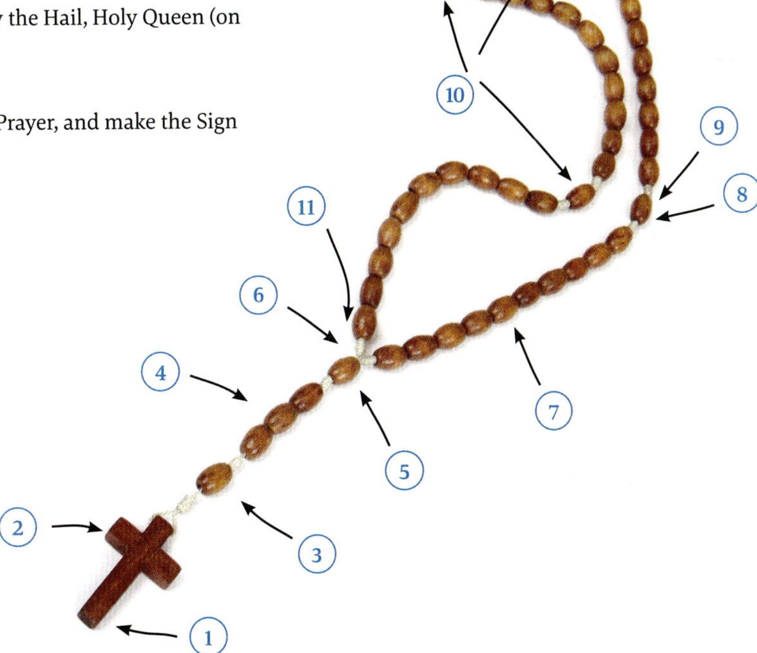


Further Resources | 133

## The Divine Mercy Chaplet

The Divine Mercy Chaplet gives us a chance to meditate on Jesus' Passion and infinite Divine Mercy. We use rosary beads to keep count as we pray.

Our Lord gave the chaplet prayers to St. Faustina in September 1935. For the text of the individual prayers, see pages 129–130.

1. Using rosary beads, begin with the Sign of the Cross, one Our Father, one Hail Mary, and the Apostles' Creed.

2. On each Our Father bead, pray, "Eternal Father, I offer you the Body and Blood, Soul and Divinity of your dearly beloved Son, our Lord Jesus Christ, in atonement for our sins and those of the whole world."

3. On each Hail Mary bead, pray, "For the sake of his sorrowful passion, have mercy on us and on the whole world."

4. Repeat these prayers on each decade. End by praying three times, "Holy God, Holy Mighty One, Holy Immortal One, have mercy on us and on the whole world."

## *Lectio Divina*
### (LEK-tsee-oh dee-VEE-nah)

*Lectio divina* (which means "divine reading" in Latin) is the traditional Catholic practice of reading and praying with Scripture. You can begin with a favorite Bible story, the "Remember This!" verse in your *Encounter* lesson, or one of the readings from "Find Out More."

With *lectio divina*, just like with the Rosary, it helps to imagine that you are in the scene. For example, you could be helping your family collect manna in the desert (Exodus 16:14–21), listening to Jesus preach the Sermon on the Mount (Luke 6:17–49), or escaping a shipwreck with St. Paul (Acts 27).

As you pray, follow these four steps:

**Step 1: *Lectio* (reading)**

Begin with the Sign of the Cross and ask the Holy Spirit to assist you in this time of prayer. Next, read a selected passage from Scripture slowly and intentionally. If possible, read the passage aloud. Listen to the words as if God is speaking to you directly, immersing yourself in the passage. If needed, you can read the passage a second time.

**Step 2: *Meditatio* (meditation)**

The second step is to meditate on the passage you just read. It is helpful to focus on particular words or verses that spoke to you or caught your attention during the reading. Like the Virgin Mary (see Luke 2:19), ponder the Word of God in your heart, seeking to encounter him and discern what he might be saying to you.

**Step 3: *Oratio* (prayer)**

In prayer, we not only speak to God but also listen to what he is saying. You can use a formal prayer from the tradition of the Church, saying the words slowly and paying attention to what the prayer is telling you about God and about your relationship with him. You may also pray in your own words, asking God for greater understanding of the Scripture passage that you just read. Ask if he wants you to make changes in your life or in your faith journey.

**Step 4: *Contemplatio* (contemplation)**

Contemplation is resting in God's presence and allowing him to arrange your thoughts and prayer. Let God enter and change your heart and mind according to his will. Like anything new, *lectio divina* may take a little practice. However, if you practice it faithfully and give God a few minutes of your time, you will start to see a real difference in your spiritual life.

## The Ten Commandments

1. I am the Lord your God: you shall not have strange gods before me.
2. You shall not take the name of the Lord your God in vain.
3. Remember to keep holy the Lord's Day.
4. Honor your father and your mother.
5. You shall not kill.
6. You shall not commit adultery.
7. You shall not steal.
8. You shall not bear false witness against your neighbor.
9. You shall not covet your neighbor's wife.
10. You shall not covet your neighbor's goods.

In their extraordinary encounters on Mount Sinai, God gave Moses the Ten Commandments (*Catechism*, following CCC 2051) and all the Law, speaking to Moses from heaven and writing the commandments on stone tablets with his own finger (Exodus 31:18). The commandments are the ground rules for human life. In them, God is telling us how to worship him and live with other people.

It is important to understand that following these commandments is the minimum expected of a Christian. Jesus reminds us of the importance of the Ten Commandments when he speaks to the rich young man (Matthew 19:16–22), and he adds that the young man must surrender everything and follow him if he wants to gain eternal life. If we want the same, we too must go beyond the bare minimum and live each day putting Jesus and our faith first.

Some Christian denominations number the Ten Commandments differently than we do as Catholics. Our Tradition uses the division listed above, given to us by St. Augustine. This list is the one established by the early Church and has been handed on to us through the centuries.

If you can commit the commandments to memory and live them out daily, you're well on your way to sainthood!

# The Beatitudes

Blessed are the poor in spirit, for theirs is the kingdom of heaven.

Blessed are those who mourn, for they shall be comforted.

Blessed are the meek, for they shall inherit the earth.

Blessed are those who hunger and thirst for righteousness, for they shall be satisfied.

Blessed are the merciful, for they shall receive mercy.

Blessed are the pure in heart, for they shall see God.

Blessed are the peacemakers, for they shall be called sons of God.

Blessed are those who are persecuted for righteousness' sake, for theirs is the kingdom of heaven.

Blessed are you when men revile you and persecute you and utter all kinds of evil against you falsely on my account. Rejoice and be glad, for your reward is great in heaven.

The word *beatitude* means "blessed." The Beatitudes are not laws or rules like the Ten Commandments; rather, they show us what God's love looks like in practice—what the Catechism calls "an order of happiness and grace, of beauty and peace" (CCC 2546).

It might already make sense to us that someone who is merciful or a peacemaker may be considered blessed. But why would we ever think of a person in mourning or a person suffering persecution as "blessed"? The answer is found in Jesus. The Beatitudes are Jesus' self-portrait. During his time on earth, Jesus embodied the Beatitudes perfectly: he was poor, humble, righteous, merciful, pure—and the Prince of Peace. He mourned the sorrows of our sinful world, and he suffered persecution for preaching the Kingdom of God. He was ultimately put to death—but through the Resurrection, Jesus reveals the reality of eternal life with the Father. As St. Paul says, "I consider that the sufferings of this present time are not worth comparing with the glory that is to be revealed to us" (Romans 8:18). The Beatitudes teach us that, though we all experience struggles and sufferings in our Christian life on earth, those who follow Jesus' example and live as faithful disciples will receive eternal glory in heaven.

If we want to live more like Jesus in our ordinary circumstances, we can look to the Beatitudes as a starting point. You can find the Beatitudes in Matthew 5:3–12; they are the opening words to Jesus' Sermon on the Mount.

## An Examination of Conscience for Middle School

An examination of conscience is a tool we use to be aware of how we have sinned since our last Confession so that we can repent and know what we need to confess. We can also use it daily before bedtime as a way to check in on our souls.

A sin is an offense against God that wounds our relationship with him and others. When we do an examination of conscience, we quiet ourselves, ask the Holy Spirit to show us how and when we fell into sin, and take time to remember our thoughts, words, and deeds. We don't do this to feel bad about ourselves or to be discouraged. We do it so we can be truly sorry for our sins and know how we want to act in the future, so we can receive the forgiveness and healing that God wants to give us.

As we examine our consciences, we also ask for the grace to avoid sin and the near occasion of sin (the situations that make it easy to fall into sin) in the future.

Remember that we must confess all mortal sins in Confession. These are sins that reject God's grace, his life in our souls. Mortal sins can mean the difference between heaven and hell. A sin is mortal if:

- We knew it was serious.
- We knew it was wrong.
- We freely chose to do it anyway.

The Ten Commandments are a clear and direct way for us to examine our consciences because when we break these commandments, we fall into sin. Here is an examination of conscience from the Ten Commandments that can help you experience God's mercy and healing in your life.*

* This examination of conscience from the Ten Commandments has been reprinted by permission from *Renewed by Jesus: My Guide to Reconciliation*, by Colin and Aimee MacIver (West Chester, PA: Ascension, 2023), 52–59. Two other examinations of conscience—from the Beatitudes and from the seven deadly sins—can also be found there.

**First Commandment: "I am the Lord your God. You shall not have strange gods before me."**

- Did I try to make God the most important thing in my life?
- Did I act like other things, activities, or people are more important than God?
- Did I spend time with God each day in prayer?
- Did I thank God for the good things he has given me?
- Did I receive Holy Communion with mortal sins that I have not confessed yet?

**Second Commandment: "You shall not take the name of the Lord your God in vain."**

- Did I always use God's name with love and respect?
- Did I use God's name out of anger or as a curse?
- Did I speak badly about God, the saints, or any other holy person or thing?
- Did I use bad language or curse words?

**Third Commandment: "Remember to keep holy the Lord's Day."**

- Did I miss Mass on a Sunday or Holy Day of Obligation on purpose without a good reason (like being sick or not having a ride)?
- Did I complain about going to Mass?
- Did I pay attention at Mass as best I could? Did I say the responses, pray, and sing?
- Did I fast (no food or drink except water) for one hour before receiving Holy Communion?
- Did I rest on Sundays?

**Fourth Commandment: "Honor your father and your mother."**

- Did I show love and respect to my parents or the adults who take care of me?
- Did I disobey them? Did I get angry or talk back to them?
- Did I try to be thankful for what my parents do for me?
- Did I help my family at home? Did I complain about chores?
- Did I argue or fight with my brothers or sisters? Am I kind to them?
- Did I respect and obey other adults in charge (priests, nuns, teachers, police, etc.)?
- Did I obey the rules at school?
- Did I do my best on homework and other schoolwork?

**Fifth Commandment: "You shall not kill."**

- Did I hurt anyone on purpose?
- Did I make fun of others or call them names?
- Did I lose my temper or get angry at anyone?

- Did I not forgive someone?
- Did I leave out anyone on purpose?
- Did I talk badly about others or gossip?
- Did I share what I can with others, especially those who have less than I do?
- Did I try to take care of my body?

**Sixth and Ninth Commandments: "You shall not commit adultery." "You shall not covet your neighbor's wife."**

- Did I try to treat my body and others' bodies with respect?
- Did I think about disrespectful things on purpose?
- Did I listen to or tell disrespectful jokes?
- Did I look at disrespectful images, videos, TV shows, or movies?

**Seventh and Tenth Commandments: "You shall not steal." "You shall not covet your neighbor's goods."**

- Did I steal anything?
- Did I take something without permission? Did I purposely not return something?
- Did I damage someone else's things?
- Was I greedy or selfish?
- Did I share what I can, especially with those who have less than I do?
- Am I thankful for what I have?
- Am I jealous of what others have or what they can do?

**Eighth Commandment: "You shall not bear false witness against your neighbor."**

- Did I lie? Did I tell half the truth?
- Did I blame others for something that I did?
- Did I spread rumors about someone?
- Did I tell secrets?
- Did I cheat on school work or in a game?
- Did I keep my promises?
- Did I keep silent when I should have said something?

## Verses to Help on Hard Days

Living the Catholic life isn't easy. Being a Christian in today's world requires a lot of patience, especially with challenges at school, on social media—even in your own family. It also requires confidence in God's loving care for you. Below are some passages from the Bible that speak to some of the feelings and struggles you may face. They are good passages to reflect on in prayer, and they can offer you hope and deepen your confidence in God's loving care for you.

*Happy reading!*

### WHY BOTHER BEING HOLY?

"You are a chosen race, a royal priesthood, a holy nation, God's own people, that you may declare the wonderful deeds of him who called you out of darkness into his marvelous light." —1 Peter 2:9

"As he who called you is holy, be holy yourselves in all your conduct; since it is written, 'You shall be holy, for I am holy.'" —1 Peter 1:15–16

"Strive for peace with all men, and for the holiness without which no one will see the Lord." —Hebrews 12:14

### NEED SOME CONFIDENCE BEFORE YOU START YOUR DAY?

"I can do all things in him who strengthens me." —Philippians 4:13

"The Lord is my light and my salvation;
whom shall I fear?
The Lord is the stronghold of my life;
of whom shall I be afraid?" —Psalm 27:1–3

"The Lord will be your confidence and will keep your foot from being caught." —Proverbs 3:26

### CAN'T FIND THE RIGHT WORDS WHEN YOU PRAY?

"[Jesus said,] 'Pray then like this:

Our Father who art in heaven,
Hallowed be thy name.
Thy kingdom come.
Thy will be done
on earth as it is in heaven.
Give us this day our daily bread;
and forgive us our trespasses

as we forgive those who trespass against us;
and lead us not into temptation,
But deliver us from evil.'" —Matthew 6:9–13

"The Spirit helps us in our weakness; for we do not know how to pray as we ought, but the Spirit himself intercedes for us with sighs too deep for words." —Romans 8:26

"The LORD is near to all who call upon him, to all who call on him in truth." —Psalm 145:18

### AFRAID THAT GOD WILL ABANDON YOU OR STOP LOVING YOU?

"God so loved the world that he gave his only-begotten Son, that whoever believes in him should not perish but have eternal life." —John 3:16

"The steadfast love of the LORD never ceases;
his mercies never come to an end;
they are new every morning;
great is your faithfulness." —Lamentations 3:22–23

"For I am sure that neither death, nor life, nor angels, nor principalities, nor things present, nor things to come, nor powers, nor height, nor depth, nor anything else in all creation, will be able to separate us from the love of God in Christ Jesus our Lord." —Romans 8:38–39

### WONDERING WHETHER GOD IS REALLY LISTENING TO YOUR PRAYERS?

"[Jesus said,] 'Ask, and it will be given you; seek, and you will find; knock, and it will be opened to you. For every one who asks receives, and he who seeks finds, and to him who knocks it will be opened.'" —Matthew 7:7–8

"You will call upon me and come and pray to me, and I will hear you. You will seek me and find me; when you seek me with all your heart, I will be found by you, says the Lord." —Jeremiah 29:12–13

"This is the confidence which we have in him, that if we ask anything according to his will he hears us." —1 John 5:14

### WORRIED ABOUT WHAT THE FUTURE HOLDS OR AFRAID OF TRUSTING GOD WITH YOUR WHOLE LIFE?

"I know the plans I have for you, says the Lord, plans for welfare and not for evil, to give you a future and a hope." —Jeremiah 29:11

"I am sure that he who began a good work in you will bring it to completion at the day of Jesus Christ." —Philippians 1:6

"We know that in everything God works for good with those who love him, who are called according to his purpose." —Romans 8:28

### WANT TO KNOW THE SECRET TO BEING GREAT IN GOD'S EYES?

"The Lord sees not as man sees; man looks on the outward appearance, but the Lord looks on the heart." —1 Samuel 16:7

"[Jesus] sat down and called the Twelve and he said to them, 'If any one would be first, he must be last of all and servant of all.' And he took a child, and put him in the midst of them; and taking him in his arms, he said to them, 'Whoever receives one such child in my name receives me; and whoever receives me, receives not me but him who sent me.'" —Mark 9:35–37

"[Jesus said,] 'Let the greatest among you become as the youngest, and the leader as one who serves.'" —Luke 22:26

### FEELING DOWN ON YOURSELF BECAUSE YOU KEEP MESSING UP?

"Since all have sinned and fall short of the glory of God, they are justified by his grace as a gift, through the redemption which is in Christ Jesus." —Romans 3:23–24

"[The Lord] said to me, 'My grace is sufficient for you, for my power is made perfect in weakness.'" —2 Corinthians 12:9

"If any one is in Christ, he is a new creation; the old has passed away, behold, the new has come." —2 Corinthians 5:17

### AFRAID TO CONFESS YOUR SINS?

"If we confess our sins, he is faithful and just, and will forgive our sins and cleanse us from all unrighteousness." —1 John 1:9

"I acknowledged my sin to you,
  and I did not hide my iniquity;
I said, 'I will confess my transgressions to the LORD';
  then you forgave the guilt of my sin." —Psalm 32:5

"He who conceals his transgressions will not prosper,
  but he who confesses and forsakes them will obtain mercy." —Proverbs 28:13

### NERVOUS ABOUT A PRESENTATION OR SOCIAL SITUATION?

"Fear not, for I am with you, be not dismayed, for I am your God; I will strengthen you, I will help you, I will uphold you." —Isaiah 41:10

"Cast all your anxieties on him, for he cares about you." —1 Peter 5:7

"Have no anxiety about anything, but in everything by prayer and supplication with thanksgiving let your requests be made known to God. And the peace of God, which passes all understanding, will keep your hearts and your minds in Christ Jesus." —Philippians 4:6–7

### UPSET ABOUT THINGS THAT PEOPLE ARE SAYING AT HOME, AT SCHOOL, OR ON SOCIAL MEDIA?

"Let all bitterness and wrath and anger and clamor and slander be put away from you, with all malice, and be kind to one another, tenderhearted, forgiving one another, as God in Christ forgave you." —Ephesians 4:31–32

"[Jesus said,] 'Judge not, and you will not be judged; condemn not, and you will not be condemned; forgive, and you will be forgiven; give, and it will be given to you. ... For the measure you give will be the measure you get back.'" —Luke 6:37–38

"[Jesus said,] 'Whatever you wish that men would do to you, do so to them.'" —Matthew 7:12

### NOT SURE WHAT TO DO ABOUT YOUR "ENEMIES" OR HOW TO DEAL WITH PEOPLE WHO HURT YOU OR MAKE YOU ANGRY?

"[Jesus said,] 'I say to you that hear, Love your enemies, do good to those who hate you, bless those who curse you, pray for those who abuse you. ... And as you wish that men would do to you, do so to them.'" —Luke 6:27–28, 31

"'If your enemy is hungry, feed him; if he is thirsty, give him drink; for by so doing you will heap burning coals upon his head.' Do not be overcome by evil, but overcome evil with good." —Romans 12:20

"Be angry but do not sin; do not let the sun go down on your anger." —Ephesians 4:26

"Let no evil talk come out of your mouths, but only such as is good for edifying, as fits the occasion, that it may impart grace to those who hear." —Ephesians 4:29

### READY TO GIVE UP HOPE THAT CERTAIN FRIENDS OR FAMILY WILL EVER FOLLOW GOD?

"[The disciples asked,] 'Who then can be saved?' But Jesus looked at them and said to them, 'With men this is impossible, but with God all things are possible.'" —Matthew 19:25–26

"God our Savior ... desires all men to be saved and to come to the knowledge of the truth." —1 Timothy 2:3–4

"The Lord is not slow about his promise as some count slowness, but is forbearing toward you, not wishing that any should perish, but that all should reach repentance." —2 Peter 3:9

### FEELING LIKE NO ONE WILL LISTEN TO YOU BECAUSE YOU'RE TOO YOUNG?

"Let no one despise your youth, but set the believers an example in speech and conduct, in love, in faith, in purity." —1 Timothy 4:12

"The LORD said to me, 'Do not say, "I am only a youth"; for to all to whom I send you you shall go, and whatever I command you you shall speak. Be not afraid of them, for I am with you to deliver you.'" —Jeremiah 1:7

### FEELING HOPELESS?

"The LORD is near to the brokenhearted, and saves the crushed in spirit." —Psalm 34:18

"Be strong and of good courage, do not fear or be in dread ... for it is the Lord your God who goes with you; he will not fail you or forsake you." —Deuteronomy 31:6

"May the God of hope fill you with all joy and peace in believing, so that by the power of the Holy Spirit you may abound in hope." —Romans 15:13

### FEELING TIRED OR WEAK?

"[Jesus said,] 'Come to me, all who labor and are heavy laden, and I will give you rest. Take my yoke upon you, and learn from me; for I am gentle and lowly in heart, and you will find rest for your souls. For my yoke is easy, and my burden is light.'" —Matthew 11: 28–30

"The LORD ... gives power to the faint,
  and to him who has no might he increases strength. ...
They who wait for the Lord shall renew their strength,
  they shall mount up with wings like eagles,
they shall run and not be weary,
  they shall walk and not faint." —Isaiah 40:28–29, 31

"I can do all things in him who strengthens me." —Philippians 4:13

### FEELING ALONE OR DOWN?

"Be strong and of good courage; be not frightened, neither be dismayed; for the LORD your God is with you wherever you go." —Joshua 1:9

"Where shall I go from your Spirit?
  Or where shall I flee from your presence?
If I ascend to heaven, you are there!
  If I make my bed in Sheol [the abode of the dead], you are there!
If I take the wings of the morning
  and dwell in the uttermost parts of the sea,
even there your hand shall lead me,

and your right hand shall hold me.
If I say, 'Let only darkness cover me,
and the light about me be night,'
even the darkness is not dark to you,
the night is bright as the day;
for darkness is as light with you." —Psalm 139:7–12

"Blessed be the God and Father of our Lord Jesus Christ, the Father of mercies and God of all comfort, who comforts us in all our affliction, so that we may be able to comfort those who are in any affliction, with the comfort with which we ourselves are comforted by God." —2 Corinthians 1:3–4

## FEELING TIRED OF DOING THE RIGHT THING?

"And let us not grow weary in well-doing, for in due season we shall reap, if we do not lose heart." —Galatians 6:9

"Do not fret because of the wicked,
be not envious of wrongdoers!
For they will soon fade like the grass,
and wither like the green herb.
Trust in the Lord, and do good;
so you will dwell in the land, and be nourished in safety.
Take delight in the Lord,
and he will give you the desires of your heart.
Commit your way to the Lord;
trust in him, and he will act." —Psalm 37:1–5

"My beloved brethren, be steadfast, immovable, always abounding in the work of the Lord, knowing that in the Lord your labor is not in vain." —1 Corinthians 15:58

## FEELING OVERWHELMED BY TEMPTATION?

"No temptation has overtaken you that is not common to man. God is faithful, and he will not let you be tempted beyond your strength, but with the temptation will also provide the way of escape, that you may be able to endure it." —1 Corinthians 10:13

"[Jesus said,] 'Watch and pray that you may not enter into temptation; the spirit indeed is willing, but the flesh is weak.'" —Matthew 26:41

"God did not give us a spirit of timidity but a spirit of power and love and self-control." —2 Timothy 1:7

## IS REMAINING PURE A STRUGGLE FOR YOU OR YOUR FRIENDS?

"Whatever is true, whatever is honorable, whatever is just, whatever is pure, whatever is lovely, whatever is gracious, if there is any excellence, if there is anything worthy of praise, think about these things." —Philippians 4:8

"This is the will of God, your sanctification: that you abstain from immorality; that each one of you know how to control his own body in holiness and honor, not in the passion of lust like heathens who do not know God. ... For God has not called us for uncleanness, but in holiness." —1 Thessalonians 4:3–5, 7

"Be content with what you have; for he has said, 'I will never fail you or forsake you.' Hence we can confidently say, 'The Lord is my helper, I will not be afraid; what can man do to me?'" —Hebrews 13:5–6

## About the Authors and Presenters

### MEET THE AUTHORS

**MARK HART,** affectionately known as the Bible Geek, is a best-selling author, award-winning producer, Catholic radio personality, and highly sought-after speaker. He proudly serves as the CIO (Chief Innovation Officer) of Life Teen International. Mark and his wife, Melanie, have four children and live in Phoenix, Arizona.

**COLIN** and **AIMEE MACIVER** teach theology at St. Scholastica Academy in Covington, Louisiana, where they serve as the campus minister and service director, respectively. Their decades of combined experience in ministry include youth ministry, Confirmation prep, speaking, training, visual art, and music ministry. Colin and Aimee have authored a number of popular programs with Ascension over the years, with *Receiving Jesus: My Guide to the Mass* and *Envision: Theology of the Body for Middle School* being two of their latest projects.

### MEET THE PRESENTERS

**CHIKA ANYANWU** is a Catholic evangelist, former Confirmation coordinator/youth and young adult minister, and the author of *My Encounter: How I Met Jesus in Prayer.* Whether speaking nationally or internationally about prayer, human dignity, or being a 30-something single woman, she always puts the love and mercy of Jesus at the forefront of her message. Chika is a member of a beautiful Nigerian family, loves her coffee black, and desires sainthood for herself and you.

**FR. FRANKIE CICERO** is a priest of the Diocese of Phoenix, where he is the parochial vicar at St. Timothy's Catholic Church in Mesa, Arizona. He attended St. John Vianney Seminary in Denver, Colorado, and was ordained eight years later on June 16, 2018.

**ASHLEY HINOJOSA** is a doctoral student in moral theology at the University of Notre Dame. She received her BA in theology with a minor in pastoral ministry at the University of Dallas, an MA in theology through ND's McGrath Institute for Church Life's Echo Program (where she served in the Archdiocese of Galveston-Houston), and an MTS at Duke Divinity School. As a Catholic speaker and writer, Ashley has worked alongside organizations such as Life Teen, The Catholic Woman, and Ascension.

**TANNER KALINA** is cofounder of the *Saints Alive* podcast, an alumnus of FOCUS (Fellowship of Catholic University Students), and a team member of the National Eucharistic Congress. He hosts Ascension's *Envision: Theology of the Body for Middle School* series and has appeared in videos on Ascension Presents. He has also contributed video projects to FOCUS, EWTN, CatholicMatch, and YDisciple.

# *Encounter: The Bible Timeline for Middle School* Program Credits

**EXECUTIVE PRODUCER & PUBLISHER**
Jonathan Strate

**GENERAL MANAGERS**
Jeffrey Cole
Dcn. John Harden

**PROJECT MANAGER**
Veronica Salazar

**PRODUCT MANAGER**
Lauren McCann

**SENIOR VIDEO PRODUCER**
Matthew Pirrall

**VIDEO CREATIVE DIRECTOR**
Matthew Longua

## *Encounter* Video Series

**PRODUCTION COMPANY**
Coronation Media

**FEATURING**
Mark Hart
Chika Anyanwu
Fr. Frankie Cicero
Ashley Hinojosa
Tanner Kalina

**THEOLOGICAL CONSULTANTS**
Jeffrey Cole
Dcn. John Harden
Carlos Taja

## *Encounter* Written Materials

**AUTHOR & WRITER**
Mark Hart

**CO-WRITERS**
Aimee and Colin MacIver

**CONTENT REVIEWERS**
Jeffrey Cole
Dcn. John Harden
Lauren McCann
Carlos Taja
Lauren Welsh

**GRAPHIC DESIGN**
Sarah Stueve
Stella Ziegler

**FEATURED ARTIST**
Chris Lewis, BARITUS Catholic

**PRINT EDITORIAL**
Christina Eberle
Rebecca Robinson

**MARKETING**
Mark Leopold
Julia Morgensai